PARAMARTHA KATHA PRASANG

Spiritual Conversations
With
Swami Muktananda

(1962 – 1966)

GURUDEV SIDDHA PEETH
GANESHPURI

PRINTED IN INDIA

Printed by P. P. Bhagwat, at Mouj Printing Bureau, Khatau Wadi, Girgaum, Bombay 400 004

Published by Shree Gurudev Siddha Peeth, Ganeshpuri, Pin 401 206, Dist. Thane, Maharashtra, INDIA

INTRODUCTION

Since the first time I had the darshan of Baba Muktananda, his divine words, which intoxicate one with the bliss of Brahman, the Absolute, touched my heart. The nectar-like drops from the ocean of his wisdom began to quench the thirst of my inner Self. The shower of his sublime teaching began to enliven my intellect by cleansing the mind.

I felt a keen desire to treasure his precious and soothing words, so that when I was not in his physical presence, I could remember him by reading what he had said. This would make me experience great joy, and would strengthen the new understanding I had acquired through the inner awakening that had taken place in me by his grace.

In the beginning I would collect Baba's words by remembering whatever wonderful things appealed to me in his informal talks. Therefore, the collection of his words of that time was small, and chosen according to my own personal interest and liking. Whenever I went for Baba's darshan, I would pick up whatever scattered gems of his words I could gather during the satsang.

From 1961 I got the privilege of being in Baba's presence all the time. The number of intellectual visitors who wished to understand the spiritual truths through words also increased. As a result, spiritual conversations began to take place in the form of questions and answers between Baba and the seekers. From these impromptu talks I would remember and later record whatever I found interesting, inspiring and enlightening. But when I saw that the treasure of his wisdom was limitless, I became more greedy and began to sit with pen and paper to take notes. I would write down as much as I could catch from the conversation. There was no tape recorder at that time. Even though in the beginning these conversations were occasional, as time passed my notebooks started filling up. On weekends the devotees would take them home to read and would experience great joy by drinking in Baba's nectar-like words. Seeing their delight, I would wish that such satsangs would occur more often so that they could be published in the form of a book. Baba knew my unexpressed desire and fulfilled it. As the satsangs became more frequent, he took the opportunity to talk at length. The drops of nectar became an ocean.

The monthly journal called *Sai Suman* began to publish them. Later the readers requested that these conversations be made available in the form of a book. As a result the book *Paramartha Katha Prasang* in Gujarati, containing Baba's spiritual conversations of the years 1962 to 1966, was published in 1972 as Part I. Later it was translated and puplished in Hindi. This book is its English translation.

The saint poet Bhartrihari has said :

परिचरितव्याः सन्तो यद्यपि कथयन्ति ते न उपदेशम् ।
यास्तेषां स्वैरकथाः ता एव भवन्ति शास्त्राणि ॥

(Even though saints do not give direct teachings, one should attend upon them, because their casual talks become scriptures).

This book of spiritual conversations is one such scripture, containing the spiritual truths revealed by Baba whenever the occasion presented itself. They are the words flowing out from a great saint's own experience. These words are Chitshakti's self-inspired mantra. They present a true perception of reality, and a guide on the path to liberation. For one who is open, this book is the revealer of spiritual mysteries; for one who is awake, it is a divine eye, and for one who is eager for Self-realization, it brings the contentment of fulfillment.

It is said, "There is no knowledge without the Guru." This is absolutely true. There is a great deal of teaching in the scriptures, but without a Guru study of the scriptures bears hardly any fruit. It becomes dry and boring. Saint Nishchaladas has said :

वेद-उदधि बिन-गुरु ळागै लौन-समान ।
बादर गुरु-मुख द्वार है अमृतसे अधिकान ॥

(Without the Guru the ocean of Vedas tastes like salt. But when the same water is showered through the cloud of Guru's mouth, it becomes sweeter than nectar).

The dry knowledge of the scriptures can at most inflate the ego, but it cannot impart the experience of inner satisfaction and peace. The state of the highest knowledge is so sublime and mysterious that it is difficult to reach it without the guidance of the Guru. It is said :

वेदान्तानामनेकत्वात् संशयानां बहुत्वतः ।
वेद्यस्याप्यतिसूक्ष्मत्वाञ्च जानाति गुरुं विना ॥

(Because Vedanta is manifold and doubts are many, and what is to be known is very subtle, without the Guru one cannot understand it).

In the short span of human life the quickest and the easiest means of attaining the spiritual goal is through the Guru. In order to acquire this knowledge from the Guru the *Bhagavad Gita* tells us :

तद्विद्धि प्रणिपातेन परिप्रश्नेन सेवया ।
उपदेक्ष्यन्ति ते ज्ञानं ज्ञानिनस्तत्त्वदर्शिनः ॥

(Learn that by humble reverence, by inquiry and by service. The men of wisdom who have seen the truth will instruct you in knowledge).

Baba Muktananda has not established any new sect or religion. He preaches only the eternal spiritual truths expounded by the great saints and enshrined in the scriptures. Thus one finds in his talks many quotations from the writings of the saints and the scriptures. However, the spiritual conversations in this book reveal his experience of the Upanishadic knowledge, his grasp of the deep mysteries of yoga, his earnest interest in the philosophy of Kashmir Shaivism, and his immense reverence for great saints like Sri Jnaneshwar Maharaj, Sant Tukaram, Sundardasji and others. Here there is no show of scholarship, but only the light of universal truth. Baba inspires everyone to realize the divine consciousness which is within themselves. He teaches that one's true religion is the actual experience of the Self; that it is the religion of the Self, or "Selfism." In this context, he has written about his own experiences in his spiritual auto-biography *Chitshaktivilas.*

All kinds of people come to Baba. Some are seekers, while others simply come out of curiosity. Some are thirsty for knowledge, while others are in search of a true Guru. Some, being tormented by the sufferings of the world, are pining for mental peace, while others want to know how to solve the problems which arise in their spiritual disciplines. Some seek advice on wordly problems, while others want guidance in their personal life. Baba satisfies everyone with answers which are always clear and to the point.

Baba's answers to people's questions are always inspired. He always gives an apt answer, and in his answers, given in the most natural and informal style, one sees his frankness, his insight into the needs of the questioner, and his knack of making a person understand the point through direct or indirect suggestions appro-priate for the occasion. Most of the questioners' problems are usually the same. Therefore, in conversations with them, the repetition of certain topics is unavoidable. Baba speaks often about the means to still the mind, about the harmony between the worldly and the spiritual, about idol worship, the significance of the 'dos' and 'don'ts' pres-cribed by the scrpitures, about recognition of a true Guru, about the qualities necessary for receiving the Guru's grace, and so on. One will find many discussions on Baba's favourite topics—the waking, dream, deep sleep, and turiya states of an individual; the unity of Jnana, Bhakti, and Yoga; the oneness of God with form and without form; the need for a Guru; true renunciation; the importance of chanting; the secret of a mantra; the technique of meditation; and so on. Yet each time he reiterates these subjects, his way of explaining the point is so unique that the readers will not find the repetitions irksome. Instead, just as one strikes a pole with a hammer to dig it into the ground, Baba's repetition acts as hammer blows which help truth penetrate into the reader's mind.

Sometimes one may find differences and contradictions in the answers given to similar questions asked by different persons at different times. But here one must keep in mind that these answers were given in a particular context and according to the need of the questioner at that time. For example, if a seeker was involved only in dry knowledge, Baba would impress upon him the greatness of the yoga of meditation. If someone was mad after yoga-siddhis, Baba would explain to him the importance of knowledge. To someone too attached to worldly things, Baba would sing the praises of renunciation. To one whose renunciation was without discrimination, Baba would explain that one can attain God even while living in the world. If a person was entangled in the worship of God only with form, Baba would lead him towards the attributeless and the formless. If a person was opposed to God with form, Baba would tell him to see the Absolute even in an idol. If a person was self-willed, caught up in his own false ideas, Baba would advise him to accept the authority of the scriptures. If a person was enslaved by old traditions and completely stuck in religious texts, Baba would urge him to perceive the Truth which is beyond all religions. To an inert Jnani, Baba would explain the dynamism of Vedanta. To one caught too much in wordly affairs, Baba would teach withdrawal from activity. Thus, Baba is more interested in the questioner than his question. He penetrates to the seeker's heart and mind. Each person is on a different level of understanding and a different state of spiritual transformation. So Baba meets each seeker on his own ground and answers appropriately. If at that time it is necessary to give him a long and loving explanation, he will do that; if a scolding is necessary he will do that; and if it is necessary to strike with harsh words, he will do even that in order to drive his point deep into the heart. In order to make clear the context in which each of these conversations took place, a brief introduction of the questioner has been given before each dialogue.

Through these talks, a general reader will get to know the true meaning of many topics. He will come to understand the theory of reincarnation, miracles, the real meaning of *yogabhrashta*, the nature of Guruseva, the saints' and sages' way of behaving, their mission and their deeds, the process of Shaktipat, and much more.

These spiritual conversations are the words of our Guru. It is not enough to say they are true and beautiful. One who wishes to turn towards God, who wants to attain something on the spiritual path, who truly desires supreme peace, should not only read this book but also contemplate it. He should absorb these teachings and act accordingly. Only then will this *Guruvani* (words of the Guru) take him across the ocean of worldly existence. In it is the Guru's divine message. It is *Gurugita*. Since Sri Guru is the embodiment of pure Consciousness, Shiva, his *vani* (word) is the power of that Consciousness. Thus the Guruvani is priceless. It is said :

एकमप्यक्षरं यस्तु गुरुः शिष्ये निवेदयेत् ।
पृथिव्यां नास्ति तद् द्रव्यं यद् दत्वा त्वनृणी भवेत् ॥

(There is no wealth on earth by which the disciple can repay his debt to the Guru for even one word of the knowledge received from him).

With folded hands, we pray to our Gurudev to speak more because his nectar-like words are never enough; we thirst for more and more, like Arjuna, who requests Lord Krishna :

भूयः कथय तृप्तिर्हि शृण्वतो नास्ति मेऽमृतम् ।

(Tell me more. I am never satiated with hearing your nectar-like words).

SWAMI PRAJNANANDA (AMMA)

Bhagawan Nityananda

Swami Muktananda

Saturday, November 24, 1962

For the past few evenings Baba has been sitting on the platform around the bilva tree in the ashram garden surrounded by devotees who came for his *darshan*. A beautiful statute of Nataraj presented by a Parsi yogi, Mr. Boman Behramjee, adorns the platform. Currently *satsangs* take place at this spot, which is very enchanting in the evening. This evening a devotee asked the following question :

THE SCRIPTURES ARE THE FORM OF GOD

Devotee: *Is it proper to consider the scriptures authoritative?*

Baba: God and the scriptures are interwoven. To doubt the scriptures is to doubt God. To help you understand this, I will relate a true incident I once read.

In North India there lived a brahmin who was a great devotee of Lord Krishna. He had deep faith in the *Bhagavad Gita,* which he studied and recited constantly. Since he had no time for any other occupation, his money dwindled to nothing. Money is like water in a pot. As you go on using it, less and less remains. Finally the poor man was reduced to such poverty that he and his family were forced to fast for three days, since he could not even receive alms from the town.

On the third day when the brahmin was reading the *Gita* as usual in a secluded place, he came across the

1

following verse in the ninth chapter: 'तेषां नित्याभियुक्तानां योगक्षेमं वहाम्यहम्' "I take up the burden of the well-being of my devotees who are always immersed in me." At this point he stopped abruptly. He began to doubt the truth of these words so he underlined them in red ink. He thought, "God promises He will take care of His devotees, but I have had no food for three days despite my long-lasting devotion. Why is this?"

While the brahmin was thinking in this manner, a handsome boy approached his wife with some food and told her to prepare a meal. His wife liked the boy so much that she invited him to stay and eat with them and she asked him to call her husband from the secluded place where he was reading the *Gita*. The boy went out and told the brahmin that his wife was calling him home for a meal.

The boy had a bleeding scratch on his arm. Pointing to it, the brahmin asked him, "What is this?" The boy replied, "It is the scratch from the line you made in the *Gita*." Overcome with remorse, the brahmin fainted and by the time he revived, the boy had vanished.

As this story strikingly illustrates, the *Gita* is God's body. It is in fact God. For this reason, the holy books used for daily chanting are worshipped and adored with sandalwood paste, *kum-kum* and flowers along with incense and lights. Only when holy books are regarded with such reverence does the knowledge contained in them bear fruit.

Sunday, November 25, 1962

Since it was Sunday many devotees were gathered at the ashram. Among them was Mr. J. L. Nain, a well-known barrister, the legal advisor to Shree Gurudev Ashram and a keen student of yoga. He asked Baba the following question :

LIVE MANTRA

Nain: *Baba, when does a mantra become alive?*

Baba: A mantra is always alive, never dead, since it is the very form of God. "Mantra is my own form, O beautiful one," Lord Shiva said to Parvati. The name and the named are identical. The *ra* and *ma* are, in fact, Sri Rama. To say that the mantra has become alive is like saying that God has become alive. God was never dead. The real question is why mantras don't bear fruit even after they are repeated for a long time. The mantra which doesn't bear fruit can be called a "dead" mantra. A "live" mantra is one which has borne fruit for the one who gives it. To give a mantra to others when one has not benefited from it oneself is just an empty ritual. It benefits neither the one who gives it nor the one who receives it. How can one who has had no experience give any experience to others ?

Those mantras by which the great sages and seers achieved tremendous power and attained Guruhood can be called live mantras or Siddha mantras. That mantra which awakens the inner consciousness, bestowing immediate results, is a live mantra.

Thursday, November 29, 1962

This afternoon Baba went to Kalyan to lay the foundation stone for the factory of Pepchemi Corporation Ltd. From there he went to Santa Cruz at 5.30 p.m., where many devotees were waiting for his *darshan* at the home

of Mr. Yogendra Trivedi. Devotees continued to arrive
throughout the evening. At 9 p.m. Mr. J. L. Nain,
barrister, lovingly invited Baba to his house in Bandra.
After being received there, Baba was asked several
questions by Mr. Nain.

NADA—BINDU—KALA

Nain: *What is meant by* nada, bindu *and* kala?
Baba: After receiving the grace bestowed by the
Guru, the seeker hears the inner sound during his
spiritual practice. This is *nada*. In the beginning the
sound is loud, but as the seeker concentrates on it, it
gradually diminishes and finally subsides altogether.
Afterwards a Blue Pearl is seen which is actually
located inside the eye even though it appears to be outside. This is *bindu*. As meditation progresses this
Blue Pearl bursts and the play of consciousness becomes
manifest. This is *kala*, which grants the experience of
realization.

THE LIFE SPAN OF A YOGI

Nain: *Can a yogi prolong his life span?*
Baba: A Siddha yogi can prolong or shorten his life
span, but for what purpose? What is the use of
experiencing the impurities of the body, which is full
of waste matter and disease? After realization of the
ultimate knowledge, the yogi might wish to give up his
body, but it is sustained by destiny and people derive
benefit from it.

Swami Ram Tirtha has called the human body a
"shit-producing factory." Composed of the five
elements, it is by nature full of impurities. The
Upanishads and *Ayurveda* describe the body in similar
terms. What sort of yogi would strive to sustain such
a body?

True happiness lies in becoming free from body-consciousness. Worldly life exists in the mind. Why would a person who has achieved the state of mind-free bliss choose to remain in the mind-enshrowded worldly state?

Siddha yogis continue living in the world only by the force of destiny. They have fully united their own will with God's universal will. The yogi who prolongs his life span beyond its destiny is indulging in "black marketeering."

Friday, November 30, 1962

Baba stayed in Bombay for two days and many devotees came for *satsang*. At this time a noteworthy answer was given to a question asked by Prajna, a graduate in philosophy and the wife of Mr. Yogendrabhai's younger brother Niranjan.

UNITY IN DIVERSITY

Prajna: *How does a realized being who experiences oneness everywhere manage to live in the world, which is full of diversity?*
Baba: In order to understand the realized being's experience of unity in diversity and diversity in unity, you should read Saint Jnaneshwar's commentary on the following verse from the fourth chapter of the *Gita*:

कर्मण्यकर्म यः पश्येदकर्मणि च कर्म यः ।
स बुद्धिमान्मनुष्येषु स युक्तः कृत्स्नकर्मकृत् ॥ ४। १८ ॥

"The *jnani* is one who sees inaction in action and action in inaction."

This subject is not easily comprehended, nor is it really a topic for discussion. It can only be understood through experience. For practical purposes, however,

the analogy of the body and its parts would be appropriate for our understanding. A person experiences his
body as one, inseparable unit, but each part has a
separate function. We don't eat with our feet or walk
on our hands. We wear shoes on our feet and put a
hat on our head. In the same way, the *jnani* (realized
being) sees oneness everywhere, but treats things
differently for the sake of practicality. Receiving a nice
hat or a pair of shoes, he would put the hat on his head,
not on his feet; the shoes would go on his feet, not on
his head. The *Gita* says that everything is the same
in the eyes of the *jnani*:

विद्याविनयसम्पन्ने ब्राह्मणे गवि हस्तिनि
शुनि चैव श्वपाके च पण्डिताः समदर्शिनः ॥ ५।१८ ॥

"The *jnanis* look upon a learned brahmin, a cow,
an elephant, a dog, or an untouchable with equal
vision." (5/18)

In spite of this perception of oneness, however, a
jnani would not receive a dog with the same deference
and respect shown to a brahmin. This is the *jnani's*
practice of diversity in unity.

Let us take another example. The *jnani* perceives the unity of the One in the apparent diversity
of the world in the same way as a mother sees no
difference between her sons and her grandsons and
considers them all her own. The *jnani* perceives
chaitanya (divine consciousness) everywhere through
his vision of the Self (*atma drishti*). Such *jnanis* are
not affected by individuality just as the sun does
not become wet when reflected in water. *Jnanis* see the
world, perform all actions, and have all sense experiences, but remain stable and unaffected within. Although
the world is not different from God, He has created it
of His own free will with many forms. Sri Krishna
says in the *Gita*, '**मद्भावा मानसा जाताः ।**' "The world

is created by my will."

The divine is one and indivisible, but diversities are created so that the world will function in a disciplined manner.

The *jnani* sees the world just as God has created it. He perceives its fundamental unity but acts in accordance with its diversity.

Saturday, December 1, 1962

This morning, returning to Ganeshpuri from Santa Cruz, Baba visited Dr. Dhirubhai Daftari, whom he once promised to visit on all return trips from Bombay. The doctor and his wife, Kanta, are deeply interested in spirituality. They are avid students of Vedanta and have great respect for *sadhus* and saints.

SHAKTIPAT GIVES RISE TO KNOWLEDGE

Dr. Daftari: *I believe that* shaktipat *calms the wayward tendencies of the mind, but that it does not give rise to knowledge.*
Baba: That is not so. While the mental tendencies become calm through *shaktipat,* a thought-free state of mind is experienced from which knowledge—pure understanding—shines forth spontaneously. When darkness is destroyed light automatically appears. One does not have to proclaim that the light will come; it is experienced. If the chimney of a lamp is covered with soot, the light inside is not clearly visible, but as one cleans the chimney, the light spreads by itself; nothing else needs to be done. It is the same with *shaktipat.*

In the evening a group of devotees came for *darshan.* One of them asked Baba a question.

WORTHINESS TO RECEIVE GURU'S GRACE

Devotee: *How do we know whether we are worthy to receive the Guru's grace or not?*

Baba: Are you not part of God? If you are sure of this, then you are as pure as God. Everyone has the right to realize God. Surrender just once to the Guru and see what happens. Let him do what he considers appropriate. He will take care of everything. In fact, the receiving of grace is in your hands. In the *Gita* it is said, '**ये यथा मां प्रपद्यन्ते तां तथैव भजाम्यहम्**' "I welcome people according to the feeling with which they surrender to me."

Monday, December 3, 1962

Divali Vrajlal Shah from Vile Parle has been staying at the ashram for the past three days with her family. She is a Jain and a keen seeker of dhyana yoga. She often has discussions with Baba.

GOOD AND BAD DEEDS OF SIDDHA SAINTS

Divali: *Do Siddha saints also have good and bad deeds?*

Baba: Those who are liberated, having become one with the Supreme Reality, are not affected by good or bad deeds, which are like drops of water on a lotus leaf for them. There are no do's or dont's for a Siddha; therefore, there are no good or bad actions for him.

Virtues and sins are experienced in a particular state. Just as the summer heat is intensely felt in Ganeshpuri but hardly at all in Ootacamand or Simla because of their higher elevation, similarly, there is a state in which the effects of actions are experienced. The Siddhas have risen much above that state to where virtues and sins don't exist.

Existence of sin is like a drop of water before the ocean of greatness of a liberated being. Just as a drop of filthy water is transformed into pure holy water after falling into the rapidly flowing Ganges, in the same way, for saints established in the Ultimate Reality, sins become virtues. If it were not so, how could a bandit become the great saint Valmiki by being with Narada ? How could the robber Naoroji become a good man after being with Chaitanya Mahaprabhu ? And how could the murderer Angulimal become a monk under Buddha's influence ? Isn't it change of sin to virtue ?

Even if Siddhas appear to be bound by pleasure and pain resulting from good and bad deeds, such pleasure and pain do not really affect them. Their liberated state never changes. In summer they experience the coolness of Ootacamand. Even though they themselves are beyond both, they praise good actions and condemn bad ones.

THE EXISTENCE OF GHOSTS AND SPIRITS

Divali: *Are there such things as ghosts and spirits?*
Baba: They don't have an independent existence like humans, animals, and birds. Those who have unfulfilled desires and meet untimely deaths become ghosts. Ghosts are not necessarily bad; and in any case, there is no reason to fear them since no one can ever harm a pure-hearted person.

The intermediate period between death and rebirth is long for some and short for others. Only a few fortunate ones are immediately reborn.

Monday, January 1, 1963

Lalbuva has lived in Ganeshpuri for the past few years and has recited the *Bhagavad Gita* daily at the *samadhi* shrine of Bhagawan Nityananda. He is known as Lalbuva, meaning "the red *sadhu*," because of his red clothes. For the past twenty days he has read the *Gita* daily at the ashram, sitting on the platform around the bilva tree. Today Baba also sat there.

VISION OF UNITY

Lalbuva: *I know the entire* Gita *by heart. I once knew its meaning as well, but now I have completely forgotten it.*

Baba: How much more do you want to know? In the *Gita,* the Lord says, 'विष्टभ्याहमिदं कृत्स्नमेकांशेन स्थितो जगत्' "I pervade the whole world with merely a fraction of my being." To know this much is enough. Whatever we see, sentient or insentient, is God's form. All our troubles arise because we see diversity in the world and are conscious of different names and forms.

A devotee had a gold statue of the deity Khandoba sitting on a horse. Unfortunately, he became so poor that he was on the verge of starvation. Someone advised him to sell the statue of Khandoba so he took it to a goldsmith who offered him 300 rupees for the deity and 700 rupees for the horse. The devotee was enraged because the value of God was less than that of the horse. The goldsmith knew no difference between the deity and the horse. To him, both were only gold. For the devotee, the deity and the horse were different. So if you acquire the vision of the goldsmith, all your troubles will end.

Tuesday, January 22, 1963

Today *satsang* was again held on the platform around the bilva tree.

THERE IS NO DISPARITY IN GOD'S CREATION

Devotee: *Why do we see so much disparity in God's creation?*

Baba: The way God is running the world is perfect. There is no mistake anywhere. I will give an example to explain this. One day a man was sitting under a berry tree smoking a pipe. Looking up at the tree, he thought, "Well, God does not seem to have much sense. Why has he given such a small fruit to this big tree and such a big fruit to that small, tender creeper bearing pumpkins? What disparity in God's creation!" After a little while, a berry fell on his head and then he came ot his senses: He exlaimed, "Oh God, no, it is not like that! You have made the world perfect! If you had given this tree a huge fruit, my head would have been crushed!"

Wednesday, January 23, 1963

Several devotees were assembled around the bilva tree platform this evening. One of the old residents of Ganeshpuri, Mr. Mardekar, and the panditji from Goregaon were among them.

THE LAW OF KARMA

Mardekar: *Tomorrow is my wife's operation. I am worried.*

Baba: Everyone has to go through the consequences of his karma. Therefore, perform good actions and live

through pleasure and pain resulting from past deeds.
All days are not the same. Bad days will continue to follow good days and good days will follow bad ones. When
an excess of sin is accumulated, we are born as animals
or birds; whereas, when good deeds predominate, we
become gods. We are born as human beings when
good and bad deeds are equal. Even gods have to take
a human birth to undergo the results of their remaining
karmas. The *Gita* says, ' क्षीणे पुण्ये मर्त्यलोकं विशन्ति '
"When their good deeds are exhausted, the gods return
to the mortal world."

One attains God-realization when all one's good
and bad *karmas* are exhausted. I will tell you a story
which illustrates this.

Once a great soul named Haridas, who was devoted
to Lord Vitthal, lived in a certain city. This was to
be his last birth. One day a devotee invited Haridas to
his home for a few days. The devotee's wife became
lustful towards the saint and urged him to sleep with
her. Haridas replied that it was against the tenets of
the scriptures to make love to a woman whose husband
was alive. Hearing this, the wife went out and killed
her husband. She returned to Haridas and said to him,
"I no longer have a husband." The saint was flabber-
gasted and shouted, "What have you done? What do
you think I am?" The woman became very angry.
Wailing and lamenting loudly, she gathered a big
crowd and accused Haridas of murdering her husband.
The case reached the court and Haridas was found
guilty. The judge did not have the heart to execute
such a saintly person. Since the murder had been committed with his hands, the judge punished Haridas by
having his arms cut off below the elbows and then
released him.

The saint continued worshipping God and

eventually Lord Vitthal appeared before him and told him to ask for a boon. Haridas said, "After having seen you, what else could I possibly desire? However, I request you to clear one doubt for me. Why was I punished by having my arms cut off even though I had done nothing wrong in my life?" The Lord replied, "Your hands were cut off. That is why you have attained me. One's destiny has to be lived out."

In order to satisfy him, the Lord showed Haridas his past life in which he was an austere yogi. One morning while he was worshipping the sun, a cow passed by. Soon afterwards a butcher ran up to him asking which way the cow had gone. "In that direction," he replied, pointing out the way with both his hands. The butcher found the cow and killed her. Then the Lord explained that in this life the cow had become the woman, the butcher, her husband and the yogi had become Haridas. The wife murdered the husband and Haridas' forearms were cut off.

God-realization is only possible after fully going through the fruits of one's past *karmas*. It is said:

अवश्यमेव भोक्तव्यं कृतं कर्म शुभाशुभम् ।
ना भुक्तं क्षीयते कर्म कल्पकोटिशतैरपि ॥

"The fruits of all the good and bad deeds performed in the past must be lived through, for the fruit of *karma* will never be destroyed in any other way even after an eternity of time."

Thursday, January 24, 1963

Jayantilal Kadakia and Lalit Sanghavi came from Secunderabad for Baba's *darshan*.

THE IMPORTANCE OF PATIENCE IN SADHANA

Lalit: *An astrologer told me that after fifteen years I would reach a certain level of spiritual attainment, but wouldn't fifteen years of my life be wasted in this way?*
Baba: Whatever has to happen according to *karma* will happen. One does not become a father the moment he is born. He must grow up, get married and then have children before he can be called a father. In the same way, one achieves results on the spiritual path at the right time. The aspirant should continue his practice with faith and patience.

Once upon a time two yogis were doing *sadhana* under a neem tree. One day Narada happened to pass by and they asked him what his destination was. Narada replied that he was going to Lord Vishnu. Both of them then requested Narada to ask the Lord how soon they would attain Self-realization. On his return journey, Narada gave each one a message from the Lord. One of the yogis was told that he would achieve his goal after 12 years. That is what the Lord had said. Hearing this, he immediately became disheartened, gave up his *sadhana* and went away. As a result, his *sadhana* remained incomplete and he gained nothing from it. The other aspirant was told that the Lord had said that he would gain Self-realization after as many lifetimes as there were leaves on the neem tree. Upon hearing this, he began to dance joyfully, knowing that he would surely attain his goal no matter how many lives it would take. This aspirant continued his *sadhana*. As a result, he speedily went through the various types of short and long births, and eventually realized the Self. Patience and contentment are essential on the spiritual path.

Mr. Albert Rudolph from New York has come to Ganeshpuri for about a week on his yearly visit for Baba's *darshan.* He has practised yoga for many years and has experienced the awakening of the Kundalini. In America he guides many people on the spiritual path.

JNANAMUDRA

Rudolph: *I have been feeling a tremendous surge of energy since I visited you here last September. The Shakti flows through both of my hands into the tips of my fingers and even seems to flow out through my fingertips. My right hand is automatically raised up in* abhaya mudra, *and I feel as though Shakti is flowing out of my palm. Is this all right?*

Baba: As far as possible, Shakti should not be allowed to flow out of the body. When such sensations are felt in the hand, the first finger should be joined with the thumb in *jnana mudra.* Conserve your energy so that it may become more powerful and you can perform great tasks through it.

Rudolph: *In America many people come to me with all kinds of problems and questions. They claim to experience peace just by sitting near me. Sometimes my Shakti flows into them, curing their diseases. Is it all right to allow the Shakti to flow into others in this way? Afterwards many times I feel tired and my body aches. Sometimes this condition lasts throughout the entire day, but after a while I feel healthy and fresh again.*

Baba: There is nothing wrong with this. Service done selflessly without desire is not wasted. The Shakti will be restored with meditation. If there is self-interest, it will be depleted.

SEAT OF THE GURU

Rudolph: *Sometimes I feel a sensation like a strong vibration between my eyebrows. I feel as though I have two eyes in my forehead from which something is*

coming out with a hissing sound. What could this be?
Baba: Between the eyebrows there is a two-petalled
lotus, the seat of the Guru. Progress beyond this point
depends entirely on the grace of the Guru. The sensations you experience are caused by the Kundalini Shakti,
which is trying to move upwards from this point.
Through concentration on the region of the two-petalled
lotus, we can know anything we desire in the world, but
it should be kept a secret as far as possible. With
increased meditation on this spot, one is inspired with
noble thoughts. A thumb-sized light is situated here
above which is a thousand-petalled lotus of brilliant
light where Shiva and Shakti become united.

Rudolph: *People who come to me have various kinds
of experiences concerning me. Sometimes they see
light, fire, etc., in place of my physical form. One person
claims that I talked to him at his home, but I know nothing about it. Sometimes when sitting in the company
of others, I have strange experiences. The breath or
prana suddenly goes up into the head resulting in deep
meditation. At other times, even while sitting on the
ground, I feel as though I am floating high in the air.*

Baba: Whatever is happening is good. Others have
experiences concerning you because the Shakti which
has passed into them from you is working in them. You
need not know about these experiences.

Rudolph: *Since I still have many impurities, I don't
like people to hold me in high esteem.*

Baba: The Self is ever pure. Since it never becomes
impure, you are pure.

Rudolph: *So you really believe that? Some of the
people who come to me seem like animals. I see besti-
ality even in the young people.*

Baba: The Self is supremely pure. What you are
seeing are their old *samskaras* and mental attitudes.

When taking leave, Rudolph again asked Baba some questions.

Rudolph: *What kind of* sadhana *should I do from now on?*
Baba: Nothing particular. Just keep meditating.
Rudolph: *I don't sit for meditation regularly. When I suddenly feel an urge, I wish to sit down calmly.*
Baba: That is all right.
Rudolph: *When will I attain perfection?*
Baba: Let the Shakti work in its own way. Everything will happen at the right time.
Rudolph: *I had a premonition when I was young that two of my disciples would become very great and world famous.*
Baba: You continue doing your duty and *sadhana;* leave the rest, the fruits, to God. Let everything happen according to His will. He will do whatever He wishes.
Rudolph: *I request your blessings for my mother and brother.*
Baba: Blessings are there, of course.

Saturday, January 26, 1963

Today the Managing Director of M/S. Mahindra and Mahindra Ltd., Mr. Harish Mahindra, came for Baba's *darshan* and *satsang*.

RECOGNITION OF ONE'S TRUE SELF

Harish: *Will I be able to make progress on the spiritual path?*
Baba: Every human being is a part of God. How can he ever change? There is no difference between God

and man. Just as mangoes alone grow on mango trees, similarly, only God is created from God. But because man, due to ignorance, has forgotten his real nature, he thinks that he is an individual being, imperfect and different from God.

In our scriptures we have a *pratyabhijnanyaya* the essence of which I will explain by telling a story.

Once a king accompanied by his young son went hunting in a forest where he saw a beautiful deer. Leaving his son under a tree, he pursued the deer for quite a long distance. After a while some tribesmen who were passing through the forest saw the young prince crying under the tree and they took him home with them, assuming that he was lost. When the king returned from hunting, his son was nowhere to be found. He went home and sent search parties in all directions, but there was no sign of the child.

After several years the king's prime minister was attending to court business and came upon the tribesmen's dwelling place. There he saw a young boy who appeared quite different from the other boys. Reminded of the lost prince, the prime minister asked him who he was. The boy replied that he was the son of a tribesman. The prime minister then asked the tribesmen about the boy, but they knew nothing except that they had found him several years ago under a tree in the forest and had brought him home. Hearing this, the prime minister was convinced that the boy was the lost prince and he took him to the palace.

Even after the boy was told that he was a prince, he still considered himself a tribesman because of his deep mental impressions of having been with tribesmen for many years. The prime minister dressed him in beautiful, princely clothes and made him view himself in a large mirror saying, "Look, this is what you really are."

Seeing his real identity, the boy's illusion vanished and he was convinced that he was really a prince. This understanding removed his former feelings of lowliness and he began to behave like a real prince.

In the same way, if we become aware of our true Self, we will realize that we are really God and all sense of imperfection will be eliminated. Man has the right to attain his Godhood and, therefore, should not despair. Keep trying, have no doubts and seek the company of saints. It is the duty of every saint to make you realize your real Self just as the prime minister helped the prince to realize his true identity.

Sunday, January 27, 1963

Mr. Dwarka Khosla, a devotee, came today for Baba's *darshan* accompanied by an elderly seeker who has lived in the Aurobindo Ashram in Pondicherry for 14 years.

ONE ENTITY PERVADES EVERYWHERE

Seeker: *Swamiji, I see Aurobindo Ghosh in you.*
Baba: Your devotion to Aurobindo Ghosh has made this whole world appear like him to you. One sees as one really feels. Aurobindo is everywhere.
Seeker: *No, not in everything. I see Aurobindo only in you.*
Baba: God is everywhere. All the different forms in the world are made of God. Just as the same artist paints different pictures of a cow, a tiger, a man and a monkey on the same canvas with the same colours and the same brush, so also this diverse and varied world is made of only one element. Only the forms are different; the substance is the same.

Mr. Yogendra Trivedi, a trustee of Shree Gurudev Ashram, and his friend, Mr. K. K. Shah, the Secretary of the All India Congress Committee, came today for Baba's *darshan*. Mr. Shah, who is a good seeker, has great love for the *Bhagavad Gita*.

K. K. Shah: *We have begun experimenting with prana-yama along with other treatments in our hospital near the Sabarkantha District in Gujarat. I believe the practice of pranayama could cure patients since prana is the most important aspect of the human body. Please give us three or four persons who will teach pranayama to the patients.*
Baba : All right.

THE SUPREME SHAKTI SUPPORTS ALL

K. K. Shah: *When the child is in the mother's womb, it receives nourishment, but does not discharge any waste matter. Breathing starts and the bowels move when the umbilical cord is cut after birth. Swamiji, who protects the child when it is in the mother's womb?*
Baba: Only one Shakti permeates the whole world, which exists only with its support. This Shakti creates, sustains, and destroys the world. It also protects the child in the womb. This energy is also called Chit Shakti or Kundalini Shakti, and is located at the base of the spine in the muladhara chakra in all human beings. When it is awakened one becomes aware of one's true Self.

This entire universe is the manifestation of Brahman. Brahman pervades everywhere and is the sole element constituting all the apparently contradictory attributes visible to us. Fire is hot and water is cool, but the coolness and the heat consist of the same element which is animate as well as inanimate. For example, the same potter makes many different pots out of the same clay on the same wheel. Likewise, this world, though having things with different names, appearances and forms, has emerged from the same Chaitanya Shakti, an energy having the power to create the many out of the one and to absorb the many back into the one.

K. K. Shah: *Man cannot comprehend this because he tries to understand it with his limited intellect.*

Baba: Very true. Man makes himself something and believes himself to be that. He learns engineering and believes himself to be an engineer; he studies law and calls himself a lawyer. Man forgets his original Self and believes he is someone whom he has created in his own mind.

Sunday, February 3, 1963

Some people from Aurangabad who had heard about Baba from the well-known Dr. A. N. Christian came for Baba's *darshan*. One of them, a doctor, began talking with Baba.

THE POWER OF WORDS

Doctor: *This lady sitting here does not keep well. No medicine has had any effect on the pain in her legs.*

Baba: Remembrance of God's name combines all medicines. It is the medicine of medicines. The power of the word is so great that the entire universe was created from it. The word, or sound, exploded and became ether, the vibrations of which created air. Friction in the air created fire. The vapour of fire became water

and the sediment in water became the earth. To cure
a disease is mere play for the mighty word that has
the power to create the world.

Doctor: *Is the power of God's name so great that it can
relieve man of all diseases and worries?*

Baba: I will relate an incident which illustrates what
power words have.

A man who had received his higher education
abroad went to a saint to discuss with him how mantra
repetition could be beneficial. The saint ignored him
and refused to talk. He lost patience and was about
to speak when the saint shouted, "Shut up, you ass!"
Enraged, the man was on the verge of exploding when
the saint said, "Now can you see the power of words?
If a bad word could cause such a violent reaction in you,
then what effect, what transformation, would God's
holy name produce?" Hearing this, the man fell at the
saint's feet.

Tuesday, February 26, 1963

Swami Vijnanananda (formerly P. R. Bhide) a journa-
list, is making an independent study of the various aspects
of yoga. He took *sannyas* on his own, calling it *"samadhi
sannyas,"* and assumed his new name. He recently came
to Vajreshwari to practise yoga and has come today for
Baba's *darshan*.

THREE KINDS OF SAMADHI

Swami Vijnananda: *No one has yet understood the
Supreme Truth.*

Baba: Everyone speaks according to his experience.
Each person's words are the reflection of his own experience. I have heard that you took *"samadhi sannyas."*

What kind of *sannyas* or *samadhi* is that?   According to the commonly understood meaning, I know only about three types of *samadhi*.   One *samadhi* is that which is built over the burial site of a saint as a memorial.   Another *samadhi* is the state of inertness in which yogis sit for hours. The third *samadhi* is the state of the Self in which one is not affected by any circumstances and remains in a state of equanimity.   This is also called *sahaj samadhi*.

(The swami did not answer Baba's question. Instead, he said:)

Swami: *I had many doubts before I started on this path.*
Baba: According to Vedanta, doubt is merely a tendency of the mind.   Doubts arise and subside, but the state of the Self always remains the same.

You must stay here in Ganeshpuri.   People would be happy to see two *sannyasis* instead of just one.
Swami: *I want to reach that state which you have attained.*
Baba: There is no such thing as attainment or non-attainment.   The one who seeks liberation is already liberated.   The Self has no bondage or liberation.   The divine Shakti is infinite.

DIVINE ENERGY IS INFINITE

Swami: *One's Shakti is depleted by giving Shakti to others and cannot be regained.   Therefore, we should not give away too much Shakti; otherwise, all of it will be irretrievably lost.   Is this true?*
Baba: When the river merges into the ocean, it becomes the ocean, giving up its separate individuality.   In the same way, how can a person's Shakti be depleted when he becomes one with the Absolute Reality, the infinite

source of Shakti? If a man who has earned a hundred
rupees keeps spending one rupee here and one rupee
there, his earnings will soon be used up, but the man
with inexhaustible wealth need not worry. Divine
wealth, divine Shakti, can never be depleted.

Saturday, March 2, 1963

Mr. V. S. Page, chairman of the Maharashtra State
Legislative Council, is a great scholar. He has made a deep
study of the *tantras* and *agamas* of Shaivism, and has assimi-
lated *Jnaneshwari*, understanding that they are both one.
Even amidst worldly affairs he lives like a true renunciate.
He comes very often for *satsang* with Baba.

Page: *When does one attain the ultimate stage on the
spiritual path?*
Baba: That stage will surely come in its own time just
as when counting, 1 is followed by 2, and 2 is followed
by 3 and so on until 100 is reached.

TRUE BLISS IS NOT RELATIVE

Page: *Some years ago I had the experience of absolute
bliss, but it has never returned despite many years of*
sadhana. *I have had many other experiences, but I always return to my initial state.*
Baba: Your present state in which you do not experience anything is higher than the experience you had.
What you experienced before was mere happiness, not
true bliss because you are now unhappy in its absence.
It means that that joy was relative. Happiness and
pain are relative, but the experience of ultimate bliss
(*satchidananda*) is unrelated and spontaneous. The

thought-free state is the true attainment. Even after attaining that state, thoughts arise, but they do not affect the fundamental state attained. The completely still state and the state with vibrations come and go. They are also known as *niramaya* and *samaya* states. In fact, if the state of stillness remains undisturbed for too long, it could prove to be a problem as in the case of Upasani Maharaj of Nasik. When his mind suddenly became still while eating, he would hold a morsel of food in his hand and remain in that state for two or three days at a time. If the state of stillness is attained even for a moment, it is sufficient. One need not remain in that state for hours.

THOUGHT-FREE STATE THROUGH SHAKTIPAT

Page: *Where should one's attention be concentrated until the thought-free state is achieved?*
Baba: One should concentrate wherever the thoughts automatically settle down: at the top of the head (*sahasrara*), heart (*hridaya*), or between the eyebrows (*ajna chakra*). The effect of *shaktipat* is like an injection of medicine that spreads automatically throughout the body. The energy transmitted by the Guru works within the seeker without any effort on his part, enabling him to attain the thought-free state. One who tries to still his mind through knowledge has to practise for a long time with constant vigilance. This is not easy, but it becomes easy after *shaktipat* is received from the Guru.
Page: *Sometimes I feel that my breathing has stopped.*
Baba: It is going on within in the *sushumna*. Yogis end their lives in the *sushumna*. The *prana* of a yogi does not go out in the ordinary manner at the time of death, but merges inside in the *sushumna*.

Baba visited Manjusar, a town near Baroda, to attend
a *yajna* called "Naukundi Vishnuyajna" at the abode of a
saint, Sri Girija-shankar Mugatramji. From there he
went to Ahmedabad where he stayed at the home of Mr.
Harsiddhashah, the grandson of the famous mill owner, Mr.
Narsinhlal. Among the many devotees who came for
darshan was Mrs. Shantagauri, the wife of the late collector, Mr. Chimanlal Kavi.

WOMEN'S RIGHT TO CHANT GAYATRI MANTRA

Shantagauri: *Is it true that women do not have the*
right to chant either om *or the Gayatri mantra?*
Baba: Who says so?
Shantagauri: *The head of our* sannyas *ashram.*
Baba: He speaks according to his interpretation of the
scriptures. But I ask you on the basis of the truth
whether Gayatri itself is female or male? Gayatri is
called *devi* (goddess). If you as a woman are jealous
of her, then don't utter her name! If women are not
allowed to repeat *om,* what about the repetition of *om*
that goes on constantly within in rhythm with your
breathing? Can anyone stop it?

MEDITATION

Shantagauri: *How should one meditate?*
Baba: Many methods of meditation are described in the
scriptures; however, the meditation that comes spontaneously through the Guru's grace is the best and
easiest. When the Sadguru bestows his grace on the
disciple, he transmits his own Shakti into him and
awakens his inner Shakti, Kundalini. With this, meditation comes spontaneously. This spiritual process of
awakening the Kundalini Shakti is called *shaktipat.* One

who has this ability to give *shaktipat* is a Guru in the true sense.

Monday, March 25, 1963

The following *satsang* took place when Baba stayed in Bombay for a few days.

DISCRIMINATION BETWEEN SPIRITUALITY AND WORLDLY LIFE

Devotee: *I cannot maintain a proper balance between the spiritual path and worldly life. What should I do?*
Baba: If a person who earns just enough for his daily bread by breaking stones and sweating suddenly comes across a diamond, should he go on breaking stones? It is appropriate to give up the ordinary after gaining the extraordinary. But don't think that I am advising you to give up the world. Do both with discrimination. People nowadays want God on the one hand and on the other, they want their businesses to be successful, their children to study properly, their health to remain perfect as well as their households and cars to run without any complications. Man should use discrimination if he wants to maintain a good balance between spiritual pursuit and worldly affairs.

Wednesday, March 27, 1963

Today in Juhu, Baba visited the home of a devotee, Shri Manilal Modi, proprietor of Gujarat Type Foundry. His son Ramendra asked Baba the following question:

REMEMBRANCE OF GOD AND FREEDOM FROM DEBT

Ramendra: *We do not have peace of mind even though we do our actions truthfully. If we are harrassed by others through no fault of our own, by what means can we keep the mind calm?*

Baba: This is known as undergoing the consequences of past actions and owing of debt. I like a person who repays the debt while remembering God. I call him a wise person.

Another Devotee: *But* karma *is inert.*

Baba: You speak merely from your reading of books. Do you know the truth? This whole world is made of one divine energy called Chiti Shakti, which is conscious. The whole world is also conscious. How can anything be inert in it?

Sunday, March 31, 1963

Today Shri Dhamankar, a long-time active Congress worker, arrived unexpectedly. He had the following conversation with Baba:

THE DETACHMENT OF AN AVADHOOT

Dhamankar: *I once asked Nityananda Baba what would happen to all the things associated with him after his death. It would be better if some arrangement for the future were made. Nityananda Baba simply replied, "All is dust."*

Baba: This is very true. He would always give the same answer. He was on the level of God. When the whole world belonged to him, then how could he have the feeling of "mine" for a small piece of land? Such great saints who are *avadhoots* are completely detached from mundane affairs.

The first meeting of the Managing Council of the ashram Trust since its formation was held today. On this occasion Baba spoke the following words :

Baba: Today the ashram Truth completes one year of its existence. It is gratifying to note that everything is running in a well-organised manner. The Charity Commissioner, Mr. Godse, has said that from the point of view of discipline, our ashram Trust is maintaining a very high standard and he has expressed the hope that it will continue to do so in the future.

THE AIM OF THE ASHRAM

God's creation is also governed by certain laws. The sun and the moon rise and set at their appointed times. We have winter, summer and the monsoon in accordance with the cycle of the seasons. If someone wishes to have another sun, or summer during the winter season, it is just not possible.

This ashram is also a part of God. Just as nobody can meddle with the laws of God's creation, likewise, nobody can disrupt the discipline of the ashram. I request the workers here to keep in view the ideal of 'परस्पर देवो भव' (*paraspara devo bhav*) and consider one another as manifestations of God Himself. If a person is incapable of doing any work, let him do none, but he should not create obstacles for others.

The aim of this ashram is to impart spiritual knowledge to sincere seekers. One cannot be completely happy through the accumulation of external knowledge. At some point in life one has to turn toward spiritual knowledge and take refuge at the feet of a Guru.

The tradition of saints has existed since time immemorial and will continue forever. This world has seen many changes and will witness many more, but

the proclamation of the saints regarding Truth will
survive as long as the sun and the moon remain in the
heavens. Falsehood may undergo change, but Truth
is eternal. Nobody can destroy the tradition of the
saints or their institutions, which are part of God.
Since God is indestructible, they too, can never be destroyed. Radhakrishnan, on the occasion of the Silver
Jubilee of the Bhartiya Vidya Bhavan in Bombay,
repeated the same Truth that spiritual knowledge is the
greatest of all knowledge. One gains this knowledge
from a Self-realized Sadguru through *gurubhakti*,
through Guru's grace. This knowledge is universal;
it knows no bounds and is, therefore, indestructible.

Tuesday, April 2, 1963

Three Sindhi women from Pune have come to stay
in Ganeshpuri for a few days. This morning they had
satsang with Baba.

WORSHIP GOD IN ANY NAME AND FORM

A Woman: *In which form should I remember the
Supreme Lord? If the Supreme Lord is one, then we
should remember Him only in one form.*
Baba: The Supreme Reality is one and yet manifests in
various forms. You can remember the Lord in any
form that you like.
Woman: *But the* Bhagavad Gita *says that God manifests as light.*

दिवि सूर्यसहस्रस्य भवेद्युगपदुत्थिता ।
यदि भाः सदृशी सा स्याद्भासस्तस्य महात्मनः ॥ ११।१२ ॥

"If the radiance of a thousand suns were to blaze out at
once in the sky, even that would not be like the splen-

dour of that Great Being." (11/12)

Baba: God is present everywhere. You may pray to Him in any form that appeals to you. If you were to consider this box as God and worship it, you would attain the same thing as by worshipping a stone idol of God. The main point is that you must remember God constantly.

Woman: *How can I know God?*

Baba: You will know Him only when He becomes pleased with you and reveals Himself to you.

Woman: *But when is He pleased?*

Baba: God is certainly pleased by your pure devotion. Remember Him constantly; chant His name all the time. You don't know about yourself, but He knows you. Leave it to Him and have faith in Him. We cannot bargain with God as we do in our worldly life. God may be pleased with one seeker who has chanted His name only seven times while He may not be pleased with another even after he has done *japa* of God's name seven million times.

Woman: *Which name of God should I repeat and how?*

Baba: You can repeat that name of God which appeals to you the most and you can chant it in any manner that is convenient for you. It is said that Valmiki was liberated even by repeating "Mara-Mara" (meaning killed-killed) instead of "Rama-Rama."

Woman: *Is it not contradictory to do* japa *and yet say "You are my mother; you are my father?"*

Baba: Do you think that praying to God saying, "You are my mother and father," is different from doing *japa* of His name or from constant remembrance of Him?

(A discussion followed in which references to the scriptures were made.)

Baba: You are discussing the scriptures through your

mental cleverness and are thus trapped by your own
cleverness. What is your ultimate goal? When you
go to the market in Pune, you don't buy all the vegetables that are available, but just those that you want.
All grains and vegetables contain nourishing substances.
Puri, bread, chapati, rice, pulses, grains—whatever you select will give you nourishment as well as
satisfaction. Similarly, the scriptures are very numerous:
*Vedas, Upanishads, Puranas, Yoga Shastras, Sankhya
Philosophy,* etc. Various methods of spiritual *sadhana*
are described in these, but your life is short so you
choose the *sadhana* that appeals to you and start doing
that. The end result of all the methods is one and the
same.

Friday, April 5, 1963

Divaliben of Vile Parle came daily for *satsang* with
Baba during his five-day stay in Santa Cruz.

Divaliben: *At one time a Jain saint who lived in Abu
was greatly respected. Wealthy people from distant
places used to visit him. He had such powers that whatever he said would come true, but after a while, he
lost his power and then the very same devotees who had
previously revered him began to slight him. What
could have caused the loss of his powers?*
Baba: During a certain period of one's *sadhana* one can
know everything; whatever one wants to know will
reveal itself. As one progresses a stage is reached in
which no thoughts or impulses arise. This stage is
higher than attainment of powers; nothing can be
known in this stage. The Jain saint at Abu used to
show off to others whatever intuitions he had and that

is why he had all that trouble. The intuitions stopped and therefore he also stopped talking about them. This does not mean he had regressed on his path.

Divaliben: *Why do the scriptures say that one should not eat tubers and that one should not eat at night?*

Baba: There is always some hidden meaning in what the scriptures say. Tubers contain a lot of sugar. At night at meal time, insects are attracted by the light. But, in any case, how far can a seeker progress even after observing all these rules?

When I was staying at Kasara Ghat, five or six Jain women *sannyasis* came to stay on the ground floor of the house. The head of the group was afflicted by a ghost. If a person cannot cure himself of an affliction caused by a wicked person's black magic, what is the use of observing rules such as whether something should or should not be done and in what manner, or whether a certain food should or should not be eaten. What kind of *tapasya* (penance) can it be that is incapable of expelling a ghost? And what sort of *tapaswini* (ascetic) is one who can be possessed by a ghost?

WITNESS CONSCIOUSNESS

Divaliben: *Kindly help me that I may remain in meditation for a longer time and that my mind may always remain calm.*

Baba: During meditation the mind may alternate between peacefulness and agitation. The Self witnesses both of these patterns of mind, but has nothing to do with either of them. The Self is not affected by anything; it is only a witness. The Self always remains in the same state without undergoing any change and that is your true nature. Remain steady in That.

Divaliben: *After attaining liberation, what is one's rela-*

tionship with the body?
Baba: After liberation, the body becomes an obstacle
rather than a help. Because everything can be known
without using the senses, the body becomes purpose-
less. When it is not necessary to hear through the ears,
what is the use of the sense of hearing? When it is not
necessary to see through the eyes, what is the use of the
sense of seeing?

Monday, May 20, 1963

Shri Anandji of the Govindji Bharmal Company has
come for a few days and is staying at the holiday camp.
He came today for *satsang* with Baba.

SERVICE TO THE GURU

Anandjibhai: *The* Bhagavad Gita *states that we can attain knowledge by doing* pranam, *by asking questions
and by serving realized beings. What is the meaning
of service here?*
Baba: It means that you should regard the lives of the
saints and the great beings as an example and behave
accordingly. Whatever work you can do for the Guru
while staying with him is service to him. Through such
service a disciple's sins are washed away and he becomes
worthy to receive the knowledge of Brahman. One
must be worthy to gain the knowledge of Brahman and
this worthiness is acquired by service to the Guru. But
in serving, one must also have an intense desire for liberation without which even service to the Guru will not
bear fruit. Many people did personal service to my
Gurudev, Nityananda, for many years, but what they
gained spiritually is best known only to themselves! A

householder saint does not give the knowledge of Brahman even to his own son if he is not worthy of it. Shvetaketu had to go to another Guru even though his own father, Uddalaka, was a knower of Brahman. Liberation is not cheap. That knowledge which leads to the state of desirelessness, free from pain, in which only permanent bliss exists, is obtained by doing service to the Guru. In order to obtain it, you must be worthy of it.

Through service to the Guru, his knowledge is attracted toward the disciple and flows into him automatically. For this reason the *Gita* says, 'तद्विद्धि प्रणिपातेन परिप्रश्नेन सेवया।' "Know It by *pranam, Satsang* and service." The meaning of service is 'करिष्ये वचनं तव।' "I shall do Thy bidding." If your Gurudev tells you to go to Benares and you go to Mecca instead, this will bring your downfall. You will not gain knowledge by asking the Guru what he has studied or what he has achieved. You will gain it only by one-pointed service to him.

THE TIME OF DEATH IS PREDETERMINED

Anandjibhai: *My doctors are advising me to undergo an operation, but I am afraid.*

Baba: Man does not die again and again; he dies only once. Death will come at its own fixed time so you need not be afraid. If the time for a man's death has not come, he cannot die even if someone should try to kill him, but he will certainly die when his time comes.

In the same village from where you come there lived a man named Shiva Pengde against whom there were forty lawsuits pending in the court. Even after a long twelve-year search, the government officials could not catch him and finally they gave up their efforts.

Eventually, he even reformed himself. He gave large sums of money in charity and built many temples and ashrams. He changed so much that the government even awarded him a title.

Shiva Pengde's mother had been a widow from childhood, but during her widowhood she became pregnant. Owing to the birth of Shiva under such circumstances, his mother dug a pit in which she buried him alive. At that very time the owner of the land happened to come there and heard a baby's cry inside the earth. He had it dug up and found the baby there. He then searched for and found the child's mother and told her to take care of it. The point of the story is that until a man's time of death has arrived, he cannot die. So do not be frightened. Go ahead with the operation.

Tuesday, May 21, 1963

Today Satchidananda, a *sannyasi* from Parle Sannyas Ashram, came to have *satsang* with Baba. Baba talked to him about *shaktipat* and about the futility of reading too many books.

KNOWLEDGE IS GAINED FROM WITHIN

Swami Satchidananda: (Presenting a book to Baba) *The author of this book is very learned and has written several books in Sanskrit.*
Baba: The books that saints and great beings wrote were inspired by their inner divine energy; for example Jnaneshwar's commentary on the *Bhagavad Gita* known as *Jnaneshwari* and Tukaram's *abhangas*.

It is not my intention to criticise learning or the

reading of books. What I want to convey is that when the same Shakti which made them write is awakened within us, all that is written is understood without effort. If the knowledge that you seek in these books can be obtained from within your Self, then you won't have to look for it outside. That knowledge and that bliss are lying within us. We are a part of God; therefore, what is in God is in us, too. It can be experienced only when the inner Shakti is awakened, and the awakening of this Shakti depends upon the grace of the Sadguru.

Thursday, June 6, 1963

During Baba's seven-day stay in Santa Cruz, *satsangs* were held.

A REALIZED BEING IS BEYOND VIRTUE OR SIN, ACCEPTANCE OR REJECTION

Divaliben: *Just as one has to reap the fruits of one's bad actions, one must also have to reap the fruits of one's good actions. In that case, isn't a realized being bound by his meritorius actions?*
Baba: Good actions with a motive are certainly binding. Good deeds done with a desire to gain merit are motivated. After God realization, the results of a realized being's good actions are enjoyed by others. He may distribute sweets or clothes, he may perform *yajnas,* he may go on pilgrimages, or he may do worship of God; the fruits of all these actions are enjoyed by others. Those who eat what he gives, those who wear the clothes, those who develop faith in God through him, those who gain knowledge through him—it is they who enjoy the fruits of his good actions.

Once a Jain saint blessed someone saying, "Go, you will win." As a result, many people were killed. Do you think that the one who gave the blessing will bear the consequences? If a saint collects funds to build a temple or a dormitory, will he himself get the fruits of these good deeds?

Divaliben: *Saints receive many offerings such as fruit, flowers, clothes, money, etc. What is the use of all these things to a realized being since he has renounced everything?*

Baba: What you say is due to lack of personal experience. Nothing binds a *jnani*. It is because the viewers are attached that they see duality between attachment and detachment. This is called misunderstanding the scriptures. Just as misunderstandings arise in mundane affairs, they also occur with regard to the scriptures. Seeing a snake in a rope is a practical illusion. Similarly, understanding just the opposite or not the real meaning of the scriptures is also an illusion.

The renunciation mentioned in the scriptures refers to a seeker's renunciation during the period of his *sadhana*. This is advised to save the seeker from obstacles and to develop detachment. For a Siddha, however, who has reached the ultimate goal of Self-realization, there is nothing to reject or accept. One who has to practise renunciation gives up his house, his possessions, his relatives, friends, everything. The reason is that he has to get rid of "I" and "mine," that is, ego. Even then, he still has to live in someone's house or under some roof; he has to retain some essential articles for daily use, and he maintains contact with some people, if not with his own relatives. He who desires liberation should destroy his ego through the attitude "all this is not mine."

In the eighteenth chapter of the *Bhagavad Gita* it is said, '**यस्य नाहंकृतो भावो बुद्धिर्यस्य न लिप्यते.**' The meaning of this verse is: What will he renounce who has completely annihilated his ego and attained true discrimination? Renunciation is possible only when the idea of mine-ness exists.

If a pot is filled with water, it can reflect the sun, moon and stars, but if the water is removed, there can be no reflection. It is a peculiarity of the mind that external objects of the world continually create images in the mind; or, in other words, thoughts of worldly objects continuously arise in the mind. These give rise to likes and dislikes, which stimulate the senses. As a result, man experiences pain and pleasure. But if a man's mind is completely dissolved, the outside objects cannot be reflected in it. Hence, for a man of realization, there is neither acceptance nor rejection. His life proceeds according to his destiny. I advise you to give up such useless thoughts. If you go on thinking excessively, your mind will become dull and disturbed, and you will not be capable of grasping the Truth.

Tuesday, July 9, 1963

Today a *sannyasi* named Swami Madhavananda came to the ashram.

KNOW VEDANTA FROM YOUR OWN EXPERIENCE

Swami Madhavananda: *At our ashram we are teaching Vedanta to the students.*
Baba: The Vedantic knowledge that is being taught in ashrams nowadays is like the academic knowledge of a college professor. Someone taught him something and

he repeated it to others. Vedanta states that there are
two things, the seer and the seen, and of these, the seer
is real and the seen is unreal. Thus from my point of
view, I am the seer, you are the seen so I am real and
you are unreal. But from your point of view, you are
the seer, I am the seen so I who was previously real have
now become unreal. Now, which of these viewpoints is
correct? The kind of Vedanta which is being learned
from books is like this while in the Vedanta of one's
experience everything is Brahman. The seer himself
appears as the seen.

A Devotee: *What is the difference between a* jnani *and
a* karma *yogi?*

Baba: The *jnani* acts considering the world as an
illusion while the karma yogi acts considering it real.
From the spiritual point of view, both are the same.

Sunday, August 11, 1963

This morning several devotees gathered in the ashram
hall for *satsang.* Among them were Mr. Nain, a barrister,
and his wife, Rukmini.

Nain: *Recently I have been reading* Ashtavakra Gita
and while reading it, I am reminded of Nirvanashatakam
of Shri Shankaracharya.

Baba: The *Ashtavakra Gita* is even greater than
Nirvanashatakam. In the scriptures, two methods of
contemplation are described: *vyatireka* and *anvaya.* "I
am not this, I am not that" is the *vyatireka* method,
which is described in *Nirvanashatakam.* When this
thought is firmly established, a stage arrives where
nothing remains of which you can say, "I am not this."
On the contrary, you begin to experience that you are

everything and everywhere, and you contemplate accordingly. This is the *anvaya* which is described in *Ashtavakra Gita*. *Sadachar* of Shri Shankaracharya and *Amritanubhava* of Jnaneshwar also describe this method of *jnana* sadhana. Another saint sang:

इस अखिल विश्व में भरा एक तू ही तू।

तुझमें–मुझमें ‘तू’, मैं–तू ‘तू’, तू ही तू ॥ १ ॥
नभ में तू, जल-थल, वायु, अतल में भी तू।

मेघध्वनि, दामिनि, वृष्टि, प्रलय में भी तू ॥ २ ॥
सागर अथाह, सरिता-प्रवाह में भी तू।

शशि-शीतलता दिनकर-प्रदाह में भी तू ॥ ३ ॥
तू पाप–पुण्य-में, नरक-स्वर्ग में भी तू।

पशु-पक्षी, सुरासुर, मनुजवर्ग में भी तू ॥ ४ ॥
है मिट्टी-लौह, पाषाण-स्वर्ण में भी तू।

चतुराश्रम में तू, चतुर्वर्ण में भी तू ॥ ५ ॥
है धनी-रंक, ज्ञानी-अज्ञानी में तू।

है निरभिमानी में अति अभिमानी में तू ॥ ६ ॥
ह शत्रु-मित्र में, बाहर-घर में तू।

है ऊपर, नीचे, मध्य, चराचर में तू ॥ ७ ॥
‘हाँ’ में ‘ना’ में तू, ‘तू’ में, ‘मैं’ में तू।

है तू-तू-तू-तू-तू-तू, बस! तू ही तू ॥ ८ ॥

This entire world is filled
By you and you alone;
You are in you;
You are in me;
You are you
And I am also you.
You are in the sky;
You are in the water and in the earth;
You are in the air
And also beneath the earth.
In the thundering of the clouds
And in the lightning,

In the showers of rain
And in the Pralaya—
What exists is only you.
In the infinite expanse of the sea
And in the flow of the river,
In the cooling moonlight
And in the sun's scorching heat—
What exists is only you.
In the virtues and in the sins,
In hell and in heaven,
In the beasts and in the birds,
In the gods and in the demons
And in all human beings—
What exists is only you.
In the earth and in iron,
In the stone and in gold,
In the four ashramas
And in the four varnas—
What exists is only you.
In the rich and in the poor,
In the wise and in the ignorant,
In the most humble
And in the proudest of all—
What exists is only you.
In the friend and in the foe,
Inside and outside of the house,
Above, below and in the middle,
In the animate and in the inanimate—
What exists is only you.
You are in yes;
You are in no;
You are in you;
You are in me;
Everywhere it is only you, you, you, **you,**
You, you and you.

Rukminiben: *Baba, what is the meaning of the word* yogabhrashta? *The* Bhagavad Gita *says,* शुचीनां श्रीमतां गेहे योगभ्रष्टोऽभिजायते (६/४१) *"a* yogabhrashta *takes birth in the family of wealthy and pious people." Is this true?*

Baba: The term *yogabhrashta* does not signify a man who has gone astray from his path of *sadhana*. If a seeker has reached the fourth or fifth stage of yoga while pursuing his *sadhana* and if his destiny requires that he leave his body before reaching the final stage of yoga, then he will be reborn in a pious and rich family, and will resume his yogic *sadhana* from the stage he had attained in his previous life. All knowledge comes to him from within spontaneously. He does not require a guru because he receives guidance from within, from his own Self. This is what is meant by *yogabhrashta*. Whether such a *yogabhrashta* seeker completes his *sadhana* with or without a Guru, his final achievement, the state of perfection he attains, will be the same. One student may obtain a master's degree in one university and transfer to another university for his Ph.D. Another student may do his entire course of study upto Ph.D. at a single university. Both will obtain the same degrees.

Nain: *Should the mind remain blank during meditation or should one see light?*

Baba: A seeker must progress beyond the lights that he sees during meditation. The experience of the bliss of the Self that springs up from within during meditation is the true light. It is the divine bliss that is signified by the word "light" in the saying, "The Self is full of light."

Tuesday, August 13, 1963

Today Shri Pratap Yande, a devotee of Baba, brought some of his friends for Baba's *darshan*.

SANYAM SIDDHI

Pratapbhai: *Two days ago I went to a friend's home. His Guru was there. He was able to materialise kumkum in a dish or a shower of flowers at will. I saw all of this with my own eyes.*

Baba: The kum-kum was already there in the dish, but because your vision was obstructed, you were unable to see it earlier. Many such varieties of magic are practised. In yoga there is a *siddhi* called *sanyam siddhi*. In order to obtain it, one must practise *tratak* (concentration on an object). One can bring forth anything by *sankalpa,* that is, just by wishing for it with a concentrated mind. Anyone can develop this ability after practising the technique for a certain period of time.

The *sanyam siddhi* is described in the *Vibhutipad* of Patanjali's *Yogadarshan* in which it is said that by practising *sanyam* on the moon, one may experience light; by doing *sanyam* on an elephant, one may acquire the elephant's strength; and by doing *sanyam* on the sun, one may obtain the sun's brightness. One may obtain the qualities of any object on which *sanyam* is practised. One can even know another's thoughts by doing *sanyam* on his mind.

Once when Swami Vivekananda was in Hyderabad, he met a man who possessed the *siddhi* of materialising whatever was requested. Swamiji asked him to demonstrate his *siddhi*. It so happened that the man had been suffering from a fever for many days and he asked Swamiji to place his hand on his head. As soon as Swamiji did so, the man's fever disappeared. Then, in

order to demonstrate his *siddhi,* the man told Swamiji
to ask for anything he wanted. Swamiji asked for
certain dishes that he had eaten in foreign countries
and which were prepared in those countries only. The
man immediately produced them and Swamiji even ate
some of the items just to satisfy himself. Swamiji
asked him about this performance and the man replied,
"What I have done is just fun; you have the real *siddhi.*"

It is possible to learn many such skills, but these
petty attainments do not lead to self-improvement; they
are simply a waste of Shakti. In Kasara, a man used
to materialise printed currency notes, but it was essential to use them immediately because the printing
would disappear after eight hours. In Borivli as well,
there was a man who could give thousands of rupees to
anyone who asked on the condition, however, that the
money be returned to him within a fixed period of
time, or else the magician would have to undergo great
trouble. In Chalisgaon there is one Nariyalbaba who
takes pieces of paper with written replies to one's
questions from the very same cocounts that one offers
to him.

Wednesday, September 11, 1963

During Baba's four-day stay at Santa Cruz, Shri
V. S. Page came for his *darshan.*

Page: *How is it possible for a realized person to describe
the state of perfection since it is beyond the grasp of the
intellect and, according to the scriptures, is attained
only by transcending the intellect? With what intellect,
then, can a realized being describe that state to us?*

Baba: If you were to descend into the depths of a well,. you would perceive a totally different world there. As long as you were there, you could not describe it to the people outside the well because you would have no means of communication. At that time the senses would not be in use and therefore no contact would be possible with the external world. After coming out of the well, you could certainly describe what you experienced there. The realized beings describe their experiences of that state of perfection in a similar manner.

Page: *The* Tantra Shastra *describes* shaktopaya, anavopaya, shambhavopaya *and* anupaya. *What is meant by* anupaya?

Baba: *Anupaya* is the *shaktipat* of Shiva.

Sunday, October 13, 1963

Today Anne Burian, a Canadian seeker, came to the ashram with Shri Sunil Damania, a devotee of Baba. After arriving in India, she changed her name to Savitri. For the past nine months she has been staying in the ashram of Swami Ramdas in Kanhangadh.

THE IMPORTANCE OF HAVING ONLY ONE GURU

Savitri: *In America I had a Mexican Guru. Because of his grace, I had a very exalted experience in which I completely lost body consciousness. I did sadhana while staying with him. For the past three years I have been in India and I have been meeting many saints and sages. Today, I have come here to obtain your grace.*

Baba: Why didn't you stay with the Mexican Guru?

Savitri: *He very much wished that I would, but I started feeling within that I should go to Tibet and so I left for India.*

Baba: Instead of going to many saints one after another, you should accept one great being as your Guru and practise your *sadhana* with him. This would be much better for you.

Savitri: *But this is not something within my control. God Himself takes me from one saint to another. My life is simply passing away in this manner. After taking me to a certain stage with one saint, God sends me to others in order to further my progress. I feel as though I have been born for a particular mission for which God is preparing me. For this reason I have no control over anything that is happening. I act as God directs me. When I was in Almora I saw Shri Ramakrishna Parama-hansa in my meditation and he told me, "Come home." So I left Almora and went to Calcutta.*

Baba: By remaining steadfastly with one Guru, his Shakti works constantly within us and takes us to perfection in due course.

Savitri: *Perhaps it may happen so when the time comes; perhaps God will make me do so. Once while medita-ting in Canada, I saw myself in India in front of a banyan tree. That was my first encounter with India. Since arriving here, however, I have not seen that banyan tree anywhere.*

Baba: It is an auspicious sign to see a banyan tree in meditation. It indicates that you will find your Guru. It is not necessary for you to actually see that banyan tree.

Savitri: *What sadhana should I do now? Please bestow your grace on me.*

Baba: The grace is there already. Remain steady in the *sahasrara;* remain intoxicated in bliss. Remember this ashram and come again whenever you can.

Shri Pranjivan Thakkar, a long time devotee, asked

Baba before leaving the ashram about the difficulties he
has been experiencing in his *sadhana*.

AGITATION OF THE MIND BEFORE IT BECOMES STILL

Thakkar: *For the past month my mind has been restless. I feel as if I have gone mad, I am frightened, I have
no desire to talk to anyone, nor am I interested in my
work at the office. I cannot sleep at night. For no reason,
all kinds of thoughts, good and bad, keep arising in my
mind.*

Baba: This is a state of the mind. Just before the mind
is about to become quiet, numerous thoughts arise.
When a whirlpool is moving very fast, it appears to be
motionless, but as its speed steadily decreases, it revolves
around a larger radius and hence appears to be increasing in speed. After moving in this manner for some
time, it suddenly comes to a halt. Similarly, when the
mind is moving very fast, it appears quiet, but as its
force starts decreasing, the mind appears to be more
agitated. Ultimately, it reaches a state of true stillness.
You need not be frightened. This stage will pass in due
course.

Thakkar: *Please continue to bestow your grace on me.*
Baba: Grace is already present; it is with you; it has not
gone anywhere. One more thing, you should try to
reduce your weight. Give up eating salt for some time.

Thursday, October 24, 1963

Swami Rameshwarananda, who has been practising
hatha yoga for the past eight years, has come to stay in
the ashram. He states that formerly he had several *siddhis*
such as the power to stop running trains, to materialise

any object just by his mere wish, to know the news before it appeared in the newspapers, to know about events that were to take place in the future and so forth. He also stayed for six months with Shri Vyasdevji (now known as Swami Yogeshwarananda) at Gangotri.

THE TRUE STATE OF LIBERATION

Swami Rameshwarananda: *I have been practising hatha yoga for the past eight or nine years, but for the last year or two, I have been feeling disturbed. How can I describe to you the wonderful powers I had in the past? Now I have lost them all.*

Baba: It seems that you are a good yogi and that you have practised hatha yoga quite thoroughly. Nothing has gone wrong and you have not lost anything. Everything is with you. Real Siddhahood is attained when one feels that one has lost everything. This is a stage just prior to becoming a real Siddha.

Now you should give up hatha yoga and sit with a quiet mind. The true supreme state is that in which nothing is being done and nothing is happening. Jnaneshwar Maharaj says:

स्तुति कांहीं न बोलणें । पूजा कांहीं न करणें ।
समिधीं कांहीं न होणें । तुझ्या ठायीं ॥

The real praise is to abide silently;
The real worship is to sit quitely.
The real *samadhi* is where nothing happens;
But remaining immersed in your own Self.

Haribhakta, a *brahmachari* from Katara, used to suffer from headache. It could not be relieved even after the application of several remedies. Someone advised him to come here and he came. He had attained a thought-free and immutable state. Still, he continued to do japa of the Gayatri mantra. This caused vibrations to arise even in his thought-free state. The resultant vibration of the subtle *nadis* in the *sahasrara* was causing his headache. I told him to stop doing *japa* and I kept him here for three days. His headache ceased immediately. Because I had given him such a simple remedy for his headache, he embraced me with overwhelming gratitude and joy.

Rameshwarananda: *I used to experience divine bliss during* sadhana. *I no longer have that experience.*
Baba: There is a state of supreme bliss even beyond the bliss of yoga. That for which you are meditating with effort, for which you are doing *sadhana,* is not in fact the supreme Self; but that which makes you meditate, that which makes you do *sadhana* is the supreme Self. The Kathopanishad says:

यन्मनसा न मनुते येनाहुर्मनो मतम् ।
तदेव ब्रह्म त्वं विद्धि नेदं यदिदमुपासते ॥

"That on which the mind cannot meditate, but which makes the mind meditate is verily Brahman. That which people worship is not Brahman."

Try to understand the real meaning of this. You did a particular *sadhana* and you think because of that you had an experience. It is not so. That from which you had the experience of bliss is the Supreme Self. That supreme bliss is not dependent upon anything.

When a seeker passes from one stage to the next, he may feel as though he has lost all his gains from the former stage, but everything is still there. For example, if I move from one bungalow to another and I do not find there the objects which were present in the previous bungalow, it doesn't mean that those objects have been destroyed.

Saturday, October 26, 1963

Rameshwarananda: *Vyasdevji used to sit in one place for a long time with a steady gaze which was not disturbed even if anyone would come or go.*
Baba: This is the stage of a seeker, not of a Siddha or a perfect being. A Siddha is one who does not get dislodged from the Self even if his vision wanders about everywhere. One who remains established steadfastly in the Self even while seeing, hearing, and smelling is the real Siddha.
Rameshwarananda: *Are there different stages of Kundalini awakening, or a* shaktipat.
Baba: No. There are three different degrees of *shaktipat,* which are *shambhavi* (mild), *mantri* (medium), and *anavi* (intense).
Rameshwarananda: *Is* shaktipat *a theme of the* Shaiva Tantra?
Baba: This science is not limited to any one book. It has descended from the Supreme Being through a lineage of Gurus.   The primordial Guru is Lord Shiva. Jnaneshwar Maharaj has said that he received this knowledge from Adinath, Matsyendranath, Goraknath, and Nivrittinath, in other words, through the Nath lineage.
Rameshwarananda: *What are* nada, bindu, *and* kala?
Baba: When the *prana* starts becoming steady, *nada,* or sound, is revealed and is heard through the ears. In *Amritanubhava,* Jnaneshwar Maharaj says that the *turiya* state is beyond *nada.* As one goes on meditating, one sees a blue spot. That is *bindu.* I can say without doubt that the great being who can describe this spot has realized God. The wise beings have described this spot in the minutest detail. The *kala* of Chiti shines in this very spot.

Today a Jewish gentleman named Samson, a retired
railway officer, came to the ashram. He has been waiting
a long time for the opportunity to speak with Baba.

TRUE REALIZATION

Samson: *I have been practising meditation for several
years, but have never had any visions of God, nor have
I attained* samadhi.

Baba: Meditation can be practised through self-effort,
but visions and *samadhi* are attained only through grace.
Visions, however, will only satisfy the eyes. Arjuna and
Lord Krishna were together for several years. Arjuna
had a constant vision of Krishna right in front of his
eyes and yet he did not have inner satisfaction or peace
of mind. This he had only when he heard the *Bhagavad Gita* from the mouth of Lord Krishna, that is, after
he had received knowledge. Similarly, Namdev used
to play and converse with Lord Vitthal, but he achieved
internal peace only after gaining knowledge from his
Guru, Visoba Kechar.

Rama, Krishna, and other avatars are incarnations
of God who come to this earth in human form in order
to fulfill a particular purpose. Having a vision of them
is not true realization. True realization is understanding their real nature. Having visions is not an attainment. The true vision is the experience of peace and
bliss in your heart. Achievement of the state of supreme bliss and peace is the real God-realization. Just as
the eyes enjoy form, the ears hear sound, and the nose
perceives smell, similarly, the heart experiences bliss.
To have visions, hear sounds or enter *samadhi* during
meditation is not the ultimate attainment. True attainment is to remain firmly established in the Self

under all circumstances. Do you practise *japa?*

Samson: *Yes, I do* japa *of so'ham. How should I proceed further?*

Baba: How do you do *japa?* Do you utter the mantra with your tongue or does it occur in the throat?

Samson: *I repeat it with my tongue.*

Baba: As you go on practising *japa* with the tongue, it will progress and start taking place in the throat. Then it is taking place in the subtle body. When it progresses to the heart, it is taking place in the causal body and when it progresses to the navel, it is said to be taking place in the supracausal body. As you go on chanting (*so'ham*), where your thoughts totally vanish, that is the abode of God. While doing *japa,* you should also experience its meaning. Keep in mind the idea, "I am That." Whatever *sadhana* you have done so far will not go to waste. Just as one has to undergo the results of bad deeds, one must also enjoy the fruits of good actions. Meeting with saints and visiting their sacred places are the fruits of that. Nothing has been wasted so you need not worry.

Saturday, November 2, 1963

This evening Shri Page and his family came to stay at the ashram for two days.

PRATEEK DARSHAN

Page: *While meditating, I often see myself in front of me. Many times I have felt myself to be separate from the body. What is the meaning of this?*

Baba: To see oneself in front of one is called *prateek darshan*. It is also called *drashtabhava*. You have reached the stage of witness consciousness. The attainment after this is not very far. The duration of the state of witness consciousness is only this much.

Saturday, December 28, 1963

Shri Pande, a college professor in Yeotmal and a representative of the *Times of India newspaper* came to the ashram today and had a discussion with Baba.

BHAGAWAN NITYANANDA WAS A DEVOTEE OF TRUTH

Pande: *To which sect did Swami Nityananda belong? Which religious order did he follow?*
Baba: He did not belong to any particular religious sect or order. He was a pure *advaitin,* that is, a believer in non-dualism.
Pande: *Which type of non-dualism did he believe in? Did he believe in the Vedanta of Shankaracharya or any other acharya?*
Baba: Non-dualism is only one. Bhagawan Nityananda was a pure Vedantin. He believed in the absolute Truth as propounded in the *Upanishads.* He did not believe in any particular Vedantic or Advaita philosophy or Shankaracharya, nor did he put forth any different path or school of philosophy. He worshipped supreme Truth and had attained perfect oneness with That.
Pande: *The Bhagavad Gita expounds four paths*: bhakti *or devotion;* jnana, *or knowledge;* karma, *or action; and* yoga. *Which of these did Swami Nityananda believe in?*
Baba: He believed in the *Gita.* He considered every word of it precious and invaluable. He did not believe in any one single path, but in all of them.

A devotee or seeker finds the path according to his own inclination and follows that path. None of these paths is wrong or imperfect, nor is one greater or lesser than the others. The *Gita* contains instruction for followers of all the paths. It is folly to consider even a single word used in the *Gita* to be wrong.

Pande: *Do you have any of Swami Nityananda's sayings?*

Baba: He always remained immersed in his own Self so when he did say something, who would be present and ready with a pencil and paper to take it down? Nevertheless, there is a book in the Kannada language called *Chidakasha Gita*. It is a compilation from memory of certain words and sentences that Nityananda Baba had spoken from time to time while staying in South India. This book cannot be considered his, nor did he wish to say anything new. A devotee once said to Nityananda Baba, "Give us some instruction." He replied, "What the poet saints Narada, Mira, Kabir, Tulsidas and others have said is just what I have said. It is not necessary for me to say any more."

Eknath Maharaj once had a desire to write a commentary on *Jnaneshwari,* but after reading it he realized that there was nothing more to be written about it. Ultimately, he wrote only the following verse:

ज्ञानेश्वरी पाठीं । जो ओवी करिल म-हाठीं ।
तेणे अमृताचे ताटीं । जाण नरोटी ठेविली ॥

If after Jnaneshwar, anyone tries
to write more on the *Gita,*
It will be like dressing a dish full of nectar with
pieces of coconut shell.

Swami Nityananda had no intention to establish a new sect. Just as in Sanskrit literature there is no poet greater than Kalidas, similarly, there is nothing

greater than the knowledge of Truth contained in the
Upanishads. How beautifully Radhakrishnan has
written about it in his book *Indian Philosophy!* Who
can write better than this? What can be greater than
that Truth?

Pande: *Yes. Radhakrishnan has not written anything
of his own. There is nothing original in it. He has
merely rewritten what is contained in the* Upanishads.

Baba: Anyone who has studied the scriptures thoroughly
will not write anything new. Only a person with one-
sided understanding starts a new sect. What is absolute
Truth existed in the past, the same exists in the present
and the same will remain in the future. The absolute
Truth never changes.

Pande: *Nowadays corruption, misconduct, etc., are prevalent all over the world. How can these be eliminated?*

Baba: Didn't much viciousness and injustice exist in
this world in the past? Ravana, Kansa, Shakuni, Man-
thara and Putana were here in earlier times. Even
righteous kings had to fight wars and respectable women
were abducted. Dushasan tried to strip Draupadi of her
clothes in the royal court. Disharmony is the very
nature of the world. It will continue. On the contrary, some people say that the present days are better
than the olden times and perhaps people are more
humane now.

Pande: *How can the world develop?*

Baba: The world is already developed. To attempt to
develop it is like developing what is already developed.
How beautiful the old buildings are! In the past, earthen
dams were made in such a way that the present-
day concrete dams cannot match them. Wasn't that
development? This world is described in the scriptures
as the universal manifested form of God. Whatever
is happening in this world today is merely a process of

transformation, which appears to us as progress. Developing what is already developed is like trying to attain that which is already attained. The same elements keep manifesting in the world in different forms and we view it as development.

Pande: *How can one attain God while living one's day-to-day life? Is it possible to enjoy material and spiritual gains at the same time?*

Baba: It is not necessary to give up this world in order to attain God-realization. One must attain it while living in this world. One must be kind and charitable. One must have a pure mind and act humanely toward others. One must not abandon truth. The truth is dear to all whether knowingly or unknowingly. For example, if a person is engaged in black marketeering, he would never proclaim it, but if he serves meals to brahmins in Benares, he would make it known to everyone. Therefore, acquire divine wealth.

Thursday, January 9, 1964

Shri Sanjay Kumar, a columnist for a Delhi newspaper, came to the ashram today. He had a discussion with Baba and asked him some questions.

RELIGION AND POLITICS

Sanjay Kumar: *Corruption is prevalent in our country. Our leaders give lots of speeches, but their words do not seem to have any effect. The public, however, is very much influenced by saints and sages. Can't they do something to remove corruption?*

Baba: In the Vedas it is said that only he who himself obeys can command others. He who has something in himself can reform others. If one has character himself, only then can he build the character of others. If one who is not detached himself tries to teach detachment to others, it will have no effect. It is the nature of this world to change. Rise and fall necessarily take place. If you perceive that society is now downfallen, progress and betterment are bound to follow. The *Bhagavad Gita* says that whenever unrighteousness prevails in the world, God will incarnate to destroy it and reestablish righteousness.

THERE IS A GOD

Sanjay Kumar: *The real saints and* sannyasis *leave society and go into isolation for meditation on the Self. The masses, therefore, do not benefit from them. Those who are* sannyasis *in name only and live among people appear to be characterless. Why is it so?*

Baba: Despite their leaving society, these saints keep working only for the world. Swami Nityananda, for example, settled down in this jungle. He had given up everything. He had nothing except a loincloth. Most of the time he remained silent, uttering only two or three words after every five or six hours. In spite of this, thousands of people visited him and obtained peace and happiness, and experienced satisfaction and contentment in their lives. The happiness and bliss for which man endlessly strives and engages in innumerable activities such as setting up factories, running about and toiling the whole day could be had easily and naturally from Swami Nityananda. Seeing him, one felt that there is God, and this made many people turn towards religion. Even rogues and scoundrels used to bow down before him. Thousands of his photographs have been sold. In homes and in shops people worship his image, offering flowers and incense, and pause for a while to pray and remember God. You must have seen photographs of Swamiji in many shops and hotels. Isn't all this his work? Did people come to him in such large numbers for no reason? There are saints and *sannyasis* of all types. Some live in isolation while some live among people. Not all saints living amidst people are impostors.

Sanjay Kumar: *The basis of our culture is its religious tradition. In the past all of life's activities were guided by religious principles, but today religion and politics are divorced. What is your opinion about this? Is it good for the country?*

Baba: Under the present political system the seeming progress is merely an outward appearance. There is no basic achievement. Take Russia, for example. Stalin was considered to be great during his lifetime, but after his death even his body was dug up and discarded. In ancient times, the sages conceived the system of government while nowadays politicians do it. Formerly, rulers were farsighted while today only expediency prevails everywhere.

As the king, so the people. If a nation's leader does not believe in God, neither will the people. Why does all this happen? In the *Bhagavad Gita*, Arjuna asked Lord Krishna the same question:

अथ केन प्रयुक्तोऽयं पापं चरति पूरुषः ।
अनिच्छन्नपि वार्ष्णेय बलादिव नियोजितः ॥ ३ । ३६ ॥

"O Varshneya! In spite of having no desire to perform bad actions, what is it that impels man to do so as if being forced?" (3/36)

Lord Krishna answered:

काम एष क्रोध एष रजोगुणसमुद्भवः ।
महाशनो महापाप्मा विद्ध्येनमिह वैरिणम् ॥ ३ । ३७ ॥

"Desires and anger arise out of rajoguna, which is never satisfied. This is the great sinner. Know this to be the greatest enemy in this world." (3/37)

TRUE PEACE COMES FROM TURNING WITHIN

Sanjay Kumar: *Many seekers are practising meditation in your ashram. How does this benefit society?*

Baba: Man's every action has as its aim the attainment of happiness, peace and satisfaction. Happiness and peace can be obtained only by controlling the mind. When the mind that wanders amidst external objects turns inward, man experiences the happiness and bliss so dear to everyone. Having worked all day, the tired man yearns for a sound night's sleep. During sleep, the mind becomes quiet and is refreshed and rejuvenated. Thus it is proven that the mind wants rest.

Seekers living in the company of a saint who has really attained the inner bliss and peace of the Self spontaneously turn inward and experience that bliss as well. It is said that on entering the ashram of Lord Buddha all one's thoughts would subside. Peace can be achieved only by abandoing all thoughts.

Sanjay Kumar: *Yes, but the entire society cannot come here.*

Baba: Whether the desire for inner bliss arises or not is an individual matter. One who has developed discrimination will certainly try to achieve that peace. It isn't possible for every individual of the society to have such discrimination. This discrimination is the supreme means to achieve peace and bliss.

Sanjay Kumar: *Just as Swami Nityananda gave you perfection and placed you here, have you prepared any-one to maintain the tradition?*

Baba: Someone will definitely get ready. Whoever is fortunate will attain it. Just as one player passes on his art, knowledge and skill to another player, a potmaker to another potmaker, a doctor to another doctor, a teacher to his student, similarly, a yogi prepares another yogi.

TRUTH IS BEYOND ALL SECTS

Sanjay Kumar: *There are photographs of saints of various sects in your ashram and you have met some of them. When meeting these saints of different sects did you encounter any feelings of hostility?*
Baba: As long as a man is bound by a particular sect, there is a possibility of feeling hostile toward other sects, but for one who has gone beyond all sects, such feelings do not arise in his mind. Sect means fence. When a plant is small, it requires a fence for its protection, but after it has become a full-grown tree, a fence is no longer necessary.

Mansur Mastana, a Muslim saint, wrote in one of his poems: मुसल्ला छोड़, तसबी तोड़, किताबें डाल पानी में ! "Give up the cloth for *namaz,* break the rosary and throw the books in the river!" Sects are created by man whereas the world is a creation of God. The world is full of diversity, but the basic principle remains the same. One who knows this secret does not feel hatred towards anyone. A Muslim will see Allah even in a temple of Rama while a Hindu will see Krishna even in a church.

There is a Sanskrit verse which says:

यं शैवाः समुपासते शिव इति ब्रह्मेति वेदान्तिनो
बौद्धा बुद्ध इति प्रमाणपटवः कर्तेति नैयायिकाः ।
अर्हन्नित्यथ जैनशासनरताः कर्मेति मीमांसकाः
सोऽयं वो विदधातु वाञ्छितफलं त्रैलोक्यनाथो हरिः ॥

"He whom the Shaivites worship as Shiva, the Vedantins call Brahman, the Buddhists call Buddha, the

Nyayakas call the doer, the Jains call Arhat, and the Mimamsakas call Karma, He is that Lord Hari who is the ruler of the three worlds. May He grant us the desired fruit."

Wednesday, January 22, 1964

Yesterday Shri Sunil Damania brought the famous Sufi saint Shri Gurdayal Mallik to the ashram. This morning Shri Mallikji, Shri Sunilbhai and others had *satsang* with Baba in Turiya Mandir.

THE INDIVIDUAL SOUL'S FOUR BODIES

Sunil: *Shardaben is ill again. For the past year she has been suffering intensely.*
Baba: Everyone must undergo his destiny. It is inescapable. One's suffering can certainly be alleviated by surrendering to a Sadguru. The individual soul has four bodies: gross, subtle, causal and supracausal. Just as these four rooms are separate from each other and, as we walk from one into another, we cease to exist in the previous room, similarly, these four bodies are quite independent of each other. When the individual soul leaves the gross body and enters the subtle body, the conditions of the former do not affect him at all. A similar situation occurs when a patient is given chloroform prior to an operation. As a result of the drug's effect, the mind becomes detached from the gross body and doesn't experience the pain suffered by it.

The *turiya* state is beyond all four bodies. In the dream state, the waking state disappears; in the state of deep sleep, both the waking and dream states disappear; but in the *turiya* state, the entire visible world disappears. In that state the happiness and misery of this world do not have any effect on the mind. Attain that state by which the burden of destiny will become light.

In the evening another *satsang* was held.

WORLDLY AFFAIRS MUST NOT BE NEGLECTED

A Devotee: *Swamiji, this man has become so engrossed in saints and* sannyasis *that he has forgotten his worldly affairs.*

Baba: (To Sunil) While you are practising spirituality, you must also do your worldly work with the same proficiency.

There was once a very wealthy and religious philanthropist named Nathkoti. The Mahadev idol was worshipped daily and bathed with cow's milk on his behalf. At one time, when he wanted to build a new monastery, Shankaracharya went to see Nathkoti at his residence. He was told that Nathkoti had gone to his shop. Shankaracharya went there, but he didn't see him. He asked someone and was told, "See, there he is." Shankaracharya saw an ordinary, simple man picking up scattered grains of wheat from the floor. He questioned a few other people to confirm that the man was actually the owner. He wondered what that man would give him. Just then, the owner approached Shankaracharya and asked the purpose of his visit. After hearing about the plans for a new monastery, Nathkoti at once asked, "How much money do you want?" Shankaracharya replied that four lakh rupees was needed. Without any hesitation, Nathkoti wrote a cheque for that amount. The moral of the story is that real wisdom lies in attending to worldly as well as spiritual work with equal efficiency.

64   Paramartha Katha Prasang

Sunday, January 26, 1964

Mr. Albert Rudolph came today from New York to
visit Baba as he does every year on his birthday. In the
afternoon he came to Baba accompanied by Barrister Nain
to act as interpreter and began asking questions.

LET EVENTS TAKE THEIR OWN COURSE

Rudolph: *For the past four or five months a lot has
been happening in my head. Sometimes it feels as
though it is going to explode. I had a similar experience
last night for the first time during the night.*
Baba: This is excellent progress. Shiva and Shakti
unite with each other in the *sahasrara* where you are
experiencing this activity. As soon as this union takes
place, you will realize God.
Rudolph: *When shall I attain that final state?*
Baba: Everything will happen in its own time. Have
patience.
Rudolph: *I often receive indications of future events
and whatever I tell anyone comes true.*
Baba: Yes, when all the tendencies of the mind subside,
you get such intuition within.
Rudolph: *I have an opportunity to obtain one hundred
four acres of forest-like land in an area near New York.
May I purchase it in order to establish an ashram there?*
Baba: What is the price?
Rudolph: *It is about one and a half lakh rupees, but I
am not in a position to pay the entire amount in cash.
I shall pay it in yearly instalments.*
Baba: Do only what comes naturally. Don't be hasty.
Whatever is going to happen will happen. Let events
take their own natural course. Look what happened
here. I never had even the slightest idea of building an

ashram here, but such a beautiful ashram spontaneously came into being.

Tuesday, January 28, 1964

Today Mr. Rudolph asked Baba about some of the experiences he is having.

KNOWLEDGE OF PAST LIVES DURING SADHANA

Rudolph: *I poured water on my head this morning while taking a bath and immediately felt as though the top portion of my head had given way. I saw a lama entering into my head. Is the Shakti of that lama working within me?*

Baba: During *sadhana* one keeps having this kind of new experience. Many dormant impressions from our innumerable past lives lie within us. These start manifesting during *sadhana* resulting in numerous visions. Sometimes past lives are seen. What you saw today was probably a vision of some previous life. It does not mean that the Shakti of any lama is working within you. During *sadhana* you will continue to have visions of worldly objects reflected in the Self. You will have many more experiences. I used to see myself riding a horse with battalions of soldiers in front of me and behind me during my *sadhana*. I concluded from this vision that I was a king during one of my previous lives. Similarly, whatever aspect of your *sadhana* remained incomplete in your previous life as a lama is being completed now.

Rudolph: *I shall return to New York in a day or two. Will you give me some special instructions regarding my sadhana?*

Baba: No, you will receive indications from within as to what you should do. However, be regular in your meditation and continue to increase your love and devotion toward your Guru.

Rudolph: *Until now my life has been full of physical suffering, which began right at the time of my birth. As I was born, the nurse who was holding me dropped me from her hands and I tumbled all the way down the staircase until I hit the last step. I was badly injured. During my childhood, I had to undergo fourteen operations, some on my chest and some on my head. Why did I have to experience all this? Was someone trying to take my Shakti away, or was God preparing me to undergo suffering in the future?*

Baba: It was neither of these. It was a way of going through your destiny. Everyone must undergo his destiny.

Rudolph: *When will all my karmas be exhausted?*

Baba: Everything will happen at the appropriate time. With the practice of yoga, one's *karmas* continue to be destroyed. Keep up your *sadhana* with sincerity and enthusiasm.

Thursday, February 6, 1964

A Parsi seeker, Mr. Kanga, has been staying in the ashram for the past few days. He received initiation from Swami Shivananda, a disciple of Sri Ramakrishna Paramahansa.

LIGHT SEEN DURING MEDITATION RADIATES FROM BRAHMAN

Kanga: *What is the nature of Brahman? I see light during meditation. What is it?*

Baba: The Supreme Brahman is changeless and still. What you are seeing is a radiation from Brahman. The true nature of Brahman is absolutely changeless and ever steady.

Saturday, February 22, 1964

About seven or eight years ago an American woman, Hilda Charlton, used to come to see Nityananda Baba now and then, and during her visits she also used to see Baba. She has been in India for the past fourteen years and has met many saints. She learned the preliminaries about kriya yoga from Yogananda Paramahansa in California. Yesterday she came to the ashram to stay for a few days to get guidance from Baba in her *sadhana*.

SIGNS OF THE AWAKENED KUNDALINI

Hilda: *My body becomes very hot when I sit for meditation. I feel intense heat within me. What should be done to cool the body down?*
Baba: Allow whatever is happening to happen. Do not try to obstruct it. It is not necessary to cool the body down. To experience heat within is a sign of the awakened Kundalini.
Hilda: *Formerly I observed fasts. Now when I sit for meditation with an empty stomach, I feel as if every cell in my body is dancing and I have a desire to dance myself. What is this?*
Baba: This is the supreme bliss. The Supreme Self pervades every cell of the body. A saint has said that Rama dwells in every particle of the body. When a seeker directs his love toward God, a feeling of happiness and bliss arises within and he starts jumping and dancing. Just as this body is formed out of every particle

of food eaten, this entire universe has come into existence because of God's presence in every particle of it.

Hilda: *During meditation and also afterwards, I have numerous visions and I hear a variety of sounds. I have many more indescribable experiences, which disturb my daily life. I feel that everything is a nuisance. What should I do about it?*

Baba: In the spine there is a *nadi* called the *sushumna* in which impressions of all one's previous lives lie dormant. While sitting for meditation or practising any other kind of *sadhana,* these impressions begin to manifest. Therefore, during the purification of the *nadis,* one has a variety of experiences. During my *sadhana,* many sounds would emerge from my throat such as those of a camel or a tiger. The noise was so loud that the cows grazing in the fields around my hut would run away!

Hilda: *Sometimes I become so still and motionless that I start to wonder whether I have gone insane. I cannot understand what is happening to me and I cannot concentrate on my routine work. At other times, so many thoughts crowd my mind that it is impossible to describe them.*

Baba: Yes, many seekers have such experiences. During my *sadhana* I also lost control of my mind, but after some time everything became all right. This is only a stage of the mind during *sadhana.* Just prior to becoming calm, innumerable thoughts arise in the mind. When all the thoughts and impressions have been expelled from the mind, it attains the *nirvikalpa* state. Before becoming still, it goes through considerable agitation. Kundalini Shakti is a live force; it is all-knowing. When we are engaged in worldly activities it protects us and makes us do things correctly. Do you get the *khechari mudra?*

Does your tongue get pulled in against your palate during *sadhana?*

Hilda: *Yes, it used to happen to me in the past and it frightened me terribly. Seven years ago I came to see you and you told me to remain calm. I believe that you know everything.*

Baba: Death comes at its preordained time so do not be afraid; have courage. Let things happen as they will. Let the Shakti do its work while you remain only as a witness. I told you the same before also.

Monday, February 24, 1964

On Friday Balwantrai Desai, a retired solicitor from Surat, came to stay at the ashram to see Baba and have *satsang* with him. He has studied Vedanta in depth and is interested in yoga. He has a keen desire to know about meditation and the awakening of the Kundalini. He has been to Pondicherry and Ramanashram, and several years ago he also met Swami Yogananda Paramahansa. Today he had a discussion with Baba.

Balwantrai: *There is a yogi named Kisan Maharaj who went into* samadhi *for eleven days. During this time, he did not eat or drink anything, nor did he excrete any urine or faeces.*

Baba: Yes, there are many such hatha yogis.

Balwantrai: *What is that state? Is that what is known as* samadhi? *Of what use is it?*

Baba: *Samadhi* is a state in which the intellect is balanced and the mind is still; it is what the *Bhagavad Gita* describes as *sthitapragna*. What can one gain by remaining in *samadhi* for eleven days? Only that people may be impressed and attracted to him.

Balwantrai: *How could he have lived without food and water?*

Baba: Have you read the *Yoga Sutras* of Patanjali? Do you know about the *sanyam siddhi* described there? One *sutra* says that by practising control over the throat, one does not feel hunger and thirst. There are also some medicines that eliminate hunger and thirst. Another method is to eat a preparation of rice that is made by soaking the rice grains in milk and then drying them. This process is repeated several times over a prescribed number of days. Consuming this kind of rice also eradicates hunger and thirst.

Balwantrai: *It is said that the body of Swami Yogananda Paramahansa did not start to decompose until several days after his death. How can this be explained?*

Baba: In the body there are ten kinds of *pranas*, or vital airs: *prana, apana, samana, vyana, udana, naga, kurma, kukara, devadatta*, and *dhananjaya*. The first five are the main, or principal, *pranas* and the next five are the subsidiary ones. Among these, the vital air called *dhananjaya* remains in the body even after death. The *Yogachudamani Upanishad* says that *dhananjaya* pervades the entire body and does not leave it even after death. The body of a yogi who has completely purified this *prana* will not undergo any disintegration for many days after death.

THE ECSTASY OF LOVE

Balwantrai: *A woman named Indiradevi stays with Shri Dilip Kumar Roy in Pune. When she goes into samadhi, Mirabai talks to her and she chants Mirabai's bhajans. Formerly, she stayed at the Aurobindo Ashram, but she left because of a difference of opinion with Mataji about this. What can we conclude about* *these experiences? Presently Indiradevi's health has greatly deteriorated.*

Baba: This kind of experience is merely a state or emotion of the mind. The real ecstasy is that in which the seeker himself becomes the object of worship and all the qualities of the worshipped object are manifested in him. Sri Ramakrishna Paramahansa and Sri Chaitanya Mahaprabhu used to get into such exalted states of love.

When I was staying in Kasara Ghat, there was a woman who used to get into that kind of state. At these times she answered correctly any questions she was asked. Many devotees of Nityananda Baba also experienced ecstatic states of love. These experiences, however, are merely manifestations of mental states. In the ecstasy of pure, divine love, the body is purified and all diseases vanish.

Balwantrai: *I have studied in great detail two or three cases of people who remember their previous lives and I have concluded that some people actually do retain such memories. I have started believing in rebirth, but how can I learn about my past life?*

Baba: You will obtain knowledge of your past births before attaining final realization.

ALLEGED INCARNATIONS OF SAI BABA OF SHIRDI

Balwantrai: *There is a sannyasi who claims to be an incarnation of Sai Baba of Shirdi. Can this be true?*

Baba: Seven other people also claim to be incarnations of Sai Baba of Shirdi. Which one can be regarded as true? This is like the story of Laila and Majnu. Laila was a beautiful princess and Majnu was a poor man. He was madly in love with her and repeated "Laila, Laila" all the time. He lost all consciousness of himself.

The king took pity on Majnu and told the chief minister to provide him with food and clothes. Seeing this, numerous impostors claimed to be Majnu and were also provided with food and clothing. Once the king enquired about the expenses of Majnu and learned that the number of Majnus had increased. He conferred with the chief minister, who shrewdly devised a solution to the problem. He sent a town crier out with the following proclamation: "Majnu has gone insane because of his love for Laila so he will be hanged tomorrow." Hearing this, all the Majnus except the real one disappeared.

I have also met two or three *sadhus* who claim to be incarnations of Sai Baba. One of them operated a factory with the money collected from his devotees and was later prosecuted by the government. I came across another incarnation of Sai Baba in Yeola. He used to put his hand on a person's eyes and give him a vision of Sai Baba. Later on, he married and led the life of a householder. A third man who claimed to be an incarnation of Sai Baba died in a car accident.

The truth is that Sai Baba of Shirdi was a completely realized being; he was a great Siddha. He became one with the Supreme Brahman and merged into the totality. He can never be reborn; God alone incarnates, no one else.

Balwantrai: *A great saint was living in the home of a householder whose daughter-in-law committed suicide. Didn't the saint have the power to advise her and avert that calamity?*

Baba: Every creature's time of death is predetermined. Providence determines the time of birth as well as death. Even great saints and sages, let alone ordinary people, must die at their destined time. No one can prevent death; no one can avert the time of death.

Balwantrai: *I have seen many saints and I have visited Nareshwar, Ramanashram, Pondicherry and other ashrams, but I never felt that any of the devotees or disciples had really achieved anything. I did not feel that anyone went there with a desire for God-realization.*

Baba: A man who has progressed in *sadhana* or who has attained something does not grow horns on his head by which you can identify his state of being. To know a *jnani* one must first attain that state oneself. One can know him by living with him for a long time. What can we understand about a person in only a day or two?

Besides, all kinds of people go to saints. Each person goes to obtain whatever he desires. A man with only two paise wants to buy a vegetable and you start advising him to buy pearls instead. First of all, he does not want pearls, nor does he have the means to purchase them. Is advising him to buy pearls wise or foolish? If a childless person goes to a saint to ask for a child and someone advises him to ask for *moksha* (liberation), of what use is it? Is that wisdom or foolishness?

Friday, February, 28, 1964

Last Sunday Shri Sunil Damania and his friend Shri Sundarrao, a devotee of Swami Ramdas of the Anandashram, came from Khar, Bombay. They presented Baba with a copy of the first issue of *The Mountain Path* published by the Ramanashram in which the magazine's editor had written an article comparing three or four saints. The devotees here read the article and today they discussed it with Baba. Many devotees were present since today is a holiday because of Holi.

NO SAINT IS SUPERIOR OR INFERIOR TO ANY OTHER

Baba: It seems that this gentleman (the editor) is capable of writing on the subject of philosophy, but he certainly cannot be an authority on saints and sages. Tukaram Maharaj says:

पाण्यामध्यें मासा झोंप घेतो कैसा ।
जावें त्याच्या वंशा तेव्हां कळे ॥

To understand
How the fish sleep under water,
You have to become a fish
And live under water.

It is childish to compare saints and sages without having been a saint and without having personally experienced their state. Doing so is neither a sign of wisdom nor good manners. How can one describe America's New York City while living in India and without ever having seen it? To try to assess the state of a saint or to compare him with others is sheer ignorance. The state of saints is not like B. A. or M.A. degrees. As a matter of fact, the final state and attainment of every saint is the same. You may call it by many names: *nirvichar, samadhi, sthitapragna, turiyatita, atmabhava,* or *ishabhava.*

All the paths and means for God-realization indicated by our saints such as the paths of knowledge, devotion and yoga are true. All the paths ultimately lead a seeker to the same goal. There are many roads leading to the same place and different means for getting there. For example, several routes lead to Delhi, but the best route for a traveller is the one from the place where he is. A man staying in Calcutta need not travel through Bombay to reach Delhi. He can reach Delhi directly via Kanpur and Allahabad. From

Calcutta he can travel by any means: train, car or airplane.   One should choose the route and means best
suited for him.   The path to God-realization best suited
to a seeker's termperament is the ideal path for him.
Whichever path he follows, his destination will be the
same.   A verse in the Shiva Mahimnah Stotram says:

रुचीनां वैचित्र्यादृजुकुटिलनानापथजुषां ।
नृणामेको गम्यस्त्वमसि पयसामर्णव इव ॥

"Just as all rivers ultimately merge into the sea, You are
the final goal for all people following different paths,
straight or crooked, according to. their temperaments
and depending on which they consider best."

A wise man will not judge saints and sages by their
paths of *sadhana* or say that one saint is superior or
inferior to another because he is *jnani, bhakta* or a yogi.
This is wrong understanding.   To think that you know
something when you do not is an illusion of knowledge.

Every seeker follows the path of God-realization
according to his own inclination.   A *jnani* has no
interest in *pranayama,* a *bhakta* is not drawn to intellectual analysis, and a yogi does not enjoy chanting.   This
does not mean that the paths of remembering God's
name, chanting and worshipping God are inferior
means of *sadhana.* Jnaneshwar Maharaj says:

तरी कीर्तनाचेनि नटनाचें । नाशिले व्यवसाय प्रायश्चित्तांचे ।
जे नामचि नाहीं पापाचें । ऐसें केलें ॥
यमदमा अवकळा आणिली । तीथैं ठायावरूनि उठविली ।
यमलोकीं खुंटिली । राहाटी आघवी ॥
यमु म्हणे काय यमावें । दमु म्हणे कवणातें दमावें ।
तीर्थें म्हणती काय खावें । दोष ओखदासि नाहीं ॥
ऐसे माझेनि नामघोषें । नाहीं करिती विश्वाची दुःखें ।
अवघें जगचि महासुखें । दुमदुमित भरलें ॥ (ज्ञानेश्वरी)

"A man who constantly chants God's name does not
have to undergo any expiation or atonement, for no trace

of sin remains in him. The yogic disciplines of *yama* and
dama become irrelevant for him. All sins are destroyed
in holy places, but his greatness is such that he surpasses
even the holy places. About such a man, *yama* says,
"Whom can I discipline?" and *dama* says, "Whom can
I control?" because by chanting God's name his mind
and senses have become one with the Self. By this
means, sinners are cleansed of their sins and need not
go to *Yamaloka*. Chanting the Lord's name removes the
misery of the whole universe and fills it with the bliss of
Brahman."

Also Tukaram Maharaj sang the following:

ब्रह्मीभूत होते काया च कीर्तनीं । भाग्य तरी ऋणी देवा ऐसा ॥
तीर्थभ्रामकासी आणीन आळस । कडु स्वर्गवास करित भोग ॥
सांडवीन तपोनिधा अभिमान । यज्ञ आणि दान लाजवीन ।
भक्तिभाग्यप्रेमा साधीन पुरुषार्थ । ब्रह्मींचा जो अर्थ निजठेवा ॥

"By chanting God's name, the body becomes the
embodiment of Brahman. Such a person becomes so
fortunate that God Himself feels indebted to him. I
shall make the pilgrims stop their roaming to holy
places; I shall make them abandon their pilgrimages and
sit in one place. I shall make the sense pleasures bitter.
I shall make the *tapasvis* (ascetics) lose their pride and
I shall make acts of ritual and charity appear small. I
shall attain the highest state of *bhakti* through chanting
with love. I shall become one with the Supreme."

After Self-realization, the *sadhana* by which one has
attained it becomes just an addiction for him. Tukaram used to chant "Vitthal, Vitthal" and Ramakrishna
Paramahansa used to repeat "Mother, Mother" even
after attaining oneness with the Supreme. Tukaram
Maharaj says in one of his verses:

विषय तो त्यांचा झाला नारायण । नावडे धन-जन माता-पिता ।

"They have no interest in society, wealth, father

or mother.   Narayana becomes their only object.

Sri Ramakrishna Paramahansa was very wise and a great *jnani*.   See how in the book *Gospel of Sri Rama-krishna* he has explained in simple and beautiful language the most intricate mysteries of *jnana*.   He may appear to be an ordinary, illiterate peasant to some, but everyone knows that highly educated and intelligent people became his disciples.   Could that have been the case if he himself were not intelligent?   If educated and highly intellectual people surrendered to him, then of what value was their learning?

Ramana Maharshi was also a great yogi.   During his *sadhana*, he experienced all the yogic *kriyas* after which he had numerous visions in meditation.   He often had such deep *samadhi* states that he would be unaware of rats biting his feet and he had to be lifted up and brought out of his cellar.   He was also a great *bhakta* and composed a song full of love and devotion for Lord Shiva of Arunachala.

Ramana Maharshi did not establish any new path because Truth is only one; it never undergoes any change or transformation.   No one can change it.   The inquiry into "Who am I?" is the path of contemplation of the Self, developing witness consciousness and dis-passion.   It would be a mistake to call it a new path, for our saints and sages expounded it thousands of years ago.   One with knowledge of the ancient Hindu scrip-tures would not consider this path new, but to one who has not studied the scriptures, it appears new.   To regard the path of Self-inquiry—"Who am I?" —as new would be like using an old Japanese technique to grow rice in America and then claiming that a new type of rice has been developed.   The Japanese people would say that this rice has existed in their land from ancient times and for them there is nothing new in it.

"India has had only one or two great saints or Gurus and all the others are inferior." Such a belief shows ignorance of Indian spiritual philosophy. India is a land of saints and sages. There is no dearth of saints and Gurus. There were brilliant *jnanis*, great *bhaktas* and saints in India in the past, they are here today and will be here in the future as well.

The realized Gurus and saints, ancient and modern, always proclaim the same Truth whether they are yogis, *jnanis*, *bhaktas* or *karma* yogis. They all have the same knowledge, realization, Shakti, love and perfection. The question of one being greater than another does not arise. The greatness of some saints comes to light while the attainment of others remains unknown, but this is no basis for arguing that one is superior to another. The greatness of saints and Gurus cannot be evaluated by such criteria as fame, *siddhis*, number of disciples, size of their ashrams, or the number of books they have written or which have been written about them. Only those with poor understanding would attempt this type of evaluation.

The Guru principle is all-pervasive; it is not limited to any one individual. The duty of every spiritual seeker is to respect the Guru principle in whatever form it has appeared, in whichever person it has manifested. It is best to surrender to only one Guru, but to disrespect the others is a great sin. To do so is like being disrespectful to the Guru principle, God and your own Guru. To say, write or proclaim that your Guru alone is great and the others in the world are false is a display of stupidity. Many disciples become so stuck in such an idea that even years after their Guru has taken *mahasamadhi* they remain prisoners of this narrow understanding and yet they consider themselves to be very wise.

There is a beautiful illustration of this. When Rama was returning from Sri Lanka with Sita and Hanuman in the Pushpak plane after defeating Ravana, the thought came to Hanuman, "There is no one like my Rama." Rama read Hanuman's thought. Just at that moment Sita was handing her ring to Rama and accidentally dropped it into the sea. Rama told Hanuman to retrieve it so he dived into the deep sea. On reaching the bottom, Hanuman was surprised to find a huge collection of rings exactly like the one Sita had dropped, all inscribed with the name "Sri Rama," and he could not recognize which of the rings was Sri Rama's. A saint was sitting there in meditation and Hanuman asked his advice about the ring. The saint replied, "Take any one of these rings. There have been many Ramas like your Rama. Each time one returns home after defeating Ravana, one ring is dropped here making this large pile."

In short, the essence of this is that all saints and sages are manifestations of Truth. They do not say anything new. If the disciple does not understand this, then by writing about his Guru merely according to his own thinking, he actually lessens rather than enhances the glory of his Guru.

Saturday, February 29, 1964

Shri B. C. Dalal, Secretary in the Ministry of Law, Maharashtra State, has been coming for some time for Baba's *darshan*. He came today accompanied by Mrs. Bharucha.

Mrs. Bharucha: *Which name of God should I use for japa?*

Baba: Actually, the Lord has no name, but nevertheless He has been given so many names. Mohammed called Him Khuda and Christ called Him God; among Hindus some call Him Rama, some call Him Krishna and some call Him Shiva. He is called by different names according to the devotees' feelings, but all these different names are of one and the same God. You may do *japa* with whichever name appeals to you.

SO'HAM IS THE ORIGINAL MANTRA

Shri Dalal: *May I use the* so'ham *mantra for* japa?
Baba: There are innumerable mantras. The Shakti is the same in all. *So'ham* (I am That) is a great mantra. It is the *ajapa-japa* mantra. Whether or not you consciously do *japa* with this mantra, it is automatically taking place with each inhalation and exhalation. The individual soul is initiated into this mantra by God while still in the womb. During the seventh month in the womb, he receives knowledge of his past and future, and repents his past *karmas*. He prays to God, and God gives him the *so'ham* mantra. At the time of birth, however, when the individual soul comes into this world, he forgets the awareness of *so'ham* and starts crying *"ko'ham"* (who am I?) instead. *So'ham* is the original mantra. Do *japa* with it.

Monday, March 16, 1964

Today Shri Yogendra Trivedi's mother, Shrimati Bhanuben, who is a keen student of Vedanta, asked Baba some questions.

KNOWLEDGE AND DESTINY

Bhanuben: *What is the relationship between* jnana *and the living out of one's* karmas?

Baba: The individual soul has different types of experiences in different states. The experiences in the waking state are different from those in the dream state. The pain of a boil is felt during the waking state, but not during sleep. If given chloroform, the individual soul does not feel any pain while undergoing an operation because the drug takes him into another state. The experience in a dream is different. If someone beats or abuses you in a dream, you feel sad; if someone praises you, you feel happy, but these emotions vanish the moment you enter the waking state. Beyond the waking and dream states is the *turiya* state in which the individual soul has no experiences.

With the knowledge of Brahman the body is burnt into ashes, but one still must undergo one's remaining destiny. During the war at Kurukshetra, Ashwathama attempted to destroy Arjuna's chariot with the *agni astra,* but it inflicted no damage at all because Lord Krishna was protecting Arjuna with his will power. Ashwathama complained to his Guru, "What sort of mantra did you teach me that does not bring forth any result?" The Guru replied, "What I taught you regarding the *astra* is absolutely true and you will definitely obtain the result of it." After seven days, the war ended whereupon Krishna told Arjuna to immediately jump out of the chariot. As soon as he had leapt out, the chariot caught fire and was reduced to ashes. Similarly, your knowledge of Brahman will certainly bear fruit as soon as you have lived out your entire destiny.

Bhanuben: *I can remain disinterested during moments*

of happiness, but I cannot do so during painful times.
Baba: In order to achieve detachment from both pain
and pleasure, you must remain steadily established in
the Self.

Tuesday, March 17, 1964

A seeker, Shri Karve, came today from Dadar to seek
Baba's clarification regarding some problems in his
sadhana.

Karve: *During meditation I have body tremors and I
perspire. I also smell a pleasant fragrance. Is this fragrance related to the tremors and sweating in any way?*
Baba: The fragrance has no relation to the tremors or
the sweating. It has its place near the two-petalled
chakra. When the *prana* becomes steady in that *chakra,*
a divine fragrance emanates from within.
Karve: *Why are there so many kinds of fragrance?*
Baba: Sometimes you will smell fragrances hitherto unknown to you. When the intensity of the fragrance
increases, it comes out through the *prana* and can also be
experienced by other people around you.
Karve: *Some people see lights of different colours during
meditation. What kind of* sadhana *enables one to see
these lights?*
Baba: One should see whatever appears naturally. One
should not make any effort to have visions nor desire
them. Why should one try to see the same thing again
and again? Meditate peacefully and you will see divine
light.
Karve: *What is the significance of lights of different
colours? Does the red light appear when one is angry?*
Baba: All these are the colours of the inner Self. Do

not think that they appear as a result of the three *gunas*, *sattva*, *rajas* and *tamas*.

The red light is not caused by anger. Tukaram Maharaj says:

रक्त श्वेत कृष्ण पीत प्रभा भिन्न ।
चिन्मय अंजन सुदलें डोळां ॥

"Because of the ointment of divinity in my eyes, I saw the different lights: red, white, black and yellow."

Wednesday, March 18, 1964

Baba has been in Santa Cruz for the past four days and will remain here for another ten days. *Satsang* is held in the morning and evening. Shri Sunil Damania came this morning with a letter.

Sunil: *Babaji, yesterday I received a letter from the editor of* The Mountain Path *published by the Rama-nashram requesting an article about Bhagawan Nitya-nanda.*

Baba: Very good. Write to him as follows:

Whenever anyone approached Nityananda Baba requesting, 'O Bhagawan! Please show us a new and easy path to suit this modern era," my revered Gurudev would reply, "This universe, which is a creation of Brahma, was created only once and since then nothing new has come into existence. The past era, which today we regard as ancient, was new then. Since each era undergoes changes according to the times, we perceive a particular age to be either ancient or new, but in fact, everything is now as it was in the beginning of creation. In a kaleidoscope, loose pieces of coloured glass are

reflected by mirrors on all four sides. As the instrument is rotated, the glass pieces keep changing position
resulting in the appearance of new patterns, but each
pattern contains the same pieces of glass. Nothing old
has disappeared, nor has anything new been added.

Again, the sun is only one, but in different countries it appears to move at different speeds. In some
countries the sun rises early while in others it rises late.
In some places it stays longer than in others. But the
sun does not have the characteristics of being late or
early, of short duration or long. The sun always is
as it is. The knowledge of God should be understood
in the same way.

It is always one, it always remains the same and
it does not become more or less.

There is no question of easy or difficult paths for
the attainment of knowledge. Man finds it difficult or
easy according to his own mental inclinations just as
some people find the English language easy to learn and
Sanskrit difficult while the reverse is the case for others.

One kind of *sadhana* may be suitable for one person and another kind for another person. None of
these different types of *sadhana* is easy or difficult in itself. The yogi finds Vedanta difficult while the *jnani*
finds yoga difficult, and for the *bhakta,* both are difficult.
The truth is that whatever appeals to a person will be
easy for him. Despite the differences in the various
paths of *sadhana* according to the seekers' inclinations,
the goal is the same. Jnaneshwar Maharaj says in
Jnaneshwari:

ज्ञानी इयेतें स्वसंविति । शैव म्हणती शक्ति । आम्ही परमभक्ति
आपुली म्हणो ॥

"That state which the *jnanis* call Brahman, yogis
call *samadhi,* and Vedantins call *nityananda* (eternal

bliss) is the *bhakta's paramabhakti,* the deepest ecstasy."

One who considers these paths to be different from each other is not wise; he is as ignorant as a child. The *Bhagavad Gita* says:

सांख्ययोगौ पृथग्बालाः प्रवदन्ति न पण्डिताः ।
एकमप्यास्थितः सम्यग् उभयोर्विन्दते फलम् ॥ ५ । ४ ॥

"The ignorant, not the wise, consider knowledge and yoga to be different.   One who establishes himself in either of these reaps the fruit of both of them."

There have been many saints in India.   They all proclaimed the same Truth.   Many years separate the times of Jnaneshwar and Vasuguptacharya, the author of the *Shiva Sutras,* yet both of them expounded the same principles. Kabir sang and Nanak spoke about the same Truth.

THERE CAN BE NO PERCENTAGES OR DEGREES OF REALIZATION

Just as all scriptures impart knowledge of the same Truth, the realization of all saints is the same.   Realization cannot be partial or of different types.   There can be disparities in worldly gains; for example, one person may have a bigger house or more money than another person.   Gains in the mundane world can be estimated in percentages, but it is not so with regard to God-realization. You cannot say that someone has attained twenty-five or fifty percent realization.   The attainment of God-realization is either complete or none at all.   There is no such thing as partial realization.

According to the Vedantic teachings, true realization is that after attaining which, nothing else remains to be attained; after seeing which, nothing else remains to be seen.   For one who has attained the supreme bliss, not even the smallest part of bliss remains to be attained.

He is known as a saint. There have been many such
saints in this era, for example, Ramakrishna Paramahansa, Sai Baba of Shirdi, Upasani Maharaj of Sakori,
Mugatram Maharaj of Manjusar, Narsimhacharya of
Baroda, Abbajan of Pune, Ramana Maharshi of Tiruvannamalai, Bhagawan Nityananda of Ganeshpuri, Sid-
dharudh Swami of Hubli and Swami Ramdas.

Even after attaining divinity, saints behave in their
daily lives according to the time and place in which they
live even though they are bound by no rules. In
Benares there lived a wealthy man who was very charitable. During the winter, he would give blankets to
the *sadhus* and during the summer, he would give them
umbrellas and water bowls.

Some *sadhus* remarked, "What sort of a philanthropist is he! Sometimes he gives us umbrellas while at
other times he gives us blankets!" But in reality, their
benefactor was being practical; it was the *sadhus* who
lacked intelligence. He provided for them according
to their needs. Similarly, saints and Gurus deal with
their disciples according to the time, place, and their
worthiness. In *ayurvedic* medicine there is an excellent remedy known as *hemagarbha,* but that does not
mean that the *vaidya* should prescribe it for every
patient. He gives each patient only the medicine that
is necessary for him. Because he doesn't give *hemagarbha* to everyone, one cannot say that the *vaidya* is
incompetent.

The goal, the state and the attainment of all saints
is the same. The bliss experienced in the thought-free
state achieved through *jnana,* the *nirvikalpa* equanimity
attained through yoga, and the ecstasy of chanting the
name of Rama are all the same.

In Maharashtra there was a great *bhakta,* Namdev,
with whom God Himself used to laugh and talk. He

proclaimed, नामा म्हणे, नाम चैतन्य निज धाम।   "God's name is God himself." Gurudev Ranade used to give the experience of peace and bliss by awakening the inner Shakti of his disciples while Swami Ramdas imparted the same experience through the use of a mantra.

Swami Nityananda's life was filled through and through with the principles of Vedanta. His greatness was amazing. He had knowledge of all the world's problems and he had the remedy for each of them. If someone complained of a stomach ache, he would advise the right treatment or administer some medicine himself. If someone asked for food, clothes or housing, he would provide those as well. To a seeker he would advise *japa*, meditation or *seva* according to the individual's capability. He belonged neither to modern nor ancient times. He always taught pure Vedanta.

When asked about any other saint, Nityananda Baba would reply, "He is my own Self." He saw no distinction among any saints.

A saint called Amritrai lived in the Aurangabad district of Maharashtra State. He had attained the supreme state and was Self-realized. One day people of different sects gathered around him and asked him for some teaching. Having realized that this universe is the form of the Supreme Self, he was always immersed in the Self and remained silent. When the people insisted, he sang the following verse:

उगा मी कोणा काय म्हणूं ॥ ध्रु० ॥
सच्चित्सुखमय एकचि असतां
कुठुनी द्वैत गणूं ?...उगा मी।
ब्रह्म विलोकुनी सोशील कैसी
जगदाभास गणूं ?...उगा मी।
अमृतसमुद्रीं अद्वैताच्या
कुठुनी कूप खणूं ?...उगा मी।

"What can I say about anything? When there is only one eternal, blissful Consciousness, where can I find duality? When I have seen and realized Brahman, how can I give any value to this world, which is only an illusion? When I am deep inside the ocean of divine nectar, why should I dig a well? What can I say about anything?"

There was no discrepancy between Swami Nityananda's philosophy and his daily life. According to him, the perception of Brahman and the practice of worldly life were the same. His teaching was that worldly life is also a manifestation of Brahman. If someone sought spiritual knowledge, he would impart that and give suitable instructions to those who discussed worldly problems. He would advise some people to become doctors, engineers or lawyers, and others to start a business or industry. He did not tell everyone to study yoga and live in an ashram. If, however, a person said that in spite of doing everything he had not found peace, then Swami Nityananda would advise him to meditate and become thought-free by turning within.

Thursday, March 19, 1964

Today Mr. Niraj, a famous Hindi poet and a professor at Aligarh University, came for Baba's *darshan* accompanied by some friends.

ALL PROBLEMS ARE SOLVED AFTER REALIZATION
Niraj: *There are so many theories about the creation of this world that one cannot easily understand which of them is correct.*
Baba: You are right. There are many theories about the creation of the universe. Which of these is true

and which are false?   How can one say that a particular
theory is false?   Those who have told us about the
creation of the world were not ordinary men.   The
Bhagavad Gita says:

ऋषिभिर्बहुधा गीतं छन्दोभिर्विविधैः पृथक्
ब्रह्मसूत्रपदैश्चैव हेतुमद्भिर्विनिश्चितैः ॥ १३।४ ॥

The *rishis* have sung about this subject in many
different metre and styles, and it has also been explained
with examples and reasons in the *Brahma Sutras*. (13/4)

In the *Yoga Vasistha* Rama asks the sage Vasishtha
a similar question.   Rama says, "You are a great seer;
you speak only Truth.   My mind is confused because
some say the world has emerged from an egg, some say
it arose from water, some say it evolved from an atom,
and some say it came into being out of the supreme
Brahman."

The fact is that whatever is visible can be described,
but how can that which is not visible be described?
About the invisible, one can only imagine in various
ways or make guesses.   Therefore, one says something
and another says something else.   The real answer to
this entire problem is revealed only with God's grace.
So far as the ultimate Truth is concerned, all saints say
the same thing.   There can certainly be different
theories about the creation of the universe, but they
are unanimous about the final attainment.

Niraj: *Bhagawan Buddha says it is the "void."*

Baba: Everyone says what he experiences.   If I were to
experience that, I would also say the same.   All paths
of *sadhana* lead to the same goal.   You may follow any
one of them; *bhakti, pranayama, jnana,* etc.

Niraj: *I certainly respect Meher Baba, but he makes
people call him God and he makes predictions about
the future. How can modern people who have cultivated*

logical thinking have faith in him?

Baba: Too much learning confuses the mind. By too much reasoning, one loses faith in God. A poet sings as follows:

बना दो बुद्धिहीन, भगवान ।
तर्कशक्ति सारी ही हर लो; हरो ज्ञान-विज्ञान ।
भर दो हृदय भक्ति-श्रद्धा से, करो प्रेम का दान ॥

"O Bhagawan, take away my intellect, take away this power of reasoning, take away my knowledge and learning. Fill my heart with devotion and faith; give me love."

Getting rid of old mental impressions is not easy. You must always strive to make your mind devoid of thoughts. You must give up dependence upon books.

Niraj: *But how can this be achieved?*

Baba: Make the mind steady. Have dispassion. Give up the sense of I-ness and my-ness. Understand that pain and pleasure are illusory. I will give you an example.

Once there were two neighbouring families who were close friends. A girl from one of the families was engaged to a boy from the other family. They developed great love for each other to such an extent that if one of them had any trouble, the other one would also become miserable. If one fell sick, the other one would not eat owing to worry. After some time, it so happened that the friendship between the two families broke up and the engagement was cancelled. Eventually, the boy and the girl each married someone else. The boy died after a year, but the girl did not feel any grief whereas previously, when she had felt that he belonged to her, his every sorrow gave her pain. This is what is known as the sense of I-ness or my-ness. When this sense disappears there is no pain.

This world has as much reality as the son of a barren woman bathing in mirage waters and wearing a garland of flowers from the sky. You should try to become one with God. He alone is real.

Niraj: *Which is the simplest and easiest way for me to do* sadhana?

Baba: Steady the mind. You can realize the Truth only by making your mind steady. Artists, scientists and musicians all excel in their work through concentration of the mind. A concentrated mind becomes one with the work. Absorb your mind in love.

Niraj: *How can I love? Shall I love God with form?*

Baba: The *Yoga Sutras* say, वीतरागविषयं वा चित्तम् ।
"Take refuge in a man who has complete dispassion. Unite your mind with him." Seek refuge in a Self-realized saint. Have love for him. As this love grows, your inner Shakti will awaken and the mind will lose its unsteadiness and become pure.

The mind is as restless as a monkey. Your mind is very restless and you are aware of it. This very recognition will help you to make it concentrated. The mind becomes steady as a result of knowledge of the Self. Understand that you neither gain nor lose anything whether your mind pursues sensual pleasures or gives them up. You do not suffer any loss when a horse that is standing near you runs away and then returns because you have no concern with its coming or going; it is the same between you and your mind. Just watch the mind. Become the witness of the mind. I also passed through a state similar to yours. I am advising you to follow the *sadhana* which benefited me.

Always contemplate the Supreme Brahman. In this way, we ourselves become Brahman. Sundardas says:

जो मन नारि कि ओर निहारत, तौ मन होत हि ताहिकु रूपा ।
जो मन काहसूं क्रोध करै, पुनि तौ मन है तब ही तद् रूपा ॥
जो मन माय हि माय रटै नित, तौ मन बूड़त माय के कूपा ।
सुन्दर जो मन ब्रह्म विचारत, तौ मन होत हि ब्रह्म स्वरूपा ॥

"The mind that always thinks of a woman becomes a woman; the mind that constantly gets angry takes on the form of anger; the mind that continually dwells in delusion drowns in the well of delusion. The mind that constantly contemplates Brahman becomes Brahman. This entire world is only an imagination of the mind."

Niraj: *Are miracles real? Is it possible to perform miracles through the practice of yoga?*

Baba: This entire world is one great miracle of the mind. It is all a play of Chiti Shakti.

Niraj: *I have heard that some yogis can make a dead man return to life. Doesn't this violate the laws of God?*

Baba: It is all according to the laws of destiny. Yogis always work according to God's laws.

Niraj: *I have heard about a twenty-two-year-old boy who can predict future events. He correctly foretells the winning numbers of race horses. Is this all the result of yogic Shakti?*

Baba: Even if one obtains such powers, they vanish after a short time. A bird flying in the air or a fish living in water—aren't these miracles or *siddhis?* There are many such miracles. Some people can acquire *siddhis* according to their desires, but they can perform them only to the extent that they have progressed. If you can believe in this kind of magic, it would be much better for you to believe in the saints and Siddhas. who can take you across this ocean of birth and death.

Niraj: *We are thinking of building an ashram for seekers in Haridwar.*

Baba: First, practise steadying your mind. Afterwards, you can do whatever work comes to you by God's will. Do what destiny makes you do. It is not necessary for you to leave this world. Realize the Truth and your concept of the world will automatically leave you.

Niraj: *We ourselves may achieve the goal, but what about our duty toward society? Wouldn't it be selfish? So many people in the world are starving and miserable.*

Baba: First realize the Truth and then you will only work to remove the misery of others. You will be working for society alone.

Saturday, March 21, 1964

Shrimati Kundanika Kapadia, a famous Gujarati writer and poetess and also editor of the Gujarati edition of the magazine 'Navneet,' came today for Baba's *darshan.*

THE PLACE OF PENANCE IN SADHANA

Kundanika: *How much bodily hardship must one undergo during* sadhana? *In other words, what is the place of penance in* sadhana?

Baba: While following a *sadhana* of *sattvic* practices, the body need not be subjected to any hardship. The body must be kept in good condition. One should do *sadhana* according to the capacity and limitations of the body. Many people practise *japa* for several hours and others chant God's name for hours while standing in water, but it is not necessary to follow these people blindly. We must progress slowly and steadily in *sadhana,* regulating our eating habits, conduct and other activities as an aid to such progress. The *Bhagavad Gita* says:

युक्ताहारविहारस्य युक्तचेष्टस्य कर्मसु ।
युक्त स्वप्नावबोधस्य योगो भवति दुःखहा ॥ ६।१८ ॥

"Yoga destroys all sorrow for him who maintains
balance in eating, waking and sleeping, and other
activities." (6/18)

Kundanika: *What should be done in order to conquer
the senses?*

Baba: There are many means to gain control over the
senses, but among them discrimination is the best. The
senses do not work on their own. They act only according to impulses received from the mind. The senses
start functioning when the mind is agitated. When the
mind becomes free from all thoughts and emotions, the
senses can easily be controlled.

THE MIND BECOMES PEACEFUL THROUGH DISCRIMINATION

Kundanika: *But the mind does not remain quiet.*

Baba: That is the nature of the mind. You must constantly discriminate. The mind becomes engaged in
the objects of its liking. It wants everything to be
pleasant. Therefore, you should always keep discriminating between what is permanent, or eternal, as opposed to what is temporary, or ephemeral; what is beneficial
to you and what is harmful. Self-mortification does not
work on the mind; the mind can only be controlled by
discrimination.

The mind is such that where nothing exists it
makes you see the whole universe as one sees a snake in
a rope or water in a mirage. It makes you see forms
in the formless. It causes relativity to manifest in the
Absolute. The *Brahmabindu Upanishad* says, '**मन एव
मनुष्याणां कारणं बन्धमोक्षयोः** ।' "The mind is the cause of
man's bondage as well as his liberation." The same mind

makes a friend into a foe and a foe into a friend. It takes you from heaven to hell, or from hell to heaven. To focus the mind outside is bondage and to focus it within is liberation. The pleasure and pain of the body do not affect the Self. The Self is free from what the body has to go through. The *Bhagavad Gita* says:

मात्रास्पर्शास्तु कौन्तेय शीतोष्ण सुखदुःखदा ।
आगमापायिनोऽनित्यास्तांस्तितिक्षस्व भारत ॥ २ । १४ ॥

"O Son of Kunti! Pleasure and pain, heat and cold arise when the senses unite themselves with the sense objects. They are temporary; they come and go. O Bharata! bear them." (2/14)

The *antahkarana* (inner psychic instrument) has two states : *chaitya* and *achaitya,* that is, live and inert. In the *achaitya* state, the individual soul does not experience the pleasure and pain of the gross body. In the *chaitya* state, however, the individual soul does experience them. Just as the rays of the sun can burn an object when focused through a convex lens, similarly, the *chaitya* state of the *antahkarana* is caused by the reflection of *chaitanya* (the life force) onto it; that is the individual soul. When the inner psychic instrument unites itself with the objects of the world, the individual soul experiences pleasure or pain and becomes disturbed. It is only in the *turiya* state that pain and pleasure are not experienced.

In the evening Shri Deshpande, a devotee, came to the ashram. He asked Baba the following question.

THE SELF IS TO BE EXPERIENCED, NOT INTELLECTUALISED

Deshpande: *My mind does not remain steady, nor can I understand God. What shall I do?*

Baba: God can never be understood by the intellect. The *Kenopanishad* says, ' यस्यामतं तस्य मतं मतं यस्य न वेद सः ' "One who says he knows God does not know Him and one who says he does not know God, in reality, knows Him."

The Supreme Brahman has no attributes and, therefore, cannot be cognised by any of the senses, nor can It be attained by the mind. The mind can contemplate the Self, but it cannot know the Self because realization of the Self is a matter of experience, not of intellectual thought.

Why do you want to steady the mind? There is one who witnesses the mind whether it is quiet or agitated. Know Him. That witness has no connection with the mind and is not dependent on the stillness of the mind. However, you must first know what the mind is. The mind is a concept that creates trouble for many people. It is good to restrain it. A mind full of desires and hopes makes a person miserable while the same mind when free from these makes a person happy. The mind that roams outside is sorrowful; the mind that turns within is peaceful. By making the mind contemplate God, it quickly becomes quiet.

Wednesday, March 25, 1964

Today Shri Niraj had a discussion with Baba.

THE INTEGRATION OF YOGA INTO DAILY LIFE

Niraj: *How can one integrate yoga into the practical life of the world?*
Baba: Yoga is already interwoven in daily life. Every creature practises yoga. Yoga is for everyone. People

generally consider it to be separate from worldly life because they do not know the true nature of yoga. They feel that it is only for *sadhus* and *sannyasis* living in jungles or caves and that the practice of yoga requires one to observe certain difficult rules, to undergo intense austerities and so forth. In fact, it is not so. Everyone unconsciously practises yoga to some extent in everyday life. For example, regulated diet and conduct is a part of yoga. Students, artists, technicians, etc., all have to fix their minds on their work; that is, the mind must be concentrated. This is also yoga. On waking up, you do not immediately cognise the outer world. For a moment the mind is devoid of any thoughts and that experience is nothing other than *samadhi*. You see yoga practised in all its aspects in the activities of daily life.

The final aim of yoga is *samadhi*. Meditation is the discipline and *samadhi* is its fruit. In *samadhi*, one achieves a thought-free state of mind and becomes united with the Supreme Self. What the yoga *shastras* call *samadhi* is called the *turiya* state in Vedanta.

Niraj: *How can the Kundalini be awakened?*

Baba: The Kundalini is already awake throughout the usual activities of worldly life, but its direction changes through the practice of *pranayama*, meditation or *japa*. Its outward focus decreases gradually and it becomes increasingly more inner-directed. Thus the Kundalini is awake in two respects: in outer activities and in the inner life. The latter is also called the awakening of the inner Shakti, which can easily be accomplished by the Guru's grace. This is known as the *siddhamarga*, or the path of the Siddhas. When the Kundalini is awakened by the Guru's grace, all the yogic practises such as *asana* (posture), concentration and meditation take place spontaneously. As soon as the mind becomes steady, *pranayama* occurs automatically; the seeker does not have to make any special effort to do it. This is the path of Guru *kripa* or Siddha Yoga. It is a great science.

Niraj: *I want to follow this yoga. Will I be able to do it?*

Baba: Why not? Everyone is a part of the Supreme Self and can, therefore, practise this yoga. Why then wouldn't it be possible for you? Try to receive the Guru's grace and thus attain it.

Niraj: *What is* nada?

Baba: Just as there is this external space, there is an inner space known as *chidakasha* in which sound arises due to the *prana*. It is called *anahat nada*. This music goes on inside ceaselessly. The divine *nada* is the vibration of the Supreme Self in the *chidakasha*.

Niraj: *I want to hear the* nada.

Baba: It is already within you. As soon as the mind becomes one-pointed, this *nada* is heard. Become one-pointed and you will surely hear it.

Thursday, April 2, 1964

Today a swami from a South Indian *math* came to see Baba and talked to him about the financial difficulties of the college he heads. After the swami's departure, Baba spoke to the devotees present.

Baba: It is not proper to approach people for the sake of money, or to go around asking for funds. In the first place, the head of a *math,* an *acharya,* or a *sannyasi* should not undertake that kind of work. This is not the *dharma,* or duty, of a *sannyasi.* The establishment and administration of institutions such as schools and colleges is the duty of the government. Despite this, if a person still wants to embark on such a project, he should first carefully assess his strength, power and resources before starting.

Worldly activities cannot proceed merely on the basis of promises such as "I shall give you money." "I shall give" is in the future tense. To have faith in such a promise is a mistake. From this, one starts getting entangled in a trap. The very nature of worldly life is such that even those who regard themselves as clever get into trouble. All work should be started only after considering one's current strength. Do not depend on the future, or your position will be like that of the bee who was once sitting on a lotus flower. Intoxicated by its nectar and fragrance, the bee was unaware that evening was quickly approaching. At sunset, the petals of the lotus closed, trapping the bee inside. The bee thought, "Well, the night will surely pass away, dawn will come, the sun will rise and as soon as its rays fall on this lotus, it will open again. Then I can escape!" But meantime, while the bee was thinking in this manner, an intoxicated elephant came by and uprooted the lotus with its trunk and put it into its mouth. The bee was crushed under the elephant's teeth along with the lotus.

If you make even the smallest error in any dealings in this world, know that you are trapped. Any activity is like a small stream in the beginning. It slowly expands and assumes the dimensions of a sea and then we drown in it. This applies not only to people living worldly lives, but also to *sannyasis,* who have taken a vow in the presence of fire that "I shall not keep anything in my hand; I renounce everything." Even they get trapped in worldly affairs. A rare one among them has received the full grace of the Guru and can escape unscathed. Only one who is free and steady-minded is

not carried away by others. In worldly affairs, he never
believes in promises.

Man becomes infatuated by words that give him
hope. This is called *maya*. The Lord says in the
Bhagavad Gita, मम माया दुरत्यया, "It is very difficult to
cross my *maya.*" The power of the Guru's grace alone
enables one to escape from the snares of *maya*. I never
tell anyone to give up anything because the temptations
of worldly life can entangle even renunciants and
sannyasis. The vast pageant of this world is very
tempting, deceptive and difficult to conquer. Hardly
anyone can escape from the clutches of this *maya*. My
advice is to have faith in the Guru and to meditate
awhile in the midst of your daily life and activities. By
remembering the Guru and spending even half an hour
daily singing God's name, their grace will take you
across this ocean.

Even in modern times, there are many instances of
seekers who have realized the Self in this very lifetime
after doing *sadhana* for a few years. What does this
indicate? Such examples demonstrate that it is not
difficult to realize God. After a while, one is sure to
attain Him. In contrast, man spends fifty or sixty years
in mundane activities and in the end does not gain any
happiness or satisfaction. After years of exhausting
effort, he remains empty. If you ask him, "Have you
obtained any peace? Have you achieved whatever you
set out to achieve?" he would reply, "I have yet to
achieve this thing and that."

Effort to attain God never goes to waste. It is
always beneficial to the individual; he is freed from the
cycle of birth and death. On the other hand, after
undergoing much hardship and expending tremendous
effort in worldly pursuits, at the end man finds himself
where he started, having achieved nothing.

Just as a manufacturer requests a shopkeeper to display his goods along with the other goods for sale in his shop in order to make them known to the public, similarly, I advise you to remember the Guru along with all your other daily concerns: your business, service, house, family, wealth and other worldly possessions. Reserve some time to remember God. That heart which has no love for God and takes no delight in singing God's name is of no value. Without Guru's grace, you get entangled in worldly life. Remember the Guru regularly and receive his grace. In that alone is the fulfillment of your life and the achievement of the supreme goal.

Sunday, April 19, 1964

Today Shri Dilip Mehta, professor of physics at K. C. College, accompanied some friends to the ashram. He regularly attends the discourses of Swami Chinmayananda. He had the following discussion with Baba.

THE GURU'S GRACE AND RECOGNITION OF A SADGURU

Dilip: *Wouldn't it be harmful for a person to receive the Guru's grace if he lacks the basic qualifications of a spiritual aspirant such as knowledge and dispassion, which are necessary in order to realize God? In other words, if a seeker begins his sadhana by obtaining Guru's grace, wouldn't it obstruct the evolution of his own inner power?*

Baba: Of all means of *sadhana,* the path of the Guru's grace is the best. The Guru's grace does not obstruct the evolution of the seeker's inner Shakti. On the contrary,

it helps his Shakti to expand. As soon as the inner
Shakti is awakened, knowledge and dispassion spontaneously arise from within. It is necessary, however,
to have a Guru who is capable of bestowing divine
grace.

Dilip: *How can one recognise such a Guru?*

Baba: This is a simple matter. How did you come
here? Someone must have aroused your curiosity by
telling you about Swami Nityananda and Ganeshpuri.
Thus you came here and had *satsang*. Similarly, you
went elsewhere and had *satsang* there. You will be able
to recognise a real Guru by meeting different Gurus.
How do you decide which college to join? First, you
make inquiries, meet the students and professors, talk
to them about the colleges and then finally decide which
college to join. In our language it is called *satsang*.
You go to a saint, remain in his company and have a
personal experience. You can truly know a Guru in
this way.

Dilip: *Many great beings change the future of their
devotees by their grace or their power. Doesn't this
violate the laws of nature?*

Baba: What is your occupation?

Dilip: *I am a professor. I teach in a college.*

Baba: When an ignorant student comes to you, you
give him knowledge and make him learned. Isn't that
so? When a student comes to you, which law tells you
whether or not to teach him? There is no such law, is
there? Similarly, saints and great beings use their divine
power or their own merits to uplift their devotees.
There is no violation of any law of nature in this.

Dilip: *Is it true that a person with unfulfilled desires
becomes a ghost after death?*

Baba: A person will always have desires until the time
of *jivanmukti*. This does not mean that all people

become ghosts. Only those who perform undesirable actions and behave contrary to the scriptures become ghosts.

Sunday, April 26, 1964

The second annual meeting of the Ashram Council was held this morning. The ashram trustees, Shri B. C. Dalal, Secretary of the Law Ministry of Maharashtra State, and some other guests were also here. They all requested Baba to say a few words. Befitting the occasion, Baba addressed them as follows:

THE NEED FOR RELIGIOUS INSTITUTIONS

My dear ones, you have all gathered here with feelings of love and brotherhood and I am very pleased to see how selflessly all of you are serving the ashram.

Before starting any work, a thorough study and understanding of it will lead to the benefit of all. The title "trustee" signifies one who is worthy of trust, in whose hands everything can be entrusted with full faith. This signifies love of the Self.

Whatever is given in charity to a religious institution belongs to God. According to the *shastras,* even one and a quarter rupee donated for a religious purpose is given to God. People donate to religious institutions purely out of love for God.

Vedanta is an unparalleled *shastra;* it is the basis for all other *shastras.* It expounds the knowledge of that Supreme Principle knowing which, man becomes God; the *jiva* becomes Shiva. After attaining that Supreme Principle, nothing else remains to be gained. In that state, one feels that he is Shiva. One who has realized the Supreme Self will always speak the truth and nothing but the truth. Tukaram Maharaj says, 'देव माझा मी देवाचा I' "God belongs to me and I belong to God." This is the doctrine of Vedanta and it is religion as well. Religious institutions exist for this purpose: to help man achieve this Truth. Such institutions must be well-managed. That is practice of religion—putting religion into practice.

Some people complain that our government is not acting according to religious principles and does not provide protection to religion, but this is not so. The government is looking after and managing many religious institutions and in this way, it is working in harmony with religion.

What is the meaning of religion? It is that by which one can know the Supreme Truth, that by which one attains eternal happiness. That is religion. Everyone undertakes activities in this world such as industry, business, politics and so on in order to obtain happiness. Vedanta says that one who has not achieved inner happiness cannot understand the true state. Religious institutions are meant for that. There man gets peace.

There is no real happiness in wearing fine clothes or eating good food, etc. True happiness is achieved only through knowledge of the Self. About this knowledge the *Bhagavad Gita* says, 'राजविद्या राजगुह्यं पवित्रमिद-मुत्तमम्' : "It is the king of all knowledges, the greatest of all secrets, the purest and the highest and it can be directly experienced. It is easy to practise and is imperishable." (9/2)

The purpose of religious institutions is to impart this knowledge and enable people to experience it. These institutions do not belong to any one individual, neither to me nor to you, nor to any swami. These

institutions are open for everyone who has love for
knowledge of the Self.

Man may progress to any extent, but he cannot
have real happiness without realizing the Truth. There
is no other way except the experience of *Shivoham* (I
am Shiva), which Mr. Dalal had the other day. The
main goal of human life is to realize the Self. Whatever
else man gains in this world is incidental whether it is
wife, sons, property or wealth. The main purpose of
a mango tree is to produce mangoes. Along with that,
it provides shade, its dried leaves and branches are used
for fuel and its trunk provides lumber. These other
uses, however, are subsidiary, or incidental. Similarly,
the main purpose of religious institutions such as
ashrams and *maths* is to remind man of the great
Vedantic proclamation तत्त्वमसि "That thou art." The
fulfillment of material desires and relief from worldly
miseries are the secondary gains of going to a saint. A
trustee is one who with selflessness and impartiality
fosters the main purpose of the religious institution.

When someone devotes himself to attaining God,
many people think that he must renounce the world,
but that isn't so. If God is all-pervading, what can be
rejected and what can be accepted? The *Taittiriya
Upanishad* says, 'तत् सृष्ट्वा तदेवानुप्राविशत्' ।"The Supreme
Lord created this cosmos and then He Himself entered
into it." This entire universe is the play of God. We
are an inseparable part of that Supreme Self. The
realization of this is liberation. The reason we greet
one another in daily life by saying "Ram Ram,"
"Namo Narayan," or "Salam 'Alequom" is that we wish
to see our own Self everywhere in everyone. The phrase
on our ashram emblem, *paraspara devo bhava* — "See
God in each other," also means the same.

Whatever work is going on in this world is, in reality, the work of God. If one understands this, one can perform any work as an offering. To cooperate selflessly in God's work is real *yajna* (sacrifice). The aim of religion is to obtain true knowledge. The *Manusmriti* advises, "Whoever protects *dharma* is protected by it. Otherwise he is destroyed."

The Lord says in the *Bhagavad Gita*:

यतः प्रवृत्तिर्भूतानां येन सर्वमिदं ततम् ।
स्वकर्मणा तमभ्यर्च्य सिद्धिं विन्दति मानवः ॥ १८।४६ ॥

"It is the Supreme Self from which the activity of all beings arises, by which everything is pervaded. One who worships that Supreme Self by performing one's own duty attains liberation." (18/46).

Work done with this understanding will be beneficial to you, to the devotees and to the religious institution.

Wednesday, April 29, 1964

Giridhari Sharad, a devotee, has returned to India after pursuing studies in the physical sciences for three years in England. While there, he maintained contact with the ashram through correspondence and read the ashram publications with great interest. He came today for Baba's *darshan* and asked some questions.

THE NATURE OF THE SELF

Giridhari: *When I was in England, I read your poem entitled "Knowledge of the Self is Easy to Attain." What is the nature of that Self? What are its attributes?*
Baba: The Self is beyond thought, cannot be seen, cannot be touched nor grasped, nor can it be described in words. These are its attributes. In other words, the

Self has no form, taste, smell, sound or texture. It can neither be comprehended by the mind nor perceived by the senses. The senses are the instruments by which we acquire knowledge of the objects and matters of the world, but they do not have the power to know the Self because they, themselves, are illumined by the Self. Those who have directly experienced the Self tell us that It is self-luminous; It cannot be the subject of questions and answers. It is to be realized or experienced through *sadhana*. The nature of the Self is not like that of any other object in the world. It cannot be described or explained through comparison with anything else. Just as there is only one sun and, therefore, you cannot say that it is like any other object or any other sun; similarly, there is nothing with which to compare the Self. In order to understand the Self, you have to realize the Self, for there is nothing similar to it.

Giridhari: *The poem also said, "Your Self is perfect light; the entire world is illumined by this light of the Self." Then is the light of the Self any different from the light of the sun? How does the light of the Self interact with that of the sun?*

Baba: There is no other light like that of the Self. It is incomparable. It is the Self that illumines the sun. Before the light of the Self, the light of the sun, moon, stars and fire is nothing. The sun and the moon shine by only an infinitesimal portion of the light of the Self. The *Kathopanishad* says :

न तत्र सूर्यो भाति न चन्द्रतारकं
नेमा विद्युतो भान्ति कुतोऽयमग्निः ।
तमेव भान्तमनुभाति सर्वं
तस्य भासा सर्वमिदं विभाति ॥

"There the sun does not shine nor the moon, the stars nor lightning, let alone fire. Where can fire shine?

By the light of the Self, all these shine. By the light of the Self, the entire universe is illumined."

Giridhari: *If the light of the Self and the light of the sun are different, there must be some evidence to prove it.*

Baba: The only evidence is the words of the Self-realized Siddhas who have themselves experienced it.

Giridhari: *How can this be explained to the modern-day scientists?*

Baba: This is not the subject of common science. In order to understand any subject, you have to follow the particular process suitable for it. For example, if some-one wants to become a doctor, he has to enter a medical college, attend the lectures of experienced doctors, and systematically undergo the clinical medical training. The knowledge of the Self cannot be taught to scientists by these academic methods. One can know the Self only after Self-realization and only a Self-realized master can make others realize it.

Giridhari: *In your book entitled* Adesh, *you stated, "That which enables you to know what happens during the waking, dream and deep sleep states is the Self." But darkness prevails in the dream and sleep states. Does this mean, therefore, that one can see objects in darkness because of the light of the Self?*

Baba: The Self illumines darkness as well as light. When the light of the Self shines, even the sun appears to be dark. Even in darkness, the Self is always shining. A man sleeping in a completely dark room sees the procession of a king in his dream. By which light does he see it? The source of that light is the Self.

Light is of two types. One is ordinary or potential light and the other is special or manifest. Ordinary light is concealed inside something as, for example, fire is concealed or potential within wood. The light of the Self is within every individual. Just as a piece of wood cannot start burning spontaneously—fire manifests only as a result of friction—similarly, only when the light of the Self emerges as a result of *sadhana,* is it fully manifest. This light is the special kind of light.

Giridhari: *Is it advisable to take these teachings for granted, or is it better to evaluate them logically?*

Baba: To accept any statement without the verification of personal experience is like accepting the stories told by one's grandmother during childhood as true. Just as, although you have not seen, you believe it when someone tells you that Dasharath, the father of Rama, was the king of Ayodhya, or that there was once an emperor called Napoleon, or that there is a city called Patna in Bihar because all this has to be believed. But how can there be any question of disbelieving or believing in the Truth, which is manifest? The Self is not a thing of the past. It is a reality that is manifest and can be directly experienced. You can see the sun with your own eyes. How can any question arise about believing in its existence when it is a reality you see yourself? The Self is the eternal Truth existing in the past, present and future. Vivekananda asked Ramakrishna, "Have you seen God?" and Ramakrishna replied, "Yes. God appears to be very far away to you, but I see him very close to me."

Saturday, May 9, 1964

Shrimati Taraben Parekh came today for Baba's *darshan* and *satsang*. She is the daughter of Brahmaleen Swami Madhavtirth, founder of the Vedanta Ashram of Valad, and was born when he was a householder.

Taraben: *What is meant by the term* "sahaj awastha"?
Baba: It is the state of witness consciousness. Just as one naturally enters the sleep or dream states, this state also comes naturally. In this state, there is no ego or I-consciousness. When we are travelling, we observe our surroundings without becoming attached to anything. This state is the same.

Taraben: *Can one meditate with eyes open?*
Baba: Certainly. One can meditate in the way that suits him best. If you try to follow a method that is not suitable for you, then difficulties will arise. In meditation with the eyes open, the eyes see the outer objects, but the mind is focused within. *Kumbhaka* does not occur even after the *prana* has become steady. Even though the eyes are open, one does not see anything; even though words enter the ears, one does not hear anything.

To become free of the awareness of knower, known and knowledge is meditation. When the mind abandons its usual nature and merges into the Self, that is meditation. The *Yoga Sutras* say the same thing about meditation: ' तत्र प्रत्ययैकतानता ध्यानम् ' (३-२) "Remaining unaffected in every situation is meditation." Being one with the Self is meditation. There are many definitions of meditation.

Saturday, June 21, 1964

Today Shri Rameshbhai Sumatilal Shah, the owner of Pannalal Silk Mills, came to the ashram for Baba's *darshan* with his family and some friends. He asked Baba the following question:

THE BLISS OF JIVANMUKTI

Rameshbhai: *Baba, what is the state in which there is neither mental nor physical suffering?*

Baba: Pleasure and pain are not experienced in the *turiya* state. In that state, everything is seen as Brahman. This is what is known as *jivanmukti,* or liberation in this very life. Waking, dream and deep sleep are the three states of the individual soul. The Self does not have any such states. The Self is the witness of these three states and the experience of this is *turiya.* Besides elimination of the non-Self, there is no other activity in *turiya.* When the mind ceases to be the mind, that is the *turiya* state.

In the waking and dream states, one sees unreality instead of Reality, while in deep sleep one sees neither. In deep sleep, the individual soul is not conscious of "I" or "you"; it is unconscious even of non-duality. In the *turiya* state, however, it sees everything as Brahman. There one sees Reality and there is an awareness of non-duality. One who has knowledge of the Self no longer sees the world as world. The various dualities such as right or wrong, the Guru and the disciple, and bondage and liberation all become one. Such a realized person does not consider the triad of doer, deed and fruit of the deed as different from the Self. He sees everything as the Self. Such a person has no mandatory duties. Since he does not experience duality, he is always non-attached. This is the fifth state in Vedanta called *asansakti.* This is *jivanmukti.*

Until one constantly experiences the bliss of *jivan-mukti,* one must repeatedly contemplate the meaning of the Vedantic teachings. If the mind has accepted that everything is nothing but Vasudev, or God, but that idea does not remain steady, and the mind and body continue to crave the pleasures of worldly objects, then faith will not become firm. If faith is not firm, the mind will remain restless and will stop the search for the Self. As a result, there will be no experience of the bliss of *jivanmukti*.

A hollow gourd normally floats in water, but sinks if filled with iron; similarly, if the mind is full of desire, hatred and so forth, it cannot remain in the continuous awareness of the Self. The company of saints and sages is an antidote to this poison of the mundane world enabling one to again experience the bliss of the Self.

In order to experience his true Self, one should remain in solitude for some time each day. If possible, he should go into complete seclusion for about seven days every two or three months. During these periods of solitude, he should abandon all thoughts and practise watching what is happening within. In this way, one gets into the state of witness consciousness.

Love for the Self arouses yearning for realization of the Self. If you want to concentrate the mind while meditating on the Self, you must not let it wander here and there. By such practice, the mind melts away and desires are eliminated.

When the inner Shakti starts expanding as a result of contemplation of the Self, many seekers have various visions, hear divine music and see different coloured lights, flames and spots of light. A seeker should not pay too much attention to these or else they will create a hindrance to his love for the Self. In order to disengage the mind from these, the best way is to continuously repeat the Vedanta *sutra* "*neti, neti*"— "not this, not this." The means to Self-realization is the Self Itself. If you remain constantly in the awareness of the Self, the mind easily becomes still. If knowledge of the Self remains steady, bliss also remains constant. This is the ideal of *sthitapragna* in the *Bhagavad Gita*. In this state, one remains undisturbed even in sorrow and adversity.

Wednesday, July 1, 1964

Miss Hilda Charlton comes to stay in the ashram now and then and has *satsang* with Baba. There was a question and answer session today.

THE LIGHTS SEEN DURING MEDITATION

Hilda: *What are the different stages in meditation? What is the sequence of the different experiences? I used to see lights and hear sounds. I also used to have visions, but I no longer have any of these experiences. I went to Rishikesh to practise meditation and there I would become one with the inner Consciousness while meditating; I would often lose awareness of the gross body. What will follow after these experiences? I ask this question because I plan to return to America and I feel I should know what to expect.*

Baba: Why? Just before leaving, won't you come to see me? Or when I go to America, won't you visit me there?

Hilda: *Yes, I shall certainly come here again and if you come to America, what more could I wish for! Babaji, please do come to America. But now, please tell me what stage will follow in my meditation.*

Baba: I will write on this subject and send you a copy of the English translation. After reading it, you will have complete understanding.

Hilda: *I can't wait for such a long time. I will lose patience. Please tell me something now.*

Baba: Then listen. In the beginning several lights are seen during meditation.

Hilda: *Yes, I used to see many lights. I even saw them with my eyes open.*

Baba: There are different kinds of lights, many of them unimportant. The main lights are red, white, black and blue. The *jivatma,* or individual soul, has four bodies: the gross, subtle, causal and supracausal. The red light represents the gross body; white, the subtle body; black, the causal body; and blue light represents the supracausal body. The red light appears as a large, expansive area within which you see a thumb-size, bright white light. Afterwards, within the white light, you see the black light. Within the black light, you see a blue spot. This shining Blue Pearl is of the nature of Brahman. Its appearance indicates the *turiya* state.

Hilda: *I see this Blue Pearl not only with closed eyes, but frequently even with my eyes open.*

Baba: This indicates that you are progressing well in meditation.

Hilda: *What should I do now?*

Baba: Nothing special. Just increase your meditation. The rest will happen spontaneously. The time will also come when nothing will happen; everything will vanish. Neither the lights nor the Blue Pearl will appear.

I have wrapped this shawl around my body. It is different from me and yet I am aware that it belongs to me. You will feel the same way about your body; that is, you will develop witness consciousness, which is also known as the *nirvikalpa* state, or *sahaj awastha,* the natural state.

Hilda: *I experience this state even now, but only occasionally; it isn't constant.*

Baba: As your bliss keeps increasing, this state will gradually become steady. Try to increase that bliss.

Hilda: *When I was in America before coming here, I used to feel during meditation that I could leave my body from the space between the eyebrows and go wherever I liked. Is this possible?*

Baba: These are all the play of *prana*. But the Blue Pearl that you see is important. It is the Supreme Self; it is the *Atma;* it is the abode of God. This Pearl appears to be outside, but actually it is within. It is located right in the centre of the eyes, ears, the vertex and the back of the head. It is the supracausal body. The entire Shakti dwells within it. With this body, we can go wherever we want. The Blue Pearl moves at tremendous speed. Its speed is such that within a fraction of a second it can go to America and return here. This Pearl appears in meditation as a scintillating, shining spot and then disappears.

Hilda: *I also see a brown light in the shape of a rupee coin. What is that light?*

Baba: That is also one of the lights, but the Blue Pearl is more important. Continue to meditate. After some time, you will acquire so much Shakti that you will be able to give others the experience of meditation. You will be able to transmit Shakti to others.

Hilda: *Oh! How beautiful! Baba, when I return to America, this is what I shall do. Here I have been able to cure some people. Should I continue to do this after returning to America? Is it advisable to do this?*

Baba: There is nothing wrong with it; however, instead of curing diseases, it would be better to guide others onto the spiritual path.

Hilda: *Baba, you have given me such clear understanding. My mind is satisfied. I used to think that Self-*

*realization would happen suddenly like a bomb
exploding, but now I understand that it comes easily
and naturally. One does not even feel it. How wonderful!*

Friday, July 3, 1964

Today Hilda Charlton again asked Baba several questions.

GREAT BEINGS ARE ONE WITH SUPREME CONSCIOUSNESS

Hilda: *Do saints like Swami Nityananda and Ramana
Maharshi continue to exist in a subtle form even after
their* mahasamadhi? *After* mahasamadhi, *some people
have had their* darshan *and have received guidance from
them.*

Baba: Before trying to comprehend this subject, it is
necessary to understand the true nature of such saints.
From the spiritual viewpoint, there are two classes of
people, limited beings and saints. You must understand how a limited being becomes a saint. According
to the *Upanishads,* that person is called a saint who has
completely merged his individuality into the attributeless, formless Chaitanya, or Supreme Consciousness,
becoming one with It. One who falls short of
completely merging with Chaitanya by even an iota remains only a limited being. He may perform any number of miracles, yet he cannot be called a saint. He may
be able to travel to Kashi or Mathura while sitting here,
he may perform many miracles or whatever he says may
come true, yet he still is imperfect. It is said:

गुपत होकर परगट होवे, जावे मथुरा कासी ।
चलता है पानी के ऊपर, मुख बोले सो होवे ॥
फिर भी कच्चा बे कच्चा, नहीं गुरु का बच्चा ॥

"He can disappear and then reappear; he can travel instantaneously to Kashi or Mathura; he can walk on water; his words may come true and yet, he is imperfect. He is not the son of a Guru."

Just as salt dissolves in water and pervades all of it, similarly, a saint is one whose consciousness pervades everywhere.

Hilda: *How is it possible for saints to maintain their individual identities after completely merging with Consciousness? How can we say, "This is Swami Nityananda" or "This is Ramana Maharshi"?*

Baba: Just as there are many mangoes on a mango tree, such saints have the same relationship with Consciousness, or just as the sea has innumerable drops of water, similarly, the saints are different forms of one Consciousness.

Hilda: *What is the special quality of the samadhi shrines of these great saints that enables many people to have their darshan even after they have left their physical bodies?*

Baba: Listen to the following story to understand this: Once, in an assembly of sages, the topic under discussion was "Which is greater, austerities (*tapasya*) or knowledge of Brahman (*Brahmajnana*)?" Vishwamitra declared, "Austerities are greater," while Vasishtha proclaimed, "Knowledge of the Self is greater." As the discussion proceeded, the arguments became increasingly heated. They could not reach any conclusion. Finally, they all went to the netherworld to seek the counsel of Sheshanaga, the king of serpents. Vishwamitra asked him to enlighten them on the subject. Being omniscient, Sheshanaga knew everything that had happened prior to their arrival. Yet he told them, "I will certainly give you the answer, but it would be helpful if you could relieve me of this heavy burden on my head." Actually, there was no burden on his head. He holds the entire earth on his head as naturally as we wear a cap.

Vishwamitra said, "For ten million years, I have done *tapasya* (austerities) and I have controlled my *pranas* for many years through the practice of *kumbhaka*. By the power of this *tapasya,* I will make the earth stand on my *yogadanda* (yoga stick). As soon as he had placed it on his *yogadanda,* the earth started to sway.

Observing this, Vasishtha said, "If I have experienced the all-pervading Supreme Self, whose nature is pure Consciousness, for even a fraction of a second, this earth will rest on my *kamandalu* (water bowl)." And, lo and behold, the earth did stand steady on his *kamandalu.*

Vishwamitra then said to Sheshanaga, "Your burden has been relieved. Now give us the answer."

Sheshanaga replied, "Where is the need for an answer now? You should all be able to understand it for yourselves."

This story gives you an idea of the great power of the *tapasya* of those great beings like Vasishtha who experienced the Supreme Self for innumerable moments rather than for just a fraction of a second. The *tapasya* of these great beings after realization of Brahman is not for their personal use because they have nothing left to attain. It is for the benefit of others. This power remains in their *samadhi* shrines. Actually, this power is the same as the all-prevading pure Consciousness. The same Consciousness is within you and it manifests in **different** forms according to your faith; thus, you have the *darshan* of saints and sages.   Just as the different objects perceived in the world are forms of the same Chaitanya Shakti, similarly, *darshan* of these saints is also a form of that same Chaitanya. When devotees visit a *samadhi* shrine offering prayers and worship, then, according to their faith, they are blessed with the *darshan* of that saint.   It is a manifestation of their own inner faith.

Hilda: *I had the* darshan *of Nityananda Baba even before I had met him in person. At that time, I didn't even know him. Therefore, I feel that even prior to meeting him, he was guiding me. How could this have happened?*

Baba: It is not at all difficult for Chaitanya Shakti to assume any form; in fact, it is very easy.   The *darshan* that you had was to foretell your eventual meeting with Baba.

THE INEQUALITIES SEEN IN THE WORLD ARE THE RESULT OF PAST ACTIONS

Hilda: *When I return to America and tell people that God is all-pervading and that He has created this world, they will ask me, "If that is so, then why is there so much misery and poverty in this world?"*

Baba: God has not created any inequalities in this world.   Pleasure and pain are seen by the individual, not by God.   Moreover, an individual's outlook is relative.   If you ask a wealthy man, "What is the world like?" in accordance with his own experiences, he would reply, "It is beautiful and full of pleasures." But if you ask a poor man the same question, he would say, "The world is full of misery."   The experiences of worldly pleasure and pain are personal and short-lived.   In the state of realization, pleasure and pain are no longer cognised.   In this regard Swami Ram Tirth used to tell a beautiful story.

There was a lords' club to which no one except lords was admitted. At the very outset, the question arose as to who would sweep, who would cook and who would perform all the other menial duties since they all had equal status. They had a meeting and decided that they would draw lots. The lord whose name was drawn for a particular task would do it for that day. In this way, they all took turns performing the various jobs required to run the club such as sweeper, errand boy, cook, secretary and president. Now, the lord who happened to be sweeping would be considered as a sweeper by passers-by, but the lord himself knew that he was a lord, not a sweeper. Thus the views of the lord and the passers-by were different.

Just as the lords in the club performed different roles according to their lots, similarly, in this world everyone lives according to his past deeds, but in essence the same Consciousness exists everywhere and in everyone; everything and everyone are equal. Pleasure and pain, wealth and poverty are all alike, but to an ordinary man they appear to be different.

Three years ago a man who had mastered the *Bhrigu Samhita* visited me. He told me that four births earlier I was a king, but now I am a monk. Similarly, man has pleasure or pain according to his past deeds. The Supreme Self, however, is always the same.

An artist paints different figures, cow, horse, man, house, river, mountain, tree and so forth, on the same wall using the same brush. These figures have different shapes and names, but in reality, they are from the same paint. Similarly, everything in this world has in fact arisen from the Supreme Self. The experience of pleasure and pain is dependent upon the thinking of the individual. The same set of circumstances will elicit different responses according to the individual's attitude.

"This is that Devadatta" is a sentence which is often quoted in Vedanta to illustrate one of its basic teachings, "Thou art That." Devadatta was the king of Benares. He developed a strong feeling of dispassion. Entrusting his kingdom to his son, he took *sannyasa*. In his wanderings, he came to a town where someone recognised him. The man told his friend, "This is that Devadatta," by which he meant, "This is the same Devadatta who was formerly the king of Benares." To others, he appeared to be a *sannyasi* and not a king because of the change in his clothes, place and status. In fact, the same person was Devadatta, the *sannyasi* as well as Devadatta, the king. Recognising the real Devadatta even in the clothes of a *sannyasi* is an example of the principle of Self-recognition according to Vedanta.

When a man is asleep, he is not aware of pleasure or pain. Even in the waking state, he forgets them when he is concentrating on some activity. This shows that pleasure and pain are not real, but are concepts of the mind and, therefore, cannot be lasting. I shall relate another story.

A fisherman once became friendly with a wealthy man. He used to take a walk everyday on the beach and the fisherman gave him fish. One day the wealthy man invited the fisherman to his home. On the appointed day, the fisherman went to the man's house, taking some fish as a gift. Both of them were very happy. They had their meals together and then the man asked the fisherman to stay overnight. He was given a beautiful bedroom filled with the fragrance of flowers and scent.

At midnight the host heard some noises in the adjacent room so he got up and looked in on the fisherman. The guest, appearing quite restless, was sitting up in bed. The host enquired, "Haven't you slept?" The fisherman replied, "There is a strange smell in this room and, therefore, I cannot go to sleep." Being perceptive, the wealthy man asked him, "Where is the cloth in which the fish you brought were wrapped?" The fisherman replied that it was outside. The host advised him to cover his face with that cloth and then go to sleep. The fisherman did so and he immediately fell asleep. Thus, what was pleasant for the wealthy man was experienced as unpleasant by the fisherman, and that which was pleasant to the fisherman was intolerable to the wealthy man. Similarly, the experiences of pleasure and pain are according to the outlook of the mind.

Saturday, July 4, 1964

A SEEKER'S EXPERIENCES

Hilda: *I see a spider-like insect when I meditate with my eyes open. As I keep looking at it, it climbs up onto the ceiling and disappears. Is something bad happening?*
Baba: What you see is not a creature, but a kind of network of light, which is actually within you although appearing to be outside. If you concentrate your mind on it, you will see spots of light. This is not a bad experience. Just be a witness to whatever you see in meditation.
Hilda: *Sometimes when I sit for meditation, I feel very dull and listless. How can I overcome this feeling?*
Baba: There is no need to do anything about it. Just

continue to sit for meditation. All these will gradually drop away. Through meditation, the mind will be purified. The feeling of disinterestedness or listlessness is a kind of state of mind. As you continue to meditate, this state will change spontaneously.

Hilda: *During meditation I sometimes have visions of divine beings. I even feel that they are giving me their blessings.*

Baba: That is good. During meditation one may see various other worlds such as Siddhaloka, Chandraloka and Indraloka. One may have visions of saints and sages. Sometimes one may also receive guidance from them.

Sunday, July 5, 1964

THE DEVELOPMENT OF SHAKTI THROUGH SELF-EFFORT AND FAITH

Nain: *Rudolph has some very exalted spiritual experiences. Are they the result of his sadhana in a previous life?*

Baba: The human body is a centre of divine energy. This energy is so powerful that, by its strength, Prahlad was able to bring God forth bodily from a pillar, Vishwamitra was able to create another world, and the Gopis were able to make Balakrishna dance in their homes. This great Shakti exists in everyone. In some people, however, it appears to be more active and in others, less. The same Chaitanya Shakti, or life force, exists in the body, mind, intellect and *prana* of every being, but the level of development of these instruments varies from one being to another. For example, some are more intellectually developed than others. Therefore,

what we must consider is how the development of the
Shakti can be accomplished. All grains of wheat are
alike. After sowing they grow with the support of the
soil. But whether they grow more or less depends upon
the skill of the farmer. Similarly, the development of
the dormant Shakti within us depends on every individual's effort. The gross bodies of man, animals, birds
and so forth are all composed of five great elements
(ether, air, fire, water and earth). The basic constituents of all bodies are the same. Sundardas says:

देह ओर देखिये तौ, देह पंचभूतन को ।
ब्रह्मा अरु कीट लग, देह ही प्रधान है ॥
प्रान ओर देखिये तौ, प्रान सब ही के एक ।
क्षुधा पुनि तृषा दोउ, व्यापत समान है ॥
मन ओर देखिये तौ, मन को स्वभाव एक ।
संकल्प-विकल्प करै, सदा ही अज्ञान है ।
आतम विचार किये, आतमा ही दीसै एक ।
सुन्दर कहत कोऊ, देखिये न आन है ॥

"If you observe the gross bodies from Brahma down
to a small insect, they are all made up of the same five
great elements. If you consider *prana,* it is the same in
all beings. Both hunger and thirst are similar for all
creatures. If you consider the nature of the mind, it is
universally the same; it is always entertaining doubts
and vacillating between one thought and another, and
thus it is steeped in ignorance. If you consider the Self,
it is also the same everywhere and at all times.
Sundardas says, 'Where can you find any difference?
One is just like another.'

In spite of the body, *pranas* and mind being similar in all beings, the development of each man's
Chaitanya Shakti depends on the subtle impressions
(*samskaras*) of his innumerable past lives and on his
own self-effort in his present life. For this development

both the awakening of the Kundalini and a deep faith are essential. Faith has great power. Faith is a great divine Shakti dwelling within you. Surdas says that by the power of their faith, the gopis milked a bull to quench the Lord's thirst! Because of the strength of her faith, Mirabai swallowed poison with no ill effects.

Faith arises as a result of one's feelings and mental tendencies, and may be placed in a worthy or unworthy object. The fruits we receive are in accordance with the object of our faith. The *Bhagavad Gita* says:

सत्त्वानुरूपा सर्वस्य श्रद्धा भवति भारत ।
श्रद्धामयोऽयं पुरुषो यो यच्छ्रद्धः स एव सः ॥ १७।३ ॥

"O Bharata! The faith of each person is according to his nature. Everyone has faith in something or in someone. Man is transformed according to his faith." (17/3)

In my early days as a monk, I went to a jungle called Anandavan in Khuldabad near Daulatabad. It was there that Eknath Maharaj had a divine vision of Lord Datta and it has since become a place of pilgrimage in Maharashtra. Janardan Swami did his *tapasya* there. I went there for the *darshan* of Bhagawan Datta. I stayed for three days. At that time I had such faith that I would meet Bhagawan there that every day I looked all around expecting Bhagawan to appear from this direction or that. Ten years later I returned to the same place, but had no desire at all to stay because, by that time, I had become a Vedantin. I had lost all interest in the manifestation of God in any form. Had I stayed in Anandavan for two or three years when I first went there, I surely would have had the *darshan* of Bhagawan Datta in a physical form. At that time I had such unshakable faith.

Sunday, July 5, 1964

Today another meeting of the ashram council was held. In addition to the council members, some other devotees were also present. After the business of the meeting was concluded, Baba spoke a few words in the form of a blessing.

Earlier in the meeting, Shri Pratap Yande had reported on his discussion with Shri Shankarrao Raut, a trustee of the Shri Bhimeshwar Sadguru Nityananda Trust, regarding the programme for the approaching Guru Purnima. Baba returned to this subject.

THE NECESSITY OF FOLLOWING THE SCRIPTURES IN RELIGIOUS CEREMONIES

Baba: What programme are you planning to have at Nityananda Baba's shrine on that day?

Pratap: *The trustees there are considering performing a* Rudrabhishek *(ritual bath given to an image of Lord Shiva)*.

Baba: Those involved in administering religious institutions should have a thorough knowledge of scriptural precepts. Charity is that which is given in the name of religion or for a religious purpose, and religion signifies God and the scriptures. Thus, knowledge of the religious scriptures is essential in order to properly administer such institutions. *Rudrabhishek* can be done on Mahashivaratri; worship of the Guru's *padukas* must be performed on Guru Purnima. On such occasions it is best to consult experts on religious rites and rituals and act according to their advice.

After the *mahasamadhi* of Nityananda Baba, an argument arose as to which day should be considered the thirteenth day. Should the days be counted from the day he left the body or from the day he was laid in the *samadhi* shrine? Swami Kuttiram, Swami Digambar and other devotees said that Baba had told them to count from the day he was put into the shrine. If I had told them the relevant scriptural rule, my plight would have been like that of the priest in the following story.

Once a group of nine fishermen went on a pilgrimage accompanied by their priest. They had a good pilgrimage, doing everything properly according to scriptural rites. Nonetheless, desire is such a peculiar thing that it is impossible to predict when and where it will lead a man. The *Bhagavad Gita* says,

इन्द्रियाणि प्रमाथीनि हरन्ति प्रसभं मनः ॥ "The turbulent senses violently carry away the mind of a wise man." (2/60)

As the group was returning home, they spotted a toddy shop. The fishermen entered the shop and drank to their hearts' content. The priest said, "Look, we have not yet completed our pilgrimage; we have not yet reached our town. What are you doing?" The fishermen became fearful that the priest would complain about them to everyone on reaching home so immediately upon arriving in town, before the priest had a chance to say a word, the fishermen told the townfolk that the priest had drunk toddy while returning from the pilgrimage. All the townspeople began to reproach him saying, "In spite of being a priest, don't you understand that you should not have behaved like that? What have you done?" In this manner, the priest got into trouble even though he had not touched a drop of toddy.

Not wanting to get into trouble like that priest, I advised them to seek the counsel of Pandit Vare Shastri of Nasik, who is a well-known and accepted authority on this subject. I told them that he had a thorough knowledge of the scriptures and that they should abide by his decision. Everyone agreed and Pandit Vare Shastri was called. He said that the thirteen days should

be counted from the day Baba had left his body and so
it was done.

Religion is not a business for idle people. It is
not a pursuit for those who have nothing else to do in
life. King Janaka ruled his vast kingdom according to
the traditions of statesmanship and, although he was not
a *sannaysi,* he was a great *tyagi* (renunciate), a great
jnani and a Siddha. One cannot live religion merely
by shaving one's head or wearing saffron clothes. These
are merely a matter of custom according to the discipline
of the four stages of life. Just by becoming a *sannyasi*
one does not acquire the authority to give judgments
on religious observances. For this, one must have
knowledge of the scriptures. Religion means friendship
with God. Religion means behaviour which is pleasing to God. Ordinarily, even in daily life, all the
actions of a person who is dear to us appear good and
pleasing. For example, followers of Nehru started
wearing a jacket like his and it became the famous
Jawahar jacket. *Tulsi* is dear to Lord Vishnu so
devotees of Vishnu wear *malas* of *tulsi.* *Rudraksha* is
dear to Lord Shankar, so his devotees wear *malas* of
rudraksha beads. In this manner, you should consider
what qualities are dear to God. These are truth, non-
violence, compassion for all creatures and a pure and
peaceful way of life. Love for these qualities is religion.
Religion is truth, the pursuit of which fructifies immediately.

One must follow the scriptural guidelines in the
performance of any religious ritual and consult one
who knows the scriptures. When we fall sick, we go to a
doctor, not a lawyer. Similarly, with regard to religious
ceremonies, we must consult a person with the appropriate expertise. The scriptural rules are quite explicit.
It is said, 'यद्यपि शुद्धं, शास्त्रविरुद्धं, न करणीयं नाचरणीयम् । '

"Any action, however good it appears, should not be carried out if it is contrary to the scriptures." This has been proven sound by experience. Guru Purnima is the Guru's day. On that day you must sing the glories of the Guru. The Guru is an essential aspect of religion. His status is great indeed. But, unless one is a true disciple, the greatness of the Guru cannot be understood. I for one am a follower of the Guru. The Guru has been considered even greater than God. Sundardas says:

गोविन्द के किये जीव वूड़त भवसागर में
सुन्दर कहत गुरु काढै दुखद्वंद्व तैं ॥
औरहू कहाँ लौं कछू मुख तें कहूँ बनाय ।
गुरु की तौ महिमा अधिक है गोविन्द तैं ॥

"The individual souls created by Govinda are drowned in the ocean of birth and death. Sundar says, 'The Guru saves them from pain and suffering. Whatever the Guru says comes true. The greatness of the Guru surpasses even that of Govinda.' "

Even the Lord is pleased by the worship of the Guru. Therefore, you should welcome, honour and worship the Guru. It is the Guru who makes you realize God. On Guru Purnima, therefore, you must perform the worship of the Guru's *padukas* and perform *rudrabhishek* on Mahashivaratri. The scriptures have outlined in detail the methods for performing these different religious ceremonies and it is our duty to follow them strictly. Even God Himself never transgresses any laws. In this connection, I remember a humorous story. King Akbar once asked Birbal, his minister, "Who is greater, God or I?" Birbal replied, "You are greater, Your Majesty, because you can rule as you like, you can transgress laws, and you can punish a person whether or not he is guilty of any offence.

God cannot do this. He has to act according to established laws and processes. God does not function
according to His every whim and fancy." God and
religion never transgress discipline or limits.

Wednesday, July 8, 1964

An American woman, Laresa Gahan, has been staying
at the ashram for the past seven or eight months. She
came after hearing about Baba from Albert Rudolph in
New York. Today she asked Baba about some doubts
which were troubling her.

DEVOTION TO THE GURU IS A GREAT SADHANA

Laresa: *Baba, two different views prevail among your
devotees. One group says that merely living in your company is sufficient; no other sadhana need be practised.
They believe that all our sadhana is done by Baba. We
do not have to make any effort. Love, devotion and
service to the Guru will take us to our goal. The second
group says that we must put forth effort without which
everything else is useless. They believe that, although
Baba may guide us and give us inspiration, we must
walk the path ourselves. Which of these two viewpoints
is correct?*

Baba: Everyone gives advice according to his own
understanding.

Laresa: *What is your opinion?*

Baba: (The first viewpoint is superior as the following
true story illustrates).

Eknath Maharaj was a great Siddha of Maharashtra.
A *bhandara*, or feast, was held every day at his place and
a special type of sweet bread, *pooranpoli*, was served.
In the same village there lived a poor woman and her

son, Gavaba, who had an insatiable desire for that particular kind of bread.   Without it, he would not eat
his meals and would create a commotion.   His mother
implored Ekanath Maharaj to let her son stay with him
because that bread was served at his place every day.
Eknath Maharaj agreed and Gavaba went to stay with
him.   Everyone started calling the boy Pooranpolia.

After a while people began asking him, "Do you
just eat pooranpolis, or do you ever do anything else
such as praying, chanting, meditating, *japa* or *tapasya?*"
Pooranpolia would reply, "Yes, I pray and worship
Eknath Maharaj.   I meditate on Eknath Maharaj.   I
repeat the name of Eknath Maharaj for *japa.*"   In this
manner the boy was fully immersed in Eknath Maharaj.
This was his only *sadhana*.

At that time Eknath Maharaj was writing a book
entitled *Bhavartha Ramayana*.   It was still incomplete
when he declared to his devotees that he would soon be
leaving his body.   The worried devotees said to him,
"Maharaj, *Bhavartha Ramayana* is still unfinished."
Eknath Maharaj replied, "Discuss the matter with Hari
Pandit.   If he cannot complete it, then Pooranpolia
will."   Hari Pandit was Eknath Maharaj's son.   He
was a learned scholar, having studied the Vedas and
Vedanta in Benares.   The devotees thought that Hari
Pandit would be able to complete the book.   What
could the illiterate Pooranpolia write? Soon after Eknath
Maharaj passed away, Hari Pandit sat down to work on
the book, but he was unable to write a single word.
Then Pooranpolia, constantly remembering his Guru,
began writing and completed the book within a short
time.

The *Mahabharata* contains another such example
of devotion to the Guru.   Dronacharya used to teach
archery to Arjuna.   Ekalavya, the son of a Bhil tribes-

man, requested Dronacharya to teach him as well. In those days the caste system was very rigidly followed and so Dronacharya refused to take this lad as his pupil. Ekalavya returned home, prepared an earthen idol of Dronacharya, placed it under a tree near his house and, considering the idol as his Guru, started practising archery on his own. Because of his unshakable faith and devotion to the Guru, he would feel himself to be Dronacharya and in that state he mastered the complete skill of archery quickly and easily. He became such an expert that he surpassed Dronacharya's other pupils.

One day a dog was passing by Ekalavya's house, barking very loudly. Ekalavya shot an arrow in such a way that it lodged right between the dog's two front teeth. The dog ran away yelping and passed Dronacharya and Arjuna. Everyone began to wonder who had the skill to shoot an arrow like that. Arjuna was not even able to remove the arrow. After some investigation, they discovered that this miraculous feat was performed by Ekalavya. This is called *gurubhakti*, devotion to the Guru. Such devotion can make a disciple even greater than his Guru. Therefore, this is the best path of God-realization.

Tuesday, July 14, 1964

In the morning the devotees were sitting in the hall around Baba. Tehmina Bharucha asked Baba some questions.

YANTRAS AND TANTRAS

Tehmina: *Are* yantras *and* tantras *valid?*
Baba: Just as there are so many other mechanical devices, similarly, *tantric yantras* are also a kind of

device. For example, the nose of a dog is equipped with an organ that enables it to track down the real criminal. Once, two servants of a Christian man were murdered here near Akloli. No one could trace the murderer. The man's son was a high official in Delhi and he brought a police officer, Mr. Kamte, to the sight of the crime. Mr. Kamte brought with him two dogs trained in England. The dogs sniffed around the site of the murder and soon afterwards led the police to the two murderers. The dogs even searched for and retrieved their shoes, which had been hidden in the river.

Similarly, there is an instrument fitted in ships that warns of rocks concealed under the water and dangerous spots in the sea. Just like these instruments, *tantric yantras* are mere tools. They are valid, but there is nothing extraordinary about them.

Tehmina: *Is it true that with the help of certain mantras, or by doing a particular type of* sadhana, *we can read other people's thoughts or acquire the power to do anything we desire?*

Baba: Patanjali's *Yogasutras* gives a description of *sanyam siddhis.* It says that by practising *sanyam,* or concentration on an object, the seeker acquires the power of that object. Some yogis are able to stop running trains. Do you know the secret behind this ability? By envisioning a mountain in the space between the eyebrows and doing *sanyam* on it, the weight of the mountain bears down on the train, forcing it to halt. Similarly, *sanyam* on an elephant enables you to acquire the strength of the elephant so that you cannot be lifted. But what is the use of learning such tricks? God is beyond all these. He can be attained only after renouncing them.

Monday, July 27, 1964

A *sannyasi*, Atmaramananda, came to the ashram today. He presented Baba with a scholarly book written in
Sanskrit by a *mahamandaleshwar*. Praising the author's
erudition, he insisted that Baba should read it. At this,
Baba said the following:

THE PRIDE OF LEARNING

Baba: The *mahamandaleshwar* is a highly learned
scholar who commands great respect. It seems that he
has set out to prove his supremacy in scholarship. Listen
to the following story.

About three or four centuries ago there lived a
great scholar named Vaman Pandit. He had proven his
supremacy seven times at the universal competition of
scholars. He had mastered all the scriptures and had
also written many books. Wherever he went, he would
carry a stack of books on the back of a mule so that
whenever anyone raised a doubt in a debate, he could
quickly provide the proof from the books. Normally,
any book, article, or discourse is considered valid only
if it can be supported by the scriptures. Without scriptural authority such works are valueless.

One day the scholar set out carrying his usual load
of books. On his way he encountered Swami Samarth
Ramdas, who asked him, "Where are you going with
that pile of books?" Vaman Pandit was very proud. He
retorted, "What can you understand anyway?" Swami
Ramdas explained to him, "Look, a person may write
any number of books, but whatever is written without
God's grace will never endure. After five hundred
years, no one will even remember your books."

Soon afterwards, Vaman Pandit again went to
Benares to participate in the universal competition of

scholars for the eighth time. One afternoon as he was passing beneath a tree, he overheard two voices quarrelling above him. One fellow shouted, "You get away from here; vacate this place at once!" The other fellow asserted, "Why should I? I am greater than you. You have won the universal competition only five times while I have won it six times." The first fellow said, "Well, anyway, a scholar who has won the competition seven times will soon be coming and you will have to vacate the place." Panditji looked up, but could not see anyone. However, he understood that the voices belonged to two Brahmin ghosts.

He was filled with remorse. He lamented, "After acquiring so much knowledge, fame and respect, is this the state I am going to achieve in the end?!" He jumped into the Ganges to drown himself, but by the grace of God, he did not die. After repenting in this way, whatever he wrote with God's grace was most beautiful and even today research is being carried out on his works.

Wednesday, July 29, 1964

Some relatives of Shri A. Shankar, a devotee from Hyderabad, came today for Baba's *darshan*. Two or three of them were seekers and asked questions.

Seeker: *Is it advisable to control the mind, or might such control have a harmful effect?*
Baba: Allowing the mind to run loose brings about misery; hence, it is better to control it and keep it in check. If you desire happiness, renounce pride in your actions and control the various waves arising in the mind. If you do not practise even one of these two, the mind will become confused and you will have to

undergo the ensuing bad consequences.

Seeker: *Are birth and death determined according to one's past deeds?*

Baba: Birth and death are determined according to one's desires.

PERFORM ONLY GOOD DEEDS

Seeker: *After death, does man obtain another human birth, or might he be born as an animal or a bird?*

Baba: A human birth is not available over and over again. An individual soul progresses or degenerates according to his actions. It keeps coming back into this world until it achieves liberation. It must reap the fruits of its actions. The fruit of good deeds is a better state and the fruit of bad actions, or sins, is an inferior state. Like man, it is also possible for animals to achieve a higher state through good actions.

Seeker: *How can animals perform good deeds?*

Baba: Animals such as dogs, cows, and donkeys eat whatever dry or stale pieces of food they are given; they eat leftover food and they lie anywhere, never complaining about their living conditions. Despite all this, they work for man and benefit him. This is their selfless service. Aren't these virtuous actions?

A DISCUSSION ON FOOD

Seeker: *Is it true that man becomes* tamasic *by consuming* tamasic *food?*

Baba: It is not by food alone that man becomes *tamasic* or *sattvic*. In ancient times many saints ate *tamasic* food and yet they were considered to be great *tapasvins* (ascetics). In spite of their non-vegetarian diets, their minds were pure and *sattvic*.

Nevertheless, it is advisable for a seeker to consume

only *sattvic* and pure food. Vegetarian food is also good for health. Someone once asked Bernard Shaw why he did not eat meat and he replied, "My stomach is not a burial ground for dead animals." Man should always remember that the purpose of eating is to maintain good health and thereby lead a happy life, not to just satisfy the sense of taste.

The food that we consume acts on our bodies in three ways. First, food nourishes our *pranas;* second, it forms the seven elements of the body; and, third, the remaining portion is excreted as fecal matter. Meat is devoid of *prana;* hence it cannot nourish our *pranas.* Its consumption only increases the fat on our bodies. Such food should be avoided.

IDOL WORSHIP

Seeker: *Swamiji, what is your opinion of idol worship?*
Baba: I do not object to idol worship, nor do I insist on it. I love my Gurudev, Nityananda Baba, so I have placed a large photograph of him here, which we worship every morning and evening. Saints such as Tukaram, Namdev, Mirabai and Eknath Maharaj were able to cross over this ocean of birth and death by performing idol worship. Even in yoga, idol worship is accepted as a means of concentrating the mind. For those people whose minds cannot remain free from thoughts or steady on the formless, idol worship is all right.

We *sannyasis* worship our own Self with the understanding, "I am Brahman"; we do not worship any other idol. Tukaram Maharaj says, '**देह देवाचे देऊळ आंत बाहिर निर्मळ**' । "This body is a temple of God. It is pure within and without." Idol worship is one of the methods of religious worship; it is a path leading to the realm of liberation. Tukaram Maharaj writes from his own experience, सगुणीं ध्यातां निर्गुणीं गेलों, आतां झालों मी नारायण । "While I was meditating on God with attributes, I reached the attributeless Absolute. I have myself become Narayan." According to Vedanta, everything is only Brahman. Thus for one who has realized the Self, God is everywhere, inside as well as outside. That which assumes the gross body is only Consciousness; that is, only the Self takes on a physical form. Then why not worship that very Consciousness Itself? We worship Gurudev considering him to be Chinmaya, the manifestation of Chiti. He can also be seen in meditation. Those who did not see him in his body see him in meditation. Some have had a direct expe₊ rience of him. Therefore, can we say that Gurudev is not here now? He was here then and he is here even now. Just as your relatives and friends feel love for your body, why shouldn't devotees of Rama, Krishna or Shiva love the idol of their deity?

Nonetheless, while performing idol worship, it is essential to consider the idol as being conscious or alive and not to look upon it as a mere piece of stone. Only then will the worship bear fruit. There was once a devotee who daily worshipped the idol of Shri Rama. Several years passed by, but Shri Rama did not become pleased with him. One day a Krishna devotee suggested that he switch to worshipping Krishna and gave him a statue of Krishna. The man put Rama's idol away in a nearby window and installed the new idol of Krishna on his altar, which he began to worship instead. One day, while he was performing *arati* to the Krishna idol, the scented smoke of the incense began wafting through the window, passing over the idol of Rama. Seeing this, the man became angry, thinking that Rama had no right to enjoy the fragrance of the incense since He had not been pleased by his many years of worship and prayer. The devotee immediately jumped up and started plugging the idol's nostrils with cottonwool. At that very moment Rama became pleased and appeared before him. The devotee wondered why Rama could not be pleased during all those years of worship and yet, now, when he was furious with Him and even hating Him, He was manifesting before him. Lord Rama explained, "Previously you considered this idol of me as mere stone, but just now, when you felt that it was alive, I manifested myself to you."

In short, if you have faith, then God is present everywhere and in everything. Whether you consider Him to be with or without attributes, it is the same. Everything has been painted with the same paint. God has no form and yet all bodies are His. God is always satisfied; idol worship is for the satisfaction of the devotee. It is he who derives fulfillment from it.

RELIGIOUS RESOLUTIONS

Seeker: *What is a religious resolution? If someone makes such a resolution and cannot fulfill it, does he commit a sin?*
Baba: A resolution is the outcome of a state of the mind. Making good resolutions is a *vedic* rite, a way of religious worship. If you resolve to feed brahmins, then you must feed them with love; or if you resolve to perform Satyanarayan Puja or Shatachandi Yajna, then you must perform these joyfully.

It is true that if someone forces you to make a resolution, it has no meaning; it is not a religious observance. If the local priests in a place of pilgrimage force you to make some resolution and give money in charity, it would have no meaning. You should tell such priests to credit your account for the amount; you should not pay them in cash.

A resolution made voluntarily such as "Henceforth
I shall not take wine," or "I shall not tell lies" is com-
mendable. There is a prayer in the Vedas, तन्मे मनः
शिवसंकल्पमस्तु । "Let the resolutions of my mind always
be auspicious." So you must cultivate the habit of having
good resolutions.

Seeker: *If a saint gives a blessing through his will, does
it come true?*

Baba: If a saint blesses you and you achieve success in
your work, it is a result of his *tapasya* and your good
fortune, but there cannot be any success without self-
effort. You should continue to perform meritorious
actions. Such actions will never go to waste. Some
karmas bear fruit immediately while others do so after
a lapse of some time.

Thursday, August 6, 1964

Shri Sunilbhai Damania came for Baba's *darshan*
accompanied by Shri Hargovinddas Jani and his wife. Shri
Jani has been staying at Ramanashram in Tiruvannamalai
for several years.

DEVOTION, KNOWLEDGE AND YOGA ARE ONE AND THE SAME

Jani: *We go every day to a friend's house in Matunga
to hear a discourse on the* Vicharasagar.

Baba: Very good. Knowledge (*jnana*), meditation
(*dhyana*) and devotion (*bhakti*) are different paths of
sadhana, but they all bestow the same final result. The
Bhagavad Gita says, ' सांख्ययोगौ पृथक् बालाः प्रवदन्ति न
पण्डिताः ।' "Only fools, not the wise, consider Sankhya and
yoga to be different."

For the followers of the path of devotion, the example of the Gopis and Narada's *Bhaktisutras* are instructive. A poet says:

श्याय श्याम रटत राधे आप हि श्याम भई ।
पूछत फिरत अपनी सखियन से, प्यारी कहाँ गई ॥

"Constantly repeating Krishna, Krishna, Radha herself became Krishna. She asked her friends, 'Where is Radha?' Radha became so completely absorbed in Krishna through the ecstasy of love and devotion that, believing herself to be Krishna, she asked her friends, 'Where is Radha?'" This is the final attainment of devotion. It is also the final achievement of the path of Self-inquiry, "Who am I?" Who is Krishna? In his commentary on the *Vishnu Sahasranam*, Shankaracharya describes who Krishna is in the first verse. He says :

सच्चिदानन्दरूपाय कृष्णायाक्लिष्टकारिणे ।
नमो वेदान्तवेद्याय गुरवे बुद्धिसाक्षिणे ॥

"I bow to that Sri Krishna who can be known with the help of Vedanta, who is the witness of the intellect, who performs actions very effortlessly, and whose nature is *sat, chit* and *ananda* (existence, knowledge and bliss) ."

For the followers of the path of knowledge, the philosophy expounded in the *Upanishads* is instructive. Sundardas says:

देखत ब्रह्म सुनै पुनि ब्रह्महि, बोलत है वहि ब्रह्म हि वानी ।
भूमिहु नीरहु तेजहु वायुहु, व्योमहु ब्रह्म जहाँ लग प्रानी ।
आदिहु अन्तहु मध्यहु ब्रह्महि, है सब ब्रह्म यहै मति ठानी ।
संुदर ज्ञेय रु ज्ञानहु ब्रह्म हि, आपहु ब्रह्म हि जानत ज्ञानी ।

"The *jnani* considers everything he sees to be Brahman; whatever he hears is Brahman; he speaks only of Brahman. For him, the earth, water, fire, air, ether and *pranas* are all Brahman. For him, the beginning, the

middle and the end of everything is Brahman. This is
his firm conviction. The *jnani* considers the known
and knowledge all to be Brahman. The phrase "Radha
became Shyam" also has the same meaning.

For the followers of yoga, Patanjali's *Yogasutras* are
authoritative. Achieving a thought-free state by controlling the mental vibrations is, in fact, *jnana*. In this
state, awareness of the universal 'I' arises; that is, the
individual 'I' becomes the universal 'I'. The great
bhakta Tukaram says, "When I understood the real
nature of Vitthal, I began to feel that Vitthal was present
in everyone and my mind became absolutely steady."
This is truly meditation, a state without thoughts.
Vedanta also gives a similar description of the final state.

Even though the spiritual practices of a *bhakta*, a
jnani and a yogi are different, the final achievement of
each is the same. You may refer to that final state as
Rama, Krishna, the Supreme Brahman or *nirvikalpa*
samadhi. It is like calling the same person by different
names.

Jani: *I am returning to Ramanashram in three months.*
I have now decided to remain there until the end of my
life.

Baba: Do not bind yourself with such resolutions or
restrictions. You should understand that whatever is
here is also elsewhere and thus you should remain
serene. Our destiny determines where we will stay; we
must not insist on any particular set of circumstances.
Saint Tulsidas says:

सब पानी गंगा भयो, सब गिरि शालिग्राम ।
सब जंगल तुलसी भयो, हृदय बसत जेहि राम ॥

"For him in whose heart Rama dwells, all waters
are the Ganges, all mountains are Shaligram, all jungles
are *tulsi*." When the mind acquires such a state, Rama

will manifest from within wherever you may be.

Sunilbhai: (observing a woman in deep meditation) *Baba, where is her Self now?*

Baba: The Self does not go anywhere, nor does it come from anywhere. Where can the Self go? The Self is all-pervasive. It pervades the entire universe. Man is seen coming to or leaving the earth, but where does the earth go? Similarly, it is the individual soul who comes and goes; the Self neither goes anywhere, nor does it come from anywhere.

Saturday, August 15, 1964

Shri Ramanbhai and Shri Harshadbhai, friends of Shri Maganbhai Hingwala, an old devotee of Nityananda Baba, came today. They had the following discussion with Baba:

MEANS OF CONQUERING MENTAL MODIFICATIONS

Ramanbhai: *It is very difficult to conquer rajasic and tamasic vrittis (thoughts). What is the easiest way to control them?*

Baba: Attend *satsang* and practise what you learn there. In this way, the heart will become purified. Saints who have gained control over their own senses are able to bring the senses of others under control. Have *satsang* with such beings and your heart will be transformed. Ordinary *satsang* improves the understanding, but does not transform. If attending *satsang* is not possible for you, then develop your discrimination and faculty of reasoning.

Ramanbhai: *Even after much reasoning, my mind cannot be controlled.*

Baba: Yes, this is a kind of internal battle in which

some skirmishes are bound to be lost and some won.
One's mental tendencies will sometimes be positive and
sometimes negative.

Ramanbhai: *But this undermines one's self-confidence.*
Baba: It is not easy to conquer *rajasic* or *tamasic*
vrittis. Even a great devotee like Arjuna had to face
this problem. He says:

चंचलं हि मनः कृष्ण प्रमाथि बलवद् दृढम् ।
तस्याहं निग्रहं मन्ये वायोरिव सुदुष्करम् ॥

"O Krishna, the mind is restless and vulnerable to
disturbances." It is very powerful and very obstinate.
The mind is as difficult to control as the wind.

Arjuna once went to a Siddha mountain called
Indraneel where he practised intense *tapasya* in
order to please Lord Shiva and thus obtain the *pashupat*
astra from him. He controlled his *pranas* and achieved
sanyam siddhis. The intensity of his *tapasya* was so
great that a fire broke out on the mountain. This
enraged the beings in Siddhaloka, who all went to
complain to Shiva. To appease them, Lord Shiva took
the form of a tribal hill-dweller and fought with Arjuna.
If a powerful person like Arjuna could not conquer
the mind, you can imagine how powerful the mind
must be. It is possible to control the wind, but to
control the mind is very difficult indeed.

Buddhiyoga, the yoga of discrimination, is an
excellent means of achieving control over the mind.
Lord Krishna also tells Arjuna, बुद्धौ शरणमन्विच्छ, और
बुद्धियोगमुपाश्रित्य "Seek refuge in the intellect. Take the
support of Buddhiyoga." So with the help of balanced
thinking, try to control the mind.
Ramanbhai: *Too much thinking leads to doubts and*
fears.

Baba: Doubts are bound to come up. Doubt is the very basis of this world. A yogi is one who has gone beyond doubt. Fear is a kind of addiction. Only one who conquers fear becomes happy. Until one attains Self-realization, fear will persist. But after Self-realization, where can there be fear? Where can there be sorrow?

Proceed steadfastly on your path. A state will ultimately arrive in which fear will drop away. Read *Yogadarshan,* attend *satsang* and also develop your discrimination. Sundardas says:

देखै तौ विचार करि, सुनै तौ विचार करि ।
बोलै तौ विचार करि, करै तौ विचार है ॥
खाय तौ विचार करि, पीवै तौ विचार करि,
सोवै तौ विचार करि, जागे तौ न टार है ॥
सुन्दर विचार कर, याही निरधार है ॥

Discriminate when you see;
Discriminate when you hear;
Discriminate when you speak;
Discriminate when you act.
Discriminate when you eat;
Discriminate when you drink;
Discriminate when you sleep;
Discriminate while you are awake.
Discriminate always; that's the surest support.

In this world everything is full of fear. In the *Vairagya Shatak,* Bhartrihari writes:

भोगे रोगभयं कुले च्युतिभयं बित्ते नृपालाद्भयं
मौने दैन्यभयं बले रिपुभयं रूपे जराया भयं ।
शास्त्रे वादभयं गुणे खलभयं काये कृतान्ताद्भयं
सर्वं वस्तुं भयान्वितं भुवि नृणां वैराग्यमेवाभयं ॥

"Sensual enjoyment creates fears of disease, a high family fears its downfall, wealth fears taxation from the king, silence fears being misunderstood as weakness, military force fears the enemy, beauty fears old age, a virtuous man fears the wicked, scriptural knowledge fears debate, and the body fears death. Thus everything in this world is full of fear. It is only *vairagya,* or dispassion, which makes you fearless."

Everything in this world has a fear of something. As man progresses materially, fear increases proportionately. For example, the discovery of the atom bomb automatically increased fear. It is the normal way of the world. Therefore, if you really want to be free of fear and attain that which is eternal, give up the idea of I-ness. A poet has said, "You cannot obtain God until you give up the idea of I-ness."

Once a man was sitting at a place where he could hear echoes. When he said something, the same words were repeated opposite him. Thinking that someone was mimicking him, he started abusing the other person. He heard the same abuse addressed to himself. He was enraged and went and complained to his Guru. The Guru understood what had happened. He said, "You become silent. Don't say anything. Then the other one will also stop abusing." That is what eventually happened. It means that, similarly, if you also forsake your individuality, then all fears and doubts will end.

Saint Janabai, who was a servant and a devotee of Saint Namdev, says:

ब्रह्मज्ञानाची किल्ली, सांगते एकच बोली ।
अभिमान निमाली, तूचि ब्रह्म ॥

"I can reveal in just one sentence the key to obtaining the knowledge of Brahman: Give up your ego and then you, yourself, will become Brahman."

Ramanbhai: *But in attempting to do this, some obstruction always crops up.*
Baba: It is like fighting with an enemy force surround-

ing you. If you want to avoid such fighting, have faith
in the Self. Become worthy of God's grace and seek
refuge in a Sadguru.

Monday, August 24, 1964

Today, Savitri Chadda came for Baba's *darshan* and
discussed some problems.

PAINT YOUR HEART WITH THE COLOUR OF GOD

Savitri: *Swamiji, I know and accept that the world is
not real; everything in this world is perishable. Nonetheless, since I live in this world, I have various worries.
I have to look after my husband and children so I
think about them constantly. What should I do about
this?*

Baba: Your heart will become saturated with whatever
colour you keep painting it. Desire, anger, greed,
attachment and egoism are the various colours for the
heart. The individual soul experiences these. Water
does not have any colour of its own, but assumes whatever colour you add to it, and if this coloured water
falls on a cloth, then the cloth also acquires the same
colour. Similarly, paint your heart with the colour of
Hari then you will see the world full of Hari. All
your worries will end and you will find happiness and
peace.

Savitri: *What must I do to paint the heart with the
colour of Hari?*

Baba: Have *satsang*, practical *satsang*. If you go to a
saint for two hours in two years, that cannot be called
satsang because for all the remaining time you are being
painted with the colour of the world. To acquire an

unfading colour, you must have the company of saints again and again.

Savitri: *The worries of worldly life constantly harass the mind. Just before leaving the house for* satsang, *some obstacle always arises. "Let me finish this work first and then I'll go. Let me finish that work also." This is what happens every time.*

Baba: Worry for the good of others is good. Worry for the welfare of your husband and children is all right. Even Gurus, who have achieved liberation, desire their disciples' liberation and think about it.

The fact is that everyone has his own destiny. Look at me. I left my home at the age of fifteen. My mother must have worried about me a lot, but I had to follow my destiny. Her worries were useless. You cannot add to or subtract from someone's destiny by worrying about him. So do your worldly work with a sense of duty and at the same time remember that everyone must live out his own destiny. Perform your duties, but paint your heart with the colour of the Lord. God alone is worthy of constant, wholehearted worship. This world is not in contradiction to God. Live in your home; look after your family, but also reserve some time for God.

Janmashtami, Sunday, August 30, 1964

This morning Barrister Nain was present for *sutsang*.

Nain: *What is meant by* uparati?
Baba: *Uparati* is the mature state of Vedantic contemplation. It is a stage. The practical aspect of dispassion is *uparati*. In this state, meditation occurs only on the Self, nothing else. Shankaracharya has explained this

in his book *Aparokshanubhuti:*

विषयेभ्यः पराव्वृत्तिः परमोपरतिर्हिसा ।

"To turn away from worldly objects and thoughts is called *uparati.*" *Uparati* is one of the six assets of a seeker.

Nain: *Many saints do not perform any action; they simply remain in one place. What is their state?*

Baba: Such lack of activity often indicates disinterestedness. True *uparati* is a state of neutrality based on the understanding that the world has no reality.

A SEEKER'S SPIRITUAL MATURITY DETERMINES HIS SADHANA

Nain: *Some people say that spirituality must be practised in a particular manner such as worship, chanting, meditation,* mantra japa, *etc., while there are others who do not even believe in visiting temples, making pilgrimages or worshipping idols.*

Baba: Advice should always be given according to the spiritual maturity of a particular seeker. Guidance is always based on the disciple's worth and ability. To advise the same type of spiritual discipline for everyone is mere obstinacy.

As soon as one listens to and understands Vedanta, one loses the desire for pilgrimages and idol worship. Immediately upon attaining knowledge of the Self, idol worship, etc., automatically drop away. Idol worship is a matter of mental inclination, a kind of mental understanding. On attaining full knowledge, all doubts about these matters automatically disappear.

I believe in the incarnations of God, but I do not say that the incarnations alone should be adored and worshipped. I would say, "Worship Him from whom the incarnations came." An incarnation is an effect that has some cause behind it. Catch hold of that cause. Everyone has his own path. Everyone has an equal right to aspire for God. Arjuna was a warrior; hence, his path was Karma Yoga. Hanuman had a preference for serving God. Although Ramakrishna Paramahansa was constantly established in the *nirvikalpa* state, he supported the worship of God as manifested in an idol. God is everywhere. Why can't he be present in an idol? Actually, a devotee sees his own Self in the idol. It is a miracle of faith that one can attain God even through an idol.

Monday, August 31, 1964

Today some followers of the Jain religion came for Baba's *darshan*. Among them was a seeker named Jayantilal.

Jayantilal: *Does a human being have another human birth after his death? If so, after how long?*
Baba: It depends upon the *karma* and desires of the person. If he has performed good actions, he has to enjoy their fruits for years in a heavenly body; if he has performed bad actions, he will be born into a lower species. A fortunate one immediately receives another human birth. If a person is doing *sadhana* and dies before completing it, he is immediately reborn as a human being.
Jayantilal: *Can one acquire the power of knowing the future in this life?*
Baba: This is not a great accomplishment. Many have acquired this ability either through yoga, palmistry or astrology. This power can also be acquired through spiritual practice. In general, such powers reside in

everyone. It occasionally happens that something we say subsequently comes true. This power can be developed further through *sadhana*. These powers relate to the *savikar* state (state with form).

The *nirvikar* state, or the state of void, is beyond these attainments. If you want to know the future, you have to disturb that *nirvikar* state. You are sitting so peacefully now, but if you wish to say or do something, you have to disturb this state.   .

Wednesday, September 9, 1964

Today Gyan Chand, a friend of Hira Nayan of the Lahera Printing Press, came for *satsang* with Baba. He has a special interest in Vedanta, which he sometimes expounds to others.

KNOWLEDGE DOES NOT BEAR FRUIT WITHOUT THE GURU'S GRACE

Gyan Chand: *Swamiji, I have read the Upanishads and various books on Vedanta such as the* Ashtavakra Gita. *I have also studied the* Yogavasishtha *and* Ramayana *with special attention and given discourses on them. Since retiring from my job as a Municipal Inspector, I have been spending my time in* satsang. *From the worldly point of view I am happy in all respects. I have been keenly interested in reading spiritual books for the past thirty years, but now I feel that despite all my reading, attending* satsangs, *and giving discourses I have achieved nothing from the point of view of spirituality. What could be the cause for this? Does my destiny come in the way?*

Baba: Destiny is always a factor. In addition, your practice may not have been thorough enough. A seeker should be perfect in practice. Knowledge bears fruit immediately for a person who has detachment, discrimination, control over the senses, self-restraint and sincere longing for Self-realization. Otherwise, his knowledge is like a parrot's repetition of words.

Gyan Chand: *How can practice become perfect?*

Baba: Understand and contemplate whatever you study. Practise meditation. Practise making your mind *nirvikalpa*, thought-free. Just as effort is required to achieve success in any worldly field, similarly, you have to do *tapasya* to go beyond *jivahood* and become Shiva. In this the Guru's grace is a very important factor; therefore, obtain that. To obtain the Sadguru's grace, you must consider him to be none other than God Himself.

In daily life, ordinary abusive terms achieve their intended effect; then why shouldn't the sacred mantra-like words of the scriptures bear fruit? If you call a person a donkey, he becomes red with anger. If simple words have so much power, then why wouldn't the words of the scriptures, which are considered to be the form of God, have power? If scriptural words do not bear fruit, you must conclude that your faith is weak. He whose mind immediately feels the effect of words can grasp any subject. He who understands the meaning of the scriptures immediately upon hearing them should be considered most worthy.

Gyan Chand: *Even after study of the scriptures and* satsang, *the mind still runs after sensual pleasures. How can this be remedied?*

Baba: Even if the mind pursues sensual pleasures, it will not necessarily be tainted. Let the mind be drowned in the ocean of the inner Self just once. Afterwards, regardless of how much it may be involved in worldly affairs, there will be no harm. It will never lose its equanimity. It is the nature of the mind to be constantly engaged in one subject or another. Therefore, keep the mind immersed in thoughts of God or the Supreme Self. It is good to have an intellect that thinks and discriminates, but at the same time, continue your *sadhana*. Have discussions with saints; this is, in fact, true *satsang*. Obtain the grace of the Guru and thereby become worthy of God's grace. The *turiya* state, described in the *Yogavasishtha,* cannot be achieved without the Guru's grace. Whatever you were unable to achieve through the path of knowledge, obtain now through yogic discipline and meditation. The path of knowledge describes the world as unreal (*mithya*). In yoga, however, it is not necessary to say that the world is unreal because it reveals itself to be so through the seeker's own experience. He who has not achieved the *turiya* state remains a slave of *prakriti*, but *prakriti* becomes the slave of one who has attained that state. Just look. Swami Nityananda established the village of Ganeshpuri in this desolate jungle without anyone's assistance, without appealing to or flattering anyone.

Divinity exists within everyone. I am always fresh, healthy and happy despite a diet of a small quantity of simple food because I have experienced my inner divinity. Although I am older than you, I appear younger, don't I? The source of this freshness is a place called Brahmananda, Satchidananda or Paramananda in which fear and sorrow are unknown. In comparison with this treasure, worldly wealth has no value. If you yearn to attain that state, remain in the company of saints. That is where the secret of attainment lies.

A DISCIPLE IS TAUGHT ACCORDING TO HIS WORTHINESS

Gyan Chand: *Is it true that saints teach disciples differently according to their worthiness?*

Baba: Rain water falls everywhere in the sea and water mixes with water, but only when a raindrop falls into a mother-of-pearl during the *swati* constellation is it transformed into a pearl. There are thousands of lecturers and they give discourses to millions of people, but for how many of them do the teachings bear fruit? Instead of giving or attending discourses, perform internal *sadhana*. Inquisitiveness is necessary, but along with it, contemplation is essential. You become like your object of constant contemplation. Ramakrishna Paramahansa contemplated Hanuman and became like him. Similarly, one who contemplates Brahman becomes Brahman.

Gyan Chand: *I have heard that you don't give discourses, but you do say something if someone asks a question.*

Baba: This is not quite correct. If I feel like speaking, I speak; otherwise I remain silent. There is no fixed time or rule in this regard. Knowledge is not an ordinary subject, nor is it cheap. The limits of a discussion are automatically determined by the worth of the listener. Nowadays knowledge has been made a subject of discourses; hence, it does not bear fruit. Teachers have given countless discourses, but how many *jnanis* have they produced? Knowledge arises only within a worthy seeker.

Gyan Chand: *Saint Jnaneshwar considers devotion* (bhakti) *and knowledge* (jnana) *to be equal.*

Baba: Both are, in fact, one. Through devotion you obtain love; through knowledge you obtain bliss. What's the difference between these two? First make yourself worthy; then you will certainly attain God.   There are many paths by which to attain Him and among them the path of Guru's grace is the best.

Gyan Chand: *Neither Ramana Maharshi nor Lord Buddha had Gurus.*

Baba: How can one become a Guru without having been a disciple?   Many seekers tell me that Ramana Maharshi is their Guru.   To have become a Guru, he himself must have been someone's disciple, if not in this life, then in his past life.   Lord Buddha had no Guru and therefore he experienced only the void, which he expounded to others.   He could only speak about that which he saw.

Sri Rama and Sri Krishna are accepted by all as incarnations of God yet even they had Gurus.   Shri Ramakrishna Paramahansa had to seek the help of Totapuri.   Even Matsyendranath has said that Adinath Parashiva was his Guru.   Vasishtha also said that he attained knowledge from another.   This is how it should be according to the scriptures.   The Guru-disciple relationship is an eternal discipline to attain knowledge.   It preserves propriety.   Why destroy it? *Jnaneshwari, Tukaram Gatha* and *Dasbodh* were written by saints who had obtained the grace of the Guru.   Even today, after the passage of so many years, these books are read in every house.

Thursday, September 10, 1964

Satish Modi, a college student in Secunderabad, comes now and then for Baba's *darshan* and has been at the ashram for the past four days.

THE IMPORTANCE OF LEADING A REGULATED LIFE

Satish: *Baba, please give me some guidance for my life.*
Baba: Very well, listen. If you want to attain any happiness in this life, then first of all, you must lead a regulated life. This means that you must arise, sleep, eat and study punctually, and that you must stay away from bad habits and vices. At the same time you must spend some time in meditation, quieting your mind. A controlled mind has such power that with it one can accomplish great works. When you need it, Truth reveals Itself within you, giving you true guidance, and you acquire competence in your work.

A river that has been obstructed by a dam gushes forth with tremendous force when the dam is suddenly opened, washing away village after village. Such power arises because of the previous containment of water. Similarly, man accumulates a storehouse of power to execute future tasks by stopping the wastage of his mental powers through control of the mind. In this way, man acquires the strength to accomplish the most difficult work.

Tuesday, September 15, 1964

Today Shri Sheshrao Wankhede, the Minister for Industries in Maharashtra, and his wife, Shrimati Kusumtai, and the wife of Lt-General S. P. Thorat came to the ashram.

SEEK PEACE WHERE IT DWELLS

Mrs. Thorat: *Babaji, from my early childhood until now, I have received tender care and comfort. I have been married for thirty-two years. I have never under-*

*gone any difficulties either at my father's house or at
my husband's. My husband is good to me. We have
status and respect in the community. My sons are also
well settled. Thus, I have every kind of happiness. I
can expect nothing more from this world. In spite of
all this, my mind is not at peace. I have read many
books; I have read the* Bhagavad Gita *and have gone on
pilgrimages. Still, I do not experience inner satisfaction. I wonder if I am unworthy of realizing God.
Isn't it possible for spiritual and practical life to coexist?*
Baba: Every human being is a part of God and is thus
worthy of knowledge of the Self and God-realization.
Worldly life is not an obstacle to pursuing spiritual
sadhana. On the contrary, it is helpful. God has
created this world with love and for the sake of love, so
how can it be an obstacle? This world is the embodiment of God. King Janaka ruled a great kingdom and
sage Yajnavalkya had two wives, and yet while living
in the world, they achieved realization of the Self; they
became *jivanmuktas.* As you can see, I am a *sannyasi,*
but can I escape the practicalities of daily life? In fact,
while living in the world and performing your duties,
you can remember and worship God.
Mrs. Thorat: *I have been trying to do just that, but
even so, I have no peace of mind.*
Baba: After attaining all his worldly goals, man still
has no peace because lack of peace is inherent in the
very nature of the things he achieves. He tries to find
peace in that which is full of agitations so how can he
get peace? You want to go north and you are running
towards the south. If you want to find peace, seek it
where it dwells.
Mrs. Thorat: *I know that the short-lived, perishable
objects of this world cannot give me inner satisfaction.
Therefore, I try to sit for meditation every day, but*

*within two or three minutes my mind becomes distracted
and rushes out toward other subjects.*

Baba: Owing to constant contemplation of the objects
and matters of the world, the mind assumes their forms
again and again. For this reason, you cannot meditate
on God for any length of time. Try to cultivate an
increasing addiction to thoughts of God in your mind.

Mrs. Thorat: *I understand this, but I cannot seem to
do it even after making an effort. What is the remedy
for this?*

Baba: *Satsang* and Guru's grace are necessary. Through
the grace of a Siddha Guru, meditation and contemplation on God occur spontaneously. He awakens the
inner Shakti of the seeker by his own spiritual power.
By this means one attains inner satisfaction and peace.

Wednesday, September 23, 1964

Today Laresa Gahan, an American asked Baba some
questions about her difficulties in *sadhana*.

ISOLATION IS NOT NECESSARY TO ATTAIN PEACE

Laresa: *Baba, I would like to have a separate room so
that I can remain in isolation. My peace is disturbed
by the constant coming and going of people where I live.*

Baba: Peace cannot be obtained by sitting in a room
behind closed doors. In fact, such seclusion sometimes
has the opposite effect. By remaining in isolation you
develop tiger-like tendencies. If anyone disturbs a
tiger in his cave, he will either leave the cave or attack
the intruder. This is not the way to attain true peace.
You must learn to remain peaceful and undisturbed in
the midst of people.

Nityananda Baba first lived in a jungle. He would throw stones at anyone who went near him, but later on, he lived among people and established a village. I, too, have established this ashram and live amidst people. Town and jungle, isolation and mingling with people:— being free from such dualistic ideas and being established in one's own Self in *nirvikalpa samadhi* is the true state.

Laresa: *I want to travel to remote places such as the Himalayas, Kashmir, Simla and Darjeeling where I feel I would be able to overcome my restlessness and obtain some peace.*

Baba: You can certainly go wherever you like, but remember that by roaming about in this way, your mind will become more agitated; your restlessness will increase. One who cannot obtain peace here cannot obtain it elsewhere either. You may go anywhere, but your mind will accompany you. How can you escape it?

Laresa: *How can I know whether I have made any spiritual progress or not, and if I have progressed, how much?*

Baba: Your progress in spirituality can be judged by the following: a) how calm you can remain in trying and difficult circumstances; b) whether or not you are less disturbed than before by the pairs of opposites such as pleasure and pain, happiness and sorrow; and c) how much inner peace and satisfaction you experience in your heart.

Sunday, September 27, 1964

Mr. Harshad and Mr. Ramnik, who are friends of Manilal Hingwala, a devotee of Nityananda Baba, came again for *satsang* today.

CHOOSING A MANTRA FOR JAPA

Ramnik: *Swamiji, I have been using the Gayatri mantra for* japa. *Is this all right?*

Baba: Who gave it to you? Which mantra were you repeating previously?

Ramnik: *I obtained the Gayatri mantra from a book. Prior to that, I was repeating the name of Krishna, but the man who gave me the book told me that the Gayatri mantra has great power. Since then I have been using it for* japa.

Baba: All mantras possess similar powers. All mantras lead you to the same final achievement.If a person claims that a particular mantra is the most powerful, he says so merely to promote and propagate a particular *math* or sect. Here at this ashram we do not have the trademark of any mantra. We are not engaged in any business. I recommend that people repeat the mantra that appeals to them most and which they have been accustomed to using. Both of you should read the biography of Ramakrishna Paramahansa. Then you will understand the unity behind all religions and all mantras. It is being unfaithful to one's *sadhana* to give up one mantra and take up another one, and then take up a third one on someone else's advice. Why did you give up a short mantra and accept a long one? You can repeat Krishna's name ten times in the span of time that is required to chant the Gayatri mantra only once. If you have to take a mantra, then take it from a Sadguru, who has the authority to give initiation. Such a mantra is alive, or conscious, and will bear fruit immediately.

Ramnik: *While doing* japa *of the Gayatri mantra, on what should the mind be concentrated? For example, while repeating Shiva's name, one thinks of Shiva; while* *repeating Krishna's name, one thinks of Krishna. In this way, who is the deity of the Gayatri mantra?*

Baba: Every mantra has its own goal. While doing *japa* of any mantra, it is better to concentrate on the letters of the mantra. Gayatri is said to be a goddess. Thus, if you so desire, you can contemplate the goddess while repeating it. There is a particular technique for doing *japa* of the Gayatri mantra. First, however, you must obtain thorough knowledge of this subject.

KNOWLEDGE MANIFESTS ITSELF FROM WITHIN; IT IS NOT OBTAINED FROM BOOKS

Harshad: *We have attended the discourses of Mahamandaleshwar on several occasions, but we were unable to comprehend them. We also read books, but we cannot distinguish between truth and untruth.*

Baba: If liberation could be obtained by reading books, all the scholars should be liberated, but in reality we find that this is not so. The knowledge contained in books is like a treasure buried underground: It is of no practical use to anyone. Do you think that knowledge is so cheap and so easily obtainable that just by listening to someone's discourse for two hours you can assimilate all the knowledge that he himself acquired after many years of *tapasya* and scriptural study? The scriptures are absolutely true. Just because you cannot understand them does not mean that they are false. It is said: शास्त्र है सब सच्चा । हम समझने में कच्चा ॥

"All scriptures are true, but our understanding is weak."

If you want to know the real meaning of the scriptures, become addicted to singing God's name. Just as a drunkard cannot live without liquor, similarly, you

should become restless without God's name. In this
way, knowledge will manifest itself from within you.

Sunday, October 4, 1964

Barrister Nain came today for Baba's *darshan*.

Nain: *Nowadays I am reading a book of questions and
answers by Shri Aurobindo.*
Baba: He was a great thinker.
Nain: *He wanted to draw the Shakti from above and
disseminate it throughout the world. It is said that the
Mother is now carrying out this work.*
Baba: The Mother has assumed the work which Aurobindo left incomplete. Now we will have to wait and
see who will be capable of succeeding her. There must
always be a disciple who is prepared to take on the work
of his Master so that it may proceed without interrup-
tion. Shankaracharya, for example, established four
maths, giving them such a firm and powerful foundation
that even 1200 years later their stature is undiminished.
Sri Ramakrishna transmitted such tremendous power
to Vivekananda that through him thousands were
transformed.
Nain: *Vivekananda propagated Hinduism very well.*
Baba: In actuality, Vivekananda propagated the
Vedanta of Shankaracharya. In particular, he protested
against the Hindu custom of untouchability, which
made his impact so great. He proclaimed the equality
of all men. He declared that everyone is worthy of
attaining God. He imparted knowledge to orphans. He
reformed the Hindu religion with a very broad outlook.
Shankaracharya was the protector of the religion

and Vivekananda was its propagator.

Nain: *Swami Vivekananda had a short life span.*

Baba: Those who have been *yogabhrashta* always have short lives. Swami Vivekananda, Swami Ram Tirth, Sri Shankaracharya and Jnaneshwar Maharaj all departed at a young age.

A group of seekers from Malad came to the ashram in the afternoon. Among them was a lawyer, Shri Chhantbar, who is a keen student of yoga and Vedanta. He had the following discussion with Baba.

THE SELF IS ALWAYS COMPLETE

Chhantbar: *We are so small and God is so great. Our power is limited while God's power is limitless. We are like a tiny well while God is like the ocean. How can we convert the well into the ocean? I cannot even understand whether the individual soul is just a part of God or is completely God.*

Baba: As long as the individual soul considers himself to be a mere portion of God, he will remain as such. As soon as he gives up his limitations, he becomes perfect. For a well to become one with the ocean, it has to merge into the ocean; that is, when its limitation as a well is destroyed, it becomes the ocean just as the space inside a pot becomes one with the total space as soon as the pot breaks. In reality, the space inside the pot is not different from the total space. It is one with the total space; it is not separate from it. Similarly, the individual Self is always complete.

Chhantbar: *How can the individual soul acquire the powers of God enabling him to create a universe?*

Baba: The universe is already created. It is foolish to talk of creating it again. It is like building what is already built. It is true that Vishwamitra demonstrated such power by creating another world. In fact, a separate world exists in every atom. You can think of innumerable universes because there is no limit to imagination.

God's world is only one existing throughout the infinity of space, but in individual souls, imaginary worlds can be countless. What we mean by the world is the expanse of the five elements; that is, everything. The world of the individual soul is included in the world of God. The individual soul builds a house on the earth and thinks that he has created a world unto himself! The fact is that when the part becomes the whole, when the *jiva* becomes Shiva, when the space inside the pot merges into the total space, when the Self becomes one with Brahman, then no separate universes can be seen.

Chhantbar: *My intellect cannot conceive of anything beyond the idea that I am only a part of the Self.*

Baba: You will be able to understand the Truth only when your "pot" has been broken. In fact, your question itself is illogical because you are complete. The Supreme Self is always in your possession, but it doesn't seem so owing to your ignorance. It is like searching everywhere for a diamond necklace that is around your neck. When you become aware that the necklace is around your own neck, would you say that you have found the lost necklace, or would you say that the necklace has never been lost?

The same thing is illustrated by the rope-snake example in Vedanta. There also, what did not exist disappears. Think about it yourself. In that example, was it the snake that was destroyed or was it that which did not exist that was destroyed?

It is a matter of wonder that one who is already liberated becomes liberated. One who is already awake has to be awakened. If consciousness never changes, then how can you undergo any change? You are what you are. Give up the thought that you are different from the Supreme Self. You are already complete. Your wrong understanding that you are incomplete, caused by your ignorance of the Self, will vanish when you obtain the knowledge of the Self. Just as a disease caused by improper diet is cured through proper diet, similarly, ignorance is eliminated by knowledge.

Wednesday, November 11, 1964

A *sannyasi* from Africa, Swami Muktananda, who has been in India for the past twelve years, came to the ashram today.

IDOL WORSHIP

Swami: *What is your opinion of idol worship?*
Baba: He who has recognised the God dwelling within his own heart will see God even in a stone idol. He who cannot find God within himself will not be able to find Him outside either; that is, he will not be able to see Him everywhere.

This reminds me of a funny story. Once Swami Ram Tirth, referring to Swami Dayananda Saraswati, said, "He is the son of a donkey." As a result, the offended party filed a libel suit against him. People advised Swami Ram Tirth to engage the services of a lawyer, but he said, "I do not require one. I shall fight the case on the strength of my own intelligence." When the case came before the court, the judge asked him, "Did you call Dayananda Saraswati the son of a donkey?" Ram Tirth replied, "Yes." Later on, in his own defence, he said, "Swami Dayananda has himself written that one who worships an idol is a donkey. Dayananda's father used to worship an idol so, according to Dayananda, his own father was a donkey. Dayananda is his father's son so doesn't it follow that he is the son of a donkey?" The judge dismissed the case.

Swami: *What is your opinion about* yajna *(sacrifice)?*
Baba: Your question is invalid. What doubt can there be about that which has been proven? What the seers, saints, Siddhas and great beings have said and written cannot be doubted. What they wrote is based on their own direct experience. Patanjali wrote the *Yogasutras* after practising and experiencing yoga. Similarly, Narada wrote the *Bhaktisutras* after experiencing the bliss of *bhakti*. We accept their teachings as authoritative. Similarly, *yajna* as described in the scriptures is authentic. It is foolish to ask someone else's opinion about it. Our scriptures are absolutely true and should not be doubted.

Thursday, December 3, 1964

Today the two sisters of Shri Pravinbhai Modi of Secunderabad, Manjula and Vasanta, came to the ashram.

Manjula: *Why is it that none of the work I undertake is ever successful?*
Baba: Divine help is essential for success in any work.

CONTEMPLATION ON GOD IS THE ONLY MEANS TO PEACE

Manjula: *Despite my efforts to calm my mind, it does not remain steady and agitations persist.*
Baba: By contemplating God, the mind becomes quiet

and concentrated. Contemplation of God is both a remedy and a blessing.

Vasanta: *Please give me knowledge. I am so deeply immersed in worldly life that I cannot find any time to worship God. I have five children and a husband to look after. We have an oil mill in Godhra and are materially prosperous, but I have not achieved anything in the realm of spirituality. My mind does not turn to God, nor do I have any opportunity to attend* satsang.

Baba: Remember God constantly. However large your family and fortune may be, they are not an obstacle to the remembrance of God. Many saints have attained God while living as householders.

Vasanta: *Whenever I try to think of God, other thoughts interfere and my mind becomes restless.*

Baba: Restlessness is the nature of the mind. It has become used to thinking about countless other subjects; therefore, it cannot suddenly become interested in God, but with practice, the mind will get used to contemplation of God.

Friday, December 11, 1964

Today Shri Pravinbhai Modi's father and his uncle, Shri Chimanlal Modi, came for Baba's *darshan* accompanied by their families. Shri Chimanlal is highly educated, well-versed in Vedanta and widely respected in Hyderabad.

THE SOCIAL SERVICE OF SAINTS

Chimanlal: *I once went to Tiruvannamalai. While there I asked Ramana Maharshi, "You have such great spiritual power. Why do you just sit in one place? Why don't you live among people and work for their uplift-*

ment? Many people would benefit from it." Ramana
Maharshi replied, *"Each individual does his own work
in his own way."*

Baba: G. N. Vaidya, a famous lawyer from Bombay,
asked me a similar question about Nityananda Baba.
He went once for *darshan* and when he arrived, there
was a long queue waiting and the front door was closed.
At the appointed time, the door was opened. After
Baba's *darshan,* the lawyer asked someone, "Why does
Swamiji sit inside with the door closed? Why doesn't
he come out?" That person replied, "I cannot answer
such questions. Go see Swami Muktananda, who lives
close by. He will clear up all your doubts." So Shri
Vaidya came to see me and we had the following conversation.

Vaidya: *People say that Swami Nityananda possesses
divine, mystical and miraculous powers. If this is so,
why doesn't he come out of seclusion and work among
people for the reformation of society? Why doesn't
he utilise his Shakti to bring about a revolution in
Hindu society? Why does he sit behind a closed door
that is only opened at a certain time despite the long
line of people seeking his* darshan?

Baba: What is your occupation?

Vaidya: *I am a lawyer.*

Baba: Do you go to court?

Vaidya: *Yes.*

Baba: Isn't there some kind of discipline in the court?
Isn't there a rule stating that the court will open at a
particular hour and that a particular case will be heard
on a certain day?

Vaidya: *Yes, of course. Without such a schedule, how
could the work proceed smoothly?*

Baba: Then why are you so surprised by the discipline
that is followed here by Swamiji? You should not find

it so peculiar. How many people had gathered for Swamiji's *darshan?*

Vaidya: *I guess there were about four thousand.*

Baba: What do you think? Did they all come for nothing, or is it possible that they benefited from Baba's *darshan?*

Vaidya: *After darshan I could see joy and satisfaction on their faces.*

Baba: Wouldn't you consider that to be the work of Nityananda Baba? Isn't he useful to the world without moving his arms and legs?

Vaidya: *Certainly he is.*

Baba: And one more thing: Have you seen Swamiji's photo anywhere?

Vaidya: *Yes, I have seen his photo in many houses, hotels and shops in Bombay.*

Baba: Isn't that also the work of Swamiji? You will find Swamiji's photos being garlanded and worshipped with lights and incense in many shops in Bombay. In spite of living behind closed doors and without giving any discourses, he has created such a tremendous feeling of devotion in the lower strata of society. Do you think this is just an ordinary accomplishment? So many people have obtained happiness from him; so many miserable people have been relieved of their troubles. Isn't this social work? Do you consider social work to be going from one place to another arranging programmes, going to courts and offices, holding meetings in parks and giving lectures? Can such activities really be called social work? These days people consider work to be only that which they can actually perceive on a gross level.

There was once a Siddha yogi named Pavahari Baba who used to remain in *samadhi* for six months at a time. One day a *sannyasi* went for his *darshan* and asked him a question similar to yours: "Why don't you go out and work to uplift society?" Pavahari Baba replied, "Do you think great Siddha Gurus should be like postmen and go from door to door distributing their discourses, advice and good wishes enclosed in envelopes?" Don't you see that God remains concealed and yet carries on the work of the whole world? Doesn't the head of a large institution sit in his office and yet handle the management of the entire institution? In the same way, Siddhas do not have to wander about in order to carry out their work. Even in the solitude of an ashram, they keep on doing their divine work.

THE SENSES ACQUIRE POWER THROUGH CONTROL

Chimanlal: *I have heard that a yogi's eyes and ears are very subtly tuned, that they can hear distant sounds and see faraway objects. Is this true?*

Baba: Yes, yogis acquire these powers through control of the senses. The subtlety of the senses increases in direct proportion to your degree of control over them and that which is more subtle is more pervasive. Therefore, through control of the senses, sounds emanating from far off places can be heard, remote objects can be seen and distant odours can be smelled. It is also possible to know another person's thoughts. Similarly, the power and effectiveness of your words increases in direct proportion to the silence that you observe. This is known as omniscience.

In general, it has become man's habit to eat as much as is available, to talk as much as possible, to see and hear whatever he can, and then later on, his thoughts are completely occupied by these experiences. In this way, he completely exhausts his energy. If he were to conserve it instead, he would be able to achieve higher goals. If you earn a thousand rupees, spend fifty and save the rest, then after some time you can become wealthy. It is the same with energy. One's power is wasted by useless thoughts, but if the mind is made steady, its power increases and the intellect becomes subtle. Electricity is so subtle that it can pass through a thin filament and yet its current is so powerful that it can burn a man.

On every path—whether *jnana, bhakti* or yoga—self-control is essential. As we turn within more and more, the senses become correspondingly subtler and more powerful, and the mind becomes one-pointed. A *jnani* continually reflects, "Not this, not this," and he goes deep inside where, finally, only Brahman remains for him. Ramana Maharshi attained Universal Consciousness through the mental inquiry, "Who am I?" A devotee becomes Krishna by constantly repeating Krishna's name. A yogi achieves the realization of *so'ham* (I am That) through meditation. In this manner, the goal and attainment of all paths is the same supreme bliss just as whatever business you have—factory, mill or shop—the goal and achievement is money.

The main objective of every path is to control the *chitta vrittis* (thoughts). Steadiness of the mind yields great power. If an engineer were to build a dam across a small stream in the jungle some distance from its source, after a while so much water would be collected that, if allowed to flow, its torrential power could wash away many villages in its path. The same applies to our mental powers. Through concentration the mind can be steadied at man's will and he thereby gains unlimited power.

Shri Anand, who is a relative of Smt. Ganagaben Shah, a devotee of Baba, came to the ashram today. He is intensely interested in *sadhana*.

PRANAYAMA

Anand: *What is the correct technique for doing pranayama?*
Baba: The aim of *pranayama* is to achieve equality between the *prana* (exhalation) and *apana* (inhalation). *Pranayama* must be learned from an expert. First, he will measure your *prana* and then recommend the appropriate length of time for practice. He will teach you how to equalise the *prana* and *apana*. The *prana* and *apana* can also be equalised through *japa,* and *pranayama* will take place spontaneously without any effort. One technique of *pranayama* is to coordinate repetition of the mantra with each inhalation and exhalation. As you inhale, you repeat the mantra once, and when you exhale, you again repeat it. After practising *japa* in this way for some time, the *prana* and *apana* become equalised. This is significant because unequal duration of inhalation and exhalation is the cause of mental unsteadiness. As soon as the *prana* and *apana* become equal, the seeker experiences great inner peace and contentment. He then understands that the mantra has begun to bear fruit for him.

Pranayama will also occur spontaneously as you keep steadying the flow of thoughts. Concentrate your mind on an idol or an image, or even a black dot on a wall; or you can concentrate on the flame of a lamp, on *Om* or any other mantra. Any technique which is an aid to steadying the mind may be used. As soon as the mind becomes steady, *pranayama* takes place automatically. These practices are not related to any particular sect. They are independent and are meant for everyone. Intelligent people do not waste time arguing about whether they are beneficial or not, but begin to practise them and attain their goal.

CONTEMPLATE THE WITNESS OF THE MIND

Anand: *Despite my best efforts to calm my mind, it remains agitated.*

Baba: Let it be agitated. It is the nature of the mind to be restless. Just as it is difficult to cool a fire, similarly, it is difficult to remove the restlessness of the mind. It is the nature of the mind to have a constantly changing flow of thoughts. From the scientific standpoint, purity or impurity of the mind is the same. We hear so many people saying, "Today such and such happened. He said this and that to me and I am feeling very upset." Next day the same people say, "Today I am experiencing great peace." The mind constantly alternates in this way between purity and impurity. Have you ever contemplated the witness who knows whether the mind has become pure or impure? Peace may be obtained by doing *pranayama*, but who cognises this peace? Have you thought about this? This knower, this seer, this cognizer has no connection with the mind regardless of whether it is pure or impure, quiet or agitated. There is no loss or damage to him if the mind is impure, nor any gain or profit for him if the mind is pure. He watches the entire play from a distance, remaining aloof. Not knowing this truth, man becomes miserable. Such an ignorant person will be unhappy even in the most favourable circumstances. A *jnani* who knows the truth will always be happy even in the most adverse circumstances. If you contemplate the witness of the mind, then *pranayama* will take place spontaneously. Such contemplation has the power to free the mind from all anxieties and worries. Therefore, give up all other thoughts and contemplate the seer. This knower is ever pure. He knows all the states of the individual soul. He is the knower of the waking, dream and deep sleep states. The mind itself is just another object; it is not the Self. Concentration on the seer of the mind is the highest type of meditation.

Choose any Siddha mantra and repeat it regularly. In this way *pranayama* will occur spontaneously and the mind will become peaceful. All mantras have the same effect. The Shakti that pervades the entire world is only one. All deities are also one. Nonetheless, ignorant people love one and hate the others. God will never be pleased by such intolerance. Allah, Christ and Shiva—all are one.

Concentrate on only one mantra. Sit in whichever *asana* is most comfortable for you such as *siddhasana, padmasana* or *sukhasana* and do *japa*. The words of the mantra have tremendous power. No mantra is separate from God; the mantra is God in the form of sound. Only a person of highly developed discrimination can understand this. If you ask for salt, you will get only salt, not sugar. If ordinary words have this much effect, imagine what power must reside in a mantra! Let go of the mind; do not be concerned about its restlessness. One who understands the mind is known as *chaitanya,* a conscious being. Try to reach that state which is the goal of human life.

Religious injunctions and prescriptions bind a man only until he realizes the Truth. After attaining the goal, after realizing the Truth, man transcends the confines of religion.

Saturday, January 2, 1965

Two months ago Harshad Panchal, a student, came to the ashram in a state of ecstatic devotion after having read an article about Baba in the Gujarati magazine *Navneet*. Baba made him eat a banana and he calmed down. He returned today for Baba's *darshan*.

SEEK GOD WITHIN YOURSELF

Harshad: *I am now attending college regularly and studying. I am experiencing peace and can concentrate better on my studies.*
Baba: Very good. First complete your studies then I will make friends with you. I like to make friends only with educated and learned people. This man sitting here is a successful engineer, that man is a doctor, that man is a lawyer and they are all seekers. So practise spirituality, but at the same time manage the practical aspect of life with equal efficiency. Who told you that you can achieve God only by leaving the world?
Harshad: *May I sing a* bhajan?
Baba: Please do.

Harshad: आँखियाँ हरि दरसन की प्यासी ।
देख्यो चाहत कमलनैन को निसिदिन रहत उदासी ॥

"My eyes are eager to see Hari;
My eyes yearn to see the lotus-eyed one.
Without seeing Him,
I feel dejected day and night."

Baba: Without knowledge of the true nature of God, you will not be able to attain Him. First, understand who God is, what His nature is and where He dwells. Then try to see Him. Now I shall also sing a *bhajan*. Listen.

क्यों बन-बन ढूँढत सांई, सांई घट माँही...क्यों...

"Why are you seeking Him in one jungle after another? He dwells right within you."

This *bhajan* was composed by a great saint of Daulatabad named Manpuri. He says that God is inside you; you need not go anywhere outside in search of Him. Make your mind steady and peaceful and you will then understand this great truth.

Harshad: *I think that I must share whatever I attain with others.*

Baba: God is already attained by everyone. What do you mean by 'I think'? Who are you? What is the validity of your thoughts? Are the Vedas, Vedanta, Narada, Vyasa, Patanjali and Shankaracharya true, or are your words true? What they say is based on their direct experience. They first experienced themselves and then taught others. Therefore, we benefit from following their advice and teachings. We achieve nothing if we proceed according to our own thoughts and feelings. On the contrary, our minds become confused. So give up your singing and crying. First complete your studies and then pursue God-realization. Seeing you, I feel like singing.

'पानी में मीन पियासी, मोहे सुनि-सुनि आवत हाँसी।'

"Hearing that the fish remain thirsty while living in water, I feel like laughing."

(handing Harshad a book entitled *Ashram Bhajanavali*) Here is another *bhajan*. Sing it.

Harshad: अगर है शौक मिलने का तो हरदम लौ लगाता जा।
           जलाकर खुदनुमाई को भसम तन पर लगाता जा॥

"If you really want to meet God, then meditate ceaselessly. Burn your ego and apply its ashes to your body."

Baba: This *bhajan* is by Mansur Mastana. He says the same thing I am saying to you. The teachings of those who have seen God are always similar. Read further.

Harshad: मुसल्ला छोड़, तसबी तोड़, किताबें डाल पानी में ।
पकड़ दस्त तू फ़रिश्तों का, गुलाम उनका कहाता जा ॥

"Throw away the prayer carpet; break the mala; throw your books in the river. Hold the hands of angels considering yourself their servant."

Baba: Angels, those who have realized God, have His authority to guide others. Mansur says not to rely on other things, but seek refuge in such beings. Do as they tell you. Give up the fancies of your own mind. Read further.

Harshad: हमेशा खा, हमेशा पी, न गफ़लत से रहो इकदम ।
नशे में सैर कर अपनी, खुदी को तू जलाता जा ॥

"Eat, drink, never neglect your Self. Revel in the intoxication of your own Self, burning your ego."

Baba: He says not to give up the routine of your daily life. Keep doing whatever you are doing. Therefore, you should complete your present engineering course. Continue your studies. A year and a half remains; complete it. Knowledge of the mundane world is essential for a monk. The scriptures also say this. Look at me. I am not only a monk, but also an Ayurvedic doctor, a farmer and an engineer. I prepared the plans for all the ashram buildings. I am also adept at cooking. Don't give up your daily life. At the same time don't be negligent; don't consider whatever you fancy to be right. Don't get stuck in the mire of your own thoughts and beliefs. Don't perform worship according to your own will. The true path is to leave your own ideas and remain intoxicated, taking refuge in saints and sages. Read further.

Harshad: न हो मुल्ला, न हो बम्मन, दुई की छोडकर पूजा ॥
हुक्म है शाह कलन्दर का, 'अनलहक' तू कहाता जा ॥
कहै मन्सूर मस्ताना, हक मैने दिल में पहचाना ॥
वही मस्तों का मयखाना उसी के बीच आता जा ॥

"Let there be neither a mullah nor a brahmin; give up worship of duality. This is the command of the King of Kings. Ceaselessly proclaim 'I am Allah; I am God.'

"Mansur Mastana says, 'I have seen Him in the heart and that is the tavern of the intoxicated ones. Enter into the midst of that tavern.' "

Baba: Mansur says that God is not outside; He is within you. I, too, have seen God within myself. He is to be worshipped within, not outside. It is God's command that you should keep repeating to yourself "I am God" and remain in the company of saints. You need not go anywhere in search of God. He will come searching for you. Have you read the life story of Chokhamela? If not, do read it. Whenever devotees would go on pilgrimage to Pandharpur, he would request them to "convey my *pranams* to Pandharinath." He himself would never go to God. Ultimately, God had to come to him.

Wednesday, January 13, 1965

For the past week Baba has been in Santa Cruz. To-day a Parsi lady named Perin came for his *darshan.* When she met Baba two days ago, she experienced great peace. Perin has been worshipping Shri Krishna for several years, and wherever she goes, she carries a small idol of the child Krishna for daily worship. She was sitting deeply engrossed in thought when Baba asked her the following question:

GOD LOVES DEVOTION, NOT CASTE

Baba: So, what did Bhagawan Krishna tell you?
Perin: *Bhagawan said, "Baba will take you to that place where you cannot go on your own."*
Baba: I also heard Him say this.
Perin: *I am not allowed in the sanctuary of the Radhakrishna Temple here. I am told, "You are a Parsi, an outcaste." Therefore, I cannot have the darshan of God.*
Baba: What is the need for you to go to such a temple? Will God be pleased only if you go to that temple? It is said, भक्तिप्रियो हि माधव : "Madhava is very fond of devotion." God is pleased by your devotion and love. He does not discriminate between caste and creed, the false divisions created by man. Devarishi Narada says in his *Bhaktisutras*, नास्ति तेषु जातिविद्यारूपकुलधनक्रियादि भेदाः "Distinctions of beauty, caste, education, family, wealth or actions do not apply to *bhaktas* (devotees)." Was the hunchback slave Kubja attractive? Was Sudama wealthy? Was Vyadh a man of good conduct? To which caste did Gajendra belong? God became pleased with all these devotees only because of their intense devotion.

When you completely understand Krishna, you will realize that He is without attributes or form; He is ever-pure and all-prevading. Krishna is not this small idol the size of your finger. The following story will illustrate this truth.

Namdev was devoted to Krishna for many years. Bhagawan would appear to him and talk with him. In spite of these exalted experiences, Gora Kumbhar, a great sage, tapped Namdev's head with a stick one day in front of a large gathering of saints saying, "This pot is not yet properly baked." Namdev complained to Krishna, but Krishna said that Gora Kumbhar was right. Namdev recognised that his understanding was incomplete and he accepted Visoba Khechar as his Guru. Under his guidance, Namdev was able to realize the all-prevasive form of Krishna and become a perfect *jnani*.

You should also remember that although Arjuna had known Krishna for many years, he did not know his true nature; he did not know that Krishna was an embodiment of the Lord. For this reason, Lord Krishna gave Arjuna the divine knowledge in the *Bhagavad Gita*.

Shri Krishna's birth is described in the *Shrimad Bhagavat Purana,* but can you say that Krishna only came into existence at that time? Vyadh shot Krishna with an arrow, but can you say that Krishna ceased to exist after that? Sri Krishna existed as the formless, attributeless Supreme Self before His birth, He exists today and He will continue to exist in the future. He is as He has been always and forever. In order to fulfill some purpose, Krishna manifested in a form. Do not cling obstinately to the idea that Krishna exists only in a photo, an idol or a temple.

The attainment of liberation is not dependent upon membership of any particular caste. It is the priests of the various sects who place all these conditions on God-realization, saying that you can attain God only if you are a Jain or a Muslim, a Vaishnavite or a Christian and so on. Isn't liberation possible apart from these sects? Love and devotion are quite sufficient for God-realization. A seeker may embrace any name of God according to his inclination. Whichever form of God you worship, the final achievement will be the same. One person will recommend that you go to Mecca; another one will advise you to go to Vrindavan while a third one will say, "Go to Jerusalem," but God is not confined within any boundaries. Never forget this truth. Pushpadanta says, "The various paths are like many different rivers that merge into the sea and become one, losing their individual names and forms." Similarly, the Supreme Self is beyond all sects. With this understanding, become intoxicated in the love and worship of God; become intoxicated with bliss.

Sunday, January 17, 1965

Chakrapani Ullal, a seeker and devotee of Baba, brought his friend Rasik Kadakia, who is a close devotee of Swami Chinmayananda, to the ashram. He discussed *shaktipat* with Baba.

Rasik: Shaktipat *is not mentioned anywhere in Vedanta.*

Baba: In Vedanta you find such sentences as 'एकमेव अद्वितीयं, एकोऽहं बहुस्याम्' "Brahman is the one without a second" or "I am one; let me become many," which indicate that That, which is without vibrations, has the power to create vibrations. The power that creates vibrations is Shakti and it is not separate from Brahman, the Supreme Self. This Shakti has such power that it can create many from one, and it can reabsorb the many back into one. This very power is the Sita of Rama, the Radha of Krishna, the Yoga-shakti of a yogi and the grace-bestowing power of a Guru. We must conclude that those who claim that Shakti is not mentioned in Vedanta have not studied Vedanta thoroughly and have no experience in this matter.

Shaktipat is not a new science of the modern age.
It is a *siddhavidya* (science of the Siddhas) that has
been described in the scriptures and handed down
according to tradition from time immemorial. Read
Sadachar of Shankaracharya or *Yogavasishtha*, or the
books of saints like Jnaneshwar and Eknath. Read what
Sri Shankaracharya says about the worship of Sri
Chakra. His Guru, Gaudapadacharya, says 'वाक्यादेव
जायते शक्तिपातः अधिकारिणाम्' । "The worthy disciple
receives *shaktipat* by just one word from his Guru."
Whatever is mentioned in the scriptures about initiation means *shaktipat*.

Even in our daily lives, we are aware of the impact
our surroundings have on us. If there is melodious
music, the listeners start swaying; if there is an atmosphere of excitement, people get excited. The same
is true of the Guru's Shakti. As soon as a person comes
into contact with the Guru, he starts undergoing mental and intellectual changes, and knowledge of the
Truth begins to manifest spontaneously from within.
Sanatkumara obtained knowledge from the silence of
Guru Dakshinamurti. That was *shaktipat*. The
meaning of the great Vedantic proclamations such as
'तत्त्वमसि' "That thou art" can be understood only
by the Guru's grace. What Sri Ramakrishna received
from Totapuri was *shaktipat*.

Some seekers follow a particular type of *sadhana*
for many years, but when they find that they have not
gained anything, they abandon their practice. This
is not so with *shaktipat diksha*. The Shakti will not
leave you until you have completed your *sadhana*.

दीयते शिवसायुज्यं क्षीयते पाशबन्धनम् ॥
अतो दीक्षेति कथिता बुधे ः सच्छास्त्रवेदिभिः ॥

Initiation, according to those who have true knowledge of the scriptures, is that by which one achieves union with Shiva and the bondage of all *karmas* is destroyed.

Shaktipat is not a religion of credit: it gives you immediate cash. It does not have to make any promises that if you perform this or that action with faith, you will someday find what you are seeking. An able Guru awakens a disciple's inner Shakti and gives him an immediate experience of God. It is improper to conclude that Shakti does not exist simply because one lacks the ability to give *shaktipat*. It is not a sign of intelligence to claim that there is no such thing as *shaktipat* because it is not mentioned in the *Bhagavad Gita* or *Srimad Bhagavat*. Guruhood is not complete without the ability to give *shaktipat*. Guruhood is not attained merely on the basis of one's learning or skills as an orator. The Guru must be able to bestow grace (*shaktipat*) on the disciple and he must also be able to control it. If something goes wrong, he should have the power to correct it.

Whether or not you believe in God, He does exist. Similarly, *shaktipat vidya* exists whether or not you know anything about it. The Truth cannot be understood simply by listening to discourses on Vedanta. That does not mean, however, that you should give up listening to Vedanta. Listen to Vedanta, but at the same time do *sadhana;* contemplate what you have heard. To contemplate day and night after listening is implicit in the Vedantic teachings. Have you read *Aparokshanubhuti* by Shankaracharya?

Rasik: . *Yes.*

Baba: You may remember that at the end of the book he describes the fifteen aspects of contemplation that he advises the seeker to practise repeatedly. Only in this way can the truth of Vedanta be grasped.

Rasik: *Can a man with an impure heart receive* shakti-pat *initiation? Wouldn't it be harmful for his Kundalini Shakti to be awakened before he has attained purity?*

Baba: Every being is a part of God; thus everyone has the right to attain liberation. Every man has some sort of impurity, but as soon as he receives *shaktipat,* the process of purification begins automatically.

Rasik: *What are the qualifications a disciple must possess in order to receive* shaktipat?

Baba: Love and devotion. The disciple's love for the Guru automatically attracts his Shakti into the disciple. *Shaktipat* doesn't have to be done intentionally. If the disciple has true love in his heart for his Guru, then he is worthy of *shaktipat* initiation.

Saturday, January 23, 1965

Mr. Sarpotdar, who is a devotee of Rangavadhut Maharaj, came with his family for *darshan.* He is the brother-in-law of Vasant Nigudkar, a long-time, sincere devotee of Baba.

NATURAL SHAKTIPAT

Sarpotdar: *When the Guru gives* shaktipat *initiation, what is he actually doing?*

Baba: There are many types of initiation. Every Guru gives initiation in his own way. In *shaktipat* initiation the Shakti dwelling within the disciple is awakened. Truly speaking, this awakening need not be done consciously because simply by remaining in the Guru's company, the disciple's Shakti is spontaneously awakened.

Sarpotdar: *What happens after that?*

Baba: This Shakti remains active in the seeker, taking him further and further in his *sadhana* until he realizes God, until he becomes one with God. With the passage of time, the Shakti increases in strength. Just as a seed, after being sown in the ground, automatically sprouts and grows into a tree bearing blossoms and fruit, Chiti Shakti continues to work within the disciple and ultimately merges with Shiva. Even before they merge, this Shakti is Shiva. Shiva and Shakti are not different. Shiva assumes the form of Shakti in order to achieve some purpose. In other words, Shakti is the active form of Shiva. In distinct form, this Shakti dwells in the *muladhara chakra,* in the heart *chakra,* and in the five *pranas.* Actually, all forms of energy are one. This Shakti is no different from any other form of Shakti.

It is not essential for a Guru to formally bestow *shaktipat* in order to awaken this Shakti. Through love and worship of the Guru, the Shakti spontaneously and naturally starts doing her work in the disciple. The Shakti has perfect understanding. She knows exactly what she must do within each individual. This same Shakti is referred to in the *Devi Bhagavat* and the *Markandeya Purana* in which it is said:

या देवी सर्वभूतेषु शक्तिरूपेण संस्थिता ।
नमस्तस्यै नमस्तस्यै नमस्तस्यै नमो नमः ॥

"I bow to that Goddess, I salute that Goddess. I worship and pray to that Goddess who dwells in all beings in the form of Shakti."

Just as a student must be worthy to learn a mundane subject from a teacher, a disciple must be worthy of receiving the Guru's grace through *shaktipat* initiation.

A German couple from South Africa, Mark and Gita Obel, accompanied Nagin Pujara, a devotee of Baba, to the ashram. When they were at Ramanashram, Ma Talyarkhan had specifically advised them to meet Baba. Earlier this morning Baba had said, "Today some German yogis will be coming." Soon after their arrival they began asking Baba questions. Since it was Republic Day, a national holiday, the ashram was crowded with devotees and they all gathered around to listen to the discussion.

YOGA IN DAILY LIFE

Mark: *Must the practice of yoga be pursued only in a specific place such as an ashram or a* math, *or can yogic* sadhana *be practised anywhere?*

Baba: Yoga may be practised anywhere and by anyone. This world was created by God through his yogic power; it is not different from yoga.

Sri Krishna, who expounded our famous religious scripture the *Bhagavad Gita,* was a great *yogeshwar* (lord of yoga). He explains in the *Gita* that he created this world through the power of his *yogamaya*. Thus, the very origin of this world is yoga.

Many people have mistaken notions about yoga and fear that it must be very difficult to practise. They believe that in order to pursue yoga one must grow a beard, live in a cave and practise severe austerities, but yoga is something that can be understood and practised by everyone. The truth is that everyone already practises yoga in daily life. Every day you practise and live the various stages and aspects of yoga as described in Patanjali's *Yogasutras*.

The first stage in yoga is *yama-niyama;* that is, disciplines that you ordinarily observe each day in one form or another. You arise at a regular hour in order to arrive at the office on time; you eat your meals and catch the train at a specified time. Offices, market places, shops, courts and schools all open and close at the appointed times. In this way, your daily life is already disciplined.

The next step in yoga is *asana*, or posture. Don't you make use of posture in your daily life? Look, you have been sitting crosslegged; this man has been squatting for such a long time and that man has been resting his chin on his arm, listening to me. I am sitting comfortably in this chair resting my feet on the floor. These are all *asanas* or postures.

Pranayama is another stage in yoga through which the *prana* (outgoing breath) and *apana* (incoming breath) become equalised. This induces a steady mental state. *Pratyahara*, the withdrawal of the mind from the senses, and *dhyana*, meditation, are also parts of yoga.

The meaning of meditation is concentration of the mind on a particular object. Is it possible for an engineer to plan the construction of a bridge without concentration? Watchmakers, mathematicians and artists focus their minds on their respective subjects thus achieving the mental concentration that enables them to be successful in their work. Meditation or yoga is always a part of daily life, but it is incomplete yoga; it is only about 75% complete.

In mundane activities, your mind is concentrated on external objects whereas the aim of spiritual practices is to transform the mind into non-mind. This is called yoga. Yesterday I met a doctor who told me that he can successfully carry out his research work only when his mind stops doing all other work. Such a thought-free state is called *samadhi* and can be easily achieved through the practice of yoga. Concentration, or meditation, is a state. The relief from tension obtained by swallowing tranquillisers can be achieved naturally without any drug through meditation.

Mark: *I am very thankful to you for explaining yoga so beautifully and using the comparison with everyday life. My second question is : we always know the purpose of our actions in worldly life, but what is the special purpose of yoga?*

Baba: The purpose of practising yoga is to eliminate the agitations that constantly arise in the mind. The main purpose of yoga is to obtain profound peace, to put an end to all sorrow and to enjoy permanent happiness and bliss.

THE YOGA OF SERVICE TO THE HUSBAND

Gita: *Would it be a sin to leave one's husband for the practice of yoga sadhana with the goal of obtaining God-realization, or is a wife's only duty to serve her husband?*

Baba: There are strong bonds between husband and wife, father and son, God and devotee, and Guru and disciple. These relationships are not based on infatuation. For a disciple, no one is greater than the Guru. He would never leave his Guru. A devotee continues to worship God even after becoming a great saint. This is called *kshetra sannyasa* or one-pointed devotion. Similarly, the relationship between a husband and wife is permanent. Just as a disciple completely surrenders himself to his Guru, a wife should serve her husband with complete devotion and self-sacrifice. Selfless service and an attitude of devotion bring profound peace. This is the judgment of the ancient high court of saints and seers as revealed in the scriptures. The scriptures proclaim that a disciple may not do any *sadhana* yet he will attain his goal if he serves his Guru wholeheartedly.

Similarly, *tapasya* in the form of service and single-minded devotion to the husband definitely bears fruit.

There lived a great saint of high and noble character in Maharashtra named Tukaram. He said, '**तुका म्हणे पतिव्रता तेची देवावरी सत्ता**' "A woman who is faithful and devoted to her husband attains peace. Not only that, she achieves the power to command God Himself." Now you can decide for yourself the relative worth of other forms of *tapasya* compared to the power acquired by a woman who faithfully serves her husband. In India a great book called *Chandipath*, which is a hymn to the goddess, is often recited by devotees. It has a prayer: "O Goddess, if you become pleased with me, grant me a wife of good character whose nature is compatible with mine so that under her influence, I shall be able to cross over this ocean of birth and death."

Thus an ideal wife can also uplift her husband. This yoga of devotion to the husband has been bestowed on you naturally and you have obtained the fruit of this *tapasya* practised over so many years. So do not worry; God is with you!

Saturday, January 30, 1965

Shri Paramananda of Sri Lanka has been staying here for the past few days. This morning he and Albert Rudolph of America came for *satsang* with Baba.

THE EFFECT OF SHAKTIPAT

Rudolph: *When does a seeker reach perfection?*
Baba: Man is born twice. His first birth takes place as a result of his father's seed. His second birth occurs

when he receives the mantra from his Guru. As he progresses in his *sadhana,* he eventually achieves complete concentration and oneness with the mantra. By the power of the mantra, he becomes an *urdhvareta;* that is, his semen starts to flow upward. The fire of yoga converts this semen into *prana* Shakti. Through *shaktipat,* the Guru initiates a revolution in this *prana* Shakti within the disciple. This is his second birth. The Guru becomes father as well as mother. Just as a fertilised ovum develops into a child within the womb, the seed in the form of the mantra that is sown within the disciple develops steadily step by step. Just as a tree is formed from a germinated seed and bears flowers and fruit, similarly, a new identity is created within the disciple by which he achieves spiritual perfection. In order to reach this state, respect for and devotion to the Guru are absolutely essential. A disciple will become only as great as he considers his Guru to be.

Rudolph: *I am thinking of buying a house in New York. Will it be possible?*

Baba: The divine energy that pervades everything in this universe from the animate to the inanimate is also functioning through you. This energy is so powerful that with its help you can achieve anything you desire. However, for this, you must possess an ever-increasing love and devotion for the Guru.

Thursday, February 11, 1965

Since morning Baba has been sitting in the compound of a spacious bungalow called "Valley View" in Mahabaleshwar reading *Pratyabhijnahridayam* with a commen-

tary by Shivanijayogi.   Shri Yogendrabhai arrived and
Baba began talking with him.

THE IMPORTANCE OF THE SHAIVITE PHILOSOPHY

Baba: What can I say Trivediji: this book is really
sublime!   The science of Shiva-Shakti, *shaktipat,* is
even superior to Vedanta.   According to Vedanta, the
world is not real; whereas in Shaivism, the world is not
only said to be real, but also filled with Consciousness.

Yogendrabhai: *Isn't it possible to explain the Truth in a
few words?   Is it necessary to read so many books to
understand it?   If it is, then those who have read the
books should all be Siddhas because they have learned
everything from the books.*

Baba: There is a great distinction between being
merely learned and being a *jnani.*   Those who have
read extensively and can give lectures are learned while
those who have realized God are *jnanis.*

Yogendrabhai: *How can God-realization be achieved?*

Baba: Not everyone can attain God-realization.   It is
the result of many lifetimes of *tapasya.* When Bhagawan
Sri Krishna was born to Devaki, she told Narada with
great pride, "You have been so devoted to Bhagawan,
but he has taken birth in my womb."   Narada replied,
"I know the truth of the matter." Saying this, he covered
her eyes with his hands and showed her several of her
past lives.   Then she understood that Krishna had been
born to her because of intense *tapasya* in previous
lives.

In our ashram, some people receive *shaktipat*
immediately upon arriving while others stay for two or
three years and yet remain unchanged.   Your friend
Bhaskarbhai Desai experienced the *khechari mudra* as
soon as he came to the ashram.   People vary in their
worthiness to obtain knowledge.

Yogendrabhai: *What is the importance of the* khechari mudra *and other such yogic* kriyas?

Baba: All these *kriyas* lead to internal purification. The passage in the *sushumna nadi* is cleared out, enabling the *prana* to travel through it without obstruction to the *sahasrara*. After becoming purified in this way, a seeker no longer experiences any pain or misery even though calamity or misfortune may befall him. He is contented and happy under all circumstances. Peace and contentment are not dependent on external circumstances, but on the inner state.

Yogendrabhai: *Can't this state be achieved through knowledge? Are yogic* kriyas *necessary in order to achieve this state?*

Baba: Even after obtaining knowledge, *shaktipat* is essential in order to preserve it.

Yogendrabhai: *Is there anything else that should be done to maintain the state of knowledge?*

Baba: Contemplate Shiva. Remember the name of God ceaselessly. Everything becomes possible with the Guru's grace. In fact, without it, all other types of *sadhana* are nothing but various kinds of exercises.

                                    Saturday, February 20, 1965

Gita and Mark Obel have been staying in the ashram since last Monday. They have *satsang* with Baba every day.

WHO IS THE EXPERIENCER OF PLEASURE AND PAIN?

Mark: *Who experiences pleasure and pain, and how is it experienced?*

Baba: The same question is raised in Vedanta. The question is asked "Who is the experiencer of pleasure and pain?" To say that pleasure and pain are experienced by the gross body is not true because the gross body is composed of the five elements and is inert. And again, if it is claimed that the Self experiences pleasure and pain, that, too, is not correct because the Self is not attached to anything. The nature of the Self is pure Consciousness, which never undergoes any change. I shall explain to you through the following analogy who it is that experiences pleasure and pain. Heat a piece of iron in the fire. By contact with the fire, it becomes hot; its colour becomes red; it melts and becomes a soft, flowing metal. On removing it from the fire, the iron again becomes solid and inert. The iron is the same as the gross body; the fire is the Self and the flowing state is the feeling or experience of pleasure and pain.

The *suryakant* gem has such a unique property that when the sun's rays pass through it and strike a piece of cloth lying beneath it, the cloth will catch fire. The same gem, however, when removed from the sunlight, lacks the power to burn anything. Suppose this gem is lying in the sun and the sun's rays pass through it and an object by chance lying near it starts burning. As a result, a fire breaks out and burns everything in the vicinity. Who is to be blamed for such a mishap, the sun or the gem? Who can be prosecuted and who declared guilty?

The gem cannot be blamed because it is inert. The sun cannot be accused because it does not burn anything with its rays and does not perform any action. The houses caught fire because of the contact between the sun and the gem. In Vedanta this phenomenon is called *pratibimbavada,* or reflection. When Consciousness is reflected in the inert, gross body, the experiencer of pleasure and pain is created in the form of the *antahkarana* (the mind, subconscious mind, intellect and ego).

Wednesday, February 24, 1965

Shri Jayakantbhai, a grandson of Sir Prabhashankar Patni, the former Chief Minister of Bhavnagar, has come to the ashram with his wife, Asha, for a one-week stay. In the evening everyone gathered in the *satsang* hall and Jayakantbhai asked Baba the following question:

EVERYONE IS WORTHY OF PRACTISING SADHANA

Jayakant: *Can everyone practise yoga?*
Baba: Through *tapasya* (austerities) and good *karmas*, man can do anything because he is a part of the Supreme Self. However, one who has turned away from God through sins or bad actions cannot practise *sadhana* just as a son born from someone else's seed cannot have the appearance or qualities of his father, nor can he act like him.

In the scriptures man is given the understanding of his true nature through the method of *pratyabhijna*, or self-recognition. Once a young prince became separated from his parents in the forest. He was found by Bhil tribesmen who raised him as one of their own children. As time passed the prince began to feel that he, too, was a tribal child even though he had been born from the seed of a king. Finally one day, the prime minister found the lost prince. When he revealed the prince's true identity to him, the prince immediately recognised the truth. Although he had mistakenly considered himself the son of a tribal man, he again became the son of his real father. He recognised his true identity. In

the same way, discover your true relationship with God
just once and then see whether everything is possible
or not, whether you understand everything or not.

Man is born only from the seed of God, but he does
not become His and therefore he is miserable. The
Lord says in the *Bhagavad Gita*:

सर्वयोनिषु कौन्तेय मूर्तयः संभवन्ति याः ।
तासां ब्रह्म महद्योनिरहं बीजप्रदः पिता ॥ १४-४ ॥

"O Son of Kunti! All the creatures born through
any womb in this universe are born out of my *prakriti,*
the supreme womb, and I am the father who casts the
seed. I am the father of all the creatures in this universe." (14/4)

Due to the powerful effect of *satsang* and a holy
place, all the glory that lies concealed within starts to
shine forth. Think for yourself about the kinds of
experiences you have been having since yesterday. The
influence of the company one keeps is very great. The
poet-saint Sundardas writes:

तात मिलै, पुनि मात मिलै, सुत-भ्रात मिलै, युवती सुखदाई ।
राज मिलै, गज-बाजि मिलै, सब साज मिलै, मनवांछित पाई ॥
लोक मिलै, सुरलोक मिलै, विधि-लोक मिलै, वैकुंठहु जाई ।
सुंदर और मिलै सब ही सुख, संत-समागम दुर्लभ भाई ॥

"You can get a father or a mother, a son or a
brother, or a pleasing young woman. You can get a
kingdom or elephants and horses, or all the precious
possessions of this world that you desire. You can
attain social status, the heavens, the realm of Brahma
or Vaikuntha (the realm of Vishnu). Sundar You can
acquire any sort of comfort and pleasure that you could
ever possibly desire, but it is extremely difficult to attain
the company of a saint."

Asha: *Is it imperative for one to undergo all the consequences of one's actions in previous lives?*

Baba: Some have to be undergone now while others will bear fruit later. For example, Narada was cursed to endure poverty for seven lifetimes. A king who was also under a curse remained childless for three lifetimes. One must undergo the consequences of one's actions either in this lifetime or in a future one. There is no escape. Only realization of the Self has the power to burn all one's past *karmas*. Knowledge reduces all of one's *karmas* to ashes. It is said in the *Bhagavad Gita*:

यथैधांसि समिद्धोऽग्निर्भस्मसात्कुरुतेऽर्जुन ।
ज्ञानाग्निः सर्वं कर्माणि भस्मसात्कुरुते तथा ॥ ४-३७ ॥

"O Arjuna! Just as a blazing fire reduces wood to ashes, similarly, the fire of knowledge burns all *karmas*." (4/37)

Jayakant: *Last Sunday when I was here, a gentleman whose son was lost came to ask for your blessings that he might be found. You assured the man that he would find his son and immediately thereafter the boy was returned to him. Today this woman informed you that after you gave her a piece of fruit and blessed her, she was able to conceive a son. How do such things happen?*

Baba: I don't know anything about it. I said he would find his son and he found him. I might have given the woman a piece of fruit—at the moment I don't remember—and she conceived a son. Mudanna here had an ulcer, but he was cured simply by living in the ashram. Pure surroundings and good actions have tremendous power.

IS AN IDOL CONSCIOUS OR INERT?

A Devotee: *Swamiji, is an idol conscious or inert?*
Baba: Heed my words. A seeker desirous of liberation must not indulge in such idle discussions. Recently

when I was in Mahabaleshwar, a spiritual camp was in progress that lasted four days. A certain gentleman gave a discourse each day. One evening two participants from the camp visited me. They told me that the lecturer was condemning idol worship, arguing that "an idol is inert; it is only stone or wood. Anyone who worships an idol is a fool. There is no reality in an idol. If you put it in fire, it will burn up without a trace." I told them, "First, put that man giving the discourse into the fire and see whether or not he burns up. If he is inert, he will burn up; if he is conscious, he will remain unaffected. After he emerges from the flames, if he retains consciousness and can still speak, then I will accept whatever he says."

It is characteristic of the common man to disrespect the scriptures while it is characteristic of the *jnanis* and saints to honour them.

TRUE RELIGION

A Devotee: *Swamiji, which is the true religion?*
Baba: There is only one religion; the rest are distinctions in the name of religion. If anyone were to say to God, "I am a Sikh," "I am a Christian," or "I am a Muslim," God would ask, "What is a Sikh? What is a Christian?" God does not differentiate between a Sikh, a Christian or a Muslim. They are all similar human beings. Christianity was not created by Christ, but by his followers. Those who coerce others into changing their religion through outrageous means are merely exploiting others in the name of religion. From the perspective of a *jnani* or a saint, all religions are identical.

Sit alone, meditate, and perceive that which arises from within. Everyone will experience the same inner

vibration: "I am Brahman," or "I am That." In
meditation the feeling of being either a Christian or a
Muslim will not arise. True religion is that wherein
one experiences "I am the Supreme Self" from within.
As long as you maintain your sense of limited individuality, you will not achieve anything. The claim that
one sect is superior to another is merely false vanity.

Thursday, February 25, 1965

This morning Jayakant and his wife, Asha, came to
the satsang hall. Baba initiated the discussion.

RENUNCIATION OF THE WORLD AND DAILY
ACTIVITIES IS NOT NECESSARY

Baba: You are a very well-matched couple as both of
you are spiritually inclined. The life of such a couple
is harmonious and free from strife. If only one of a
pair is interested in spirituality, he or she will have to
undergo some suffering. A judge of the High Court
used to come here often. His wife feared that he would
turn into a sannyasi one day so she would always argue
with him, trying to dissuade him from visiting the
ashram. A professor's wife also used to come here
despite her husband's disapproval, but after meeting
me, he also developed feelings of love and devotion.

A spiritual seeker need not leave the world. Whatever you have to renounce can be renounced while
living in the world. It is only a matter of changing
your mental attitude. If one is incapable of doing this
while living in the world, how will he be able to accomplish it by running away from the world? If one cannot
renounce while living in his own home, what will he be

able to renounce by living in a jungle?

Sri Ramachandra and Sri Krishna did not give up the world. Both Saint Yajnavalkya and Saint Tukaram had two wives each and had to look after their homes and families. Worldly life and spirituality are not incompatible. Understand this truth, worship and sing the glories of God with love, and continue to perform your worldly duties. In this way, you will attain happiness and peace.

Friday, February 26, 1965

This morning Gita and Mark Obel and five other devotees came to the ashram. Later in the afternoon they all gathered around Baba in the *satsang* hall.

THE IMPORTANCE OF THE GURU

Gita: *Why is it necessary to have a Guru on one's spiritual journey?*
Baba: In spirituality the Guru occupies the highest position. It is very difficult to obtain a Guru. Nonetheless, nothing is impossible in this world of God. As long as the sun, the moon, the stars, the Himalayas and the Ganges endure; Gurus, Paramahansas, Siddhas and great beings will continue to appear in this world. Their tradition will never be lost nor broken. Chandraloka, Indraloka, Siddhaloka—there are many such lokas and numberless Siddhas dwell in such regions. One who has obtained the grace of the Guru and who follows the path shown by the Guru can have visions of these Siddhas. Such visions may not appear immediately after receiving the Guru's grace, but you will certainly see Siddhaloka before the final realization. Siddhas

dwelling in Siddhaloka also give initiation. In order to obtain the knowledge of Brahman, it is esssential to have a Guru in one form or another. Without the Guru's grace, one remains deprived of the supreme knowledge.

One must have devotion for the Guru to obtain his grace. You can understand its greatness from the famous example of Ekalavya. The devotion of Eknath Maharaj for his Guru, Janardan Swami, was also exemplary.

Once all the fellow devotees of Eknath Maharaj were about to set out on a pilgrimage and they earnestly requested Eknath to accompany them. He declined saying, "I am fully occupied in service to my Guru. Take this coin and offer it to the Ganges on my behalf." When the devotees reached Haridwar, they prayed and meditated according to the scriptural rites. Then they tossed Eknath's coin toward the Ganges and Mother Ganges herself stretched out her hand to receive it. Beholding this amazing sight, the devotees were wonder-struck. Then they heard a voice saying, "Mother Ganges is always eager to accept any gift from one who considers his Guru to be the mantra, the centre of pilgrimage and God."

Perhaps a Guru may be found, but it is extremely difficult for a Guru to find a worthy disciple with correct understanding of the Guru principle. The fruits of worshipping the Guru will vary depending on whether you consider him to be mortal or divine. To think of anything besides the Guru is infidelity. The Guru is the essence of Brahma, Vishnu and Mahesh. He who surrenders himself completely in body, mind and speech to the Guru becomes the Guru himself. Just as after merging with the sea, the river itself becomes the sea, similarly, such a devotee does not remain separate from the Guru. He who remains separate from God cannot truly be called a devotee, and he who remains separate from the Guru cannot truly be called a disciple.

.

Tuesday, March 2, 1965

Prior to the departure of Gita and Mark Obel for South Africa today, everyone gathered in the *satsang* hall. A child who was playing happily in the hall suddenly started crying, and the next moment was laughing again. After a short while he became angry with his mother and started hitting her. Observing the child, Mark asked Baba the following question:

THE EIGHT-PETALLED HEART LOTUS

Mark: *Why is this child's mind fluctuating so rapidly?*
Baba: The knowers of yoga speak of an eight-petalled lotus situated in man's heart. Each petal has a different colour and a distinctive quality: love, hatred, anger, fear, attachment, desire, compassion and peace. The *Dhyanabindu Upanishad* says:

"हृदिस्थाने अष्टदलपद्मं वर्तते तन्मध्ये रेखावलयं कृत्वा जीवात्मरूपं ज्योतिरूपमणुमात्र वर्तते ।"

"There is an eight-petalled lotus in the heart. The *jivatma* (individual soul) dwells at its centre in a subtle form of light."

The individual being keeps rotating over these petals assuming the quality of the petal on which it dwells. As he wanders about on these petals, he indulges in such notions as "I am the doer, I am the enjoyer; I am happy, I am sorrowful, I am black, I am white." For example, when the individual soul dwells on the white petal, he is full of devotion and tends to be religious; when he dwells on the red petal, he becomes lazy and inactive.

You can understand this from your own experience. You may have noticed that sometimes when someone approaches you, you may feel love or anger toward that person for no apparent reason. Sometimes you feel sad and pessimistic without any cause. You have surely experienced the fluctuating states of your mind in this way. The aim of meditation is to disengage the individual soul from all these tendencies and make him steady in his own Self. When one becomes established in the centre of the heart lotus, he experiences bliss and recognises his true nature. Even a seeker who meditates regularly remains subject to mental instability until he attains perfection. Until then, he will vacillate between love and anger, dispassion and desire.

You should understand, however, that although the individual soul may be subject to changing moods and states according to the quality of the petal on which he dwells, in reality, these are not the essential qualities of the Self. The Self is beyond all qualities. Just as a man may be identified as the man wearing red clothes or the man wearing yellow clothes, in the same way, the qualities of the petals are superimposed on the Self and then he is said to be angry or kind, lazy or energetic and so forth.

Further evidence to support the view that the individual soul is separate from all these attributes is that when he is experiencing one quality, he does not simultaneously experience any of the other ones. If all the qualities actually belonged to him then he would possess them all at all times, but this is not the case. For example, when one is in a state of anger, he does not experience love. When one is in a mood of dispassion, he has no desires. These various experiences that the individual soul undergoes are the result of the merits and demerits he has earned by his own previous actions.

The essential nature of the Self is Satchidananda (existence, knowledge and bliss). The true feeling arising from within him is अहं ब्रह्मास्मि "I am Brahman." "I am God; God is mine"—this is the individual soul's real inspiration. Have you understood this properly? I have explained it in this way just for your sake.

Mark: *You have explained it very clearly and I am very happy to have learned all this. (addressing Dr. J. C. Mehta, a devotee of Baba) Kindly translate Baba's discourse into English and send it to my son in South Africa. It would definitely appeal to him. He is a well-known heart specialist there.*

Gita: *Baba, why does the individual soul keep rotating on those petals?*

Baba: In order to undergo the results of past actions. This is his nature.

Thursday, March 4, 1965

Draupadi Singh, a West Indian lady, has been staying in the ashram for seven weeks. She has studied yoga at many other ashrams in India during the past ten years. After meeting Baba and receiving his grace in the form of *shaktipat*, she finally feels satisfied. Baba gave her the book *Pratyabhijnahridayam*, which she read twice, and today she discussed it with him.

Draupadi: *Babaji, I read in* Pratyabhijnahridayam *that Shiva Himself becomes the individual soul, but I do*

*not understand how this transformation occurs. The
ninth sutra says, "By the contraction of Shakti, That
which is of the form of Consciousness is covered with
impurities and becomes a* samsari *(worldly soul)."
What is the meaning of "the contraction of Shakti"?*
Baba: Once in a while, in a transcendent state of bliss,
don't you feel that you are Shiva? And again at other
times, don't you feel that you are Draupadi? This is
known as the contraction of Shakti. This is the result
of changes in attitude.

Sunday, March 7, 1965

   This morning Shri Ishwarlal Barot came to the
ashram accompanied by some Sindhi friends. They asked
Baba a few questions.

Devotee: *I have been in India since the formation of
Pakistan. I have been to many places in the country.
During these travels I have observed that the migrants
from Pakistan may try any number of places, but they
earn the best in Bombay. Why is that?*
Baba: It may appear to you that they earn very well in
Bombay, but every person earns money according to his
own destiny. What he is destined to have never goes
wrong.
Devotee: *I stayed for a month in the ashram of Shri
Vinoba Bhave. While there, I noticed that about
seventy-five per cent of his devotees were government
officers and ministers. Why should saints become entangled with ministers?*
Baba: In the olden days there were Raj Gurus, or Gurus
to the kings. The kings consulted them regarding

political and personal affairs. This was beneficial to
both the king and his subjects. The royal Gurus were
adept in all arts and sciences. They possessed the
strength of *tapasya*. Because of their selflessness and
impartial outlook, they could recognise the truth in any
situation and give the correct advice. Vinobaji is a
saint and has faith in Brahman. What harm can there
be in ministers seeking his company or advice?
Devotee: *I have too much anger. How can I subdue it?*
Baba: Apply your faculties of reflection and discrimination each time anger arises and it will automatically
decrease.

                                  Sunday, March 14, 1965

    This morning Shri Virendrakumar Jain, editor of
Bharati, the periodical of Bharatiya Vidya Bhavan, came
to the ashram. He is also a well-known Hindi poet. He
had a discussion with Baba in the *satsang* hall.

Virendra Kumar: *Since Shakti is formless and all-pervading, is it proper to see Her in the form of a gross body
or to worship Her with attributes?*
Baba: This entire world is a manifestation of that formless, all pervasive Shakti.   It is said:

या सा तु मातृका देवि परतेजः समन्विता ।
तया व्याप्तमिदं विश्वं सब्रह्म भुवनान्तकम् ॥
सा नित्या मुक्ता सनातनी ॥

"The entire universe from Brahmaloka down to this
earth is pervaded entirely by the supreme glory of
Mother Shakti, who is eternal and free."
The entire universe has been created by that Shakti.
Can't She who has created rivers, mountains, trees, birds

and animals assume a form? It is a very simple matter
for Her. Shakti is both with and without attributes.
She is one and also many. She possesses the unique
power of being able to convert one into many and many
into one.

MATERIAL ENJOYMENTS AND LIBERATION

Virendrakumar: *Lord Shiva is said to be the giver of
both worldly enjoyments and liberation. How does he
give material enjoyment?*
Baba: Lord Shiva is the giver of the fruits of action and
He presides over all actions. Whatever actions you perform, whether good or bad, the Lord is the owner of
all those actions. If you continuously act with this
understanding you will attain liberation, but if you do
not have this understanding, you will attain only
material enjoyments, the fruits of the mundane world.
Whatever action you perform, do it for the sake of God.
If you act with the understanding that Parashiva is the
final reaper of the fruits of all actions, then you will
attain liberation. The *Bhagavad Gita* says:

कर्मजं बुद्धियुक्ता हि फलं त्यक्त्वा मनीषिणः ।
जन्मबन्धविनिर्मुक्ताः पदं गच्छन्त्यनामयम् ॥ २-५१ ॥

"The wise, possessed of knowledge and action without desire for fruits, are freed from the bondage of
birth and achieve liberation." (2-51)
The *Gita* also says, ' किं कर्म किमकर्मेति कवयोऽप्यत्र मोहिताः ।'
"Even the wise become confused about what action is
and what inaction is." Many great beings tried to get
rid of the fruits of action through renunciation, but the
results would not leave them! Sai Baba of Shirdi, for
example, was a great *tyagi* (ascetic), but today his
samadhi shrine is worshipped. Lakhs of rupees are offered there and it is covered with costly shawls and other

valuable items. Similarly, the photograph of Nityananda Baba, a great *avadhut,* is carried in procession in
a silver palanquin. Siddharudha Swami of Hubli used
to wear gold-embroidered clothes and a crown studded
with diamonds and precious stones. If someone commented on it, he used to say, "I do it knowingly.
Instead of my *samadhi* stone being polished (worshipped) after I am gone as is the case of other saints, I am
polishing it myself."

Even great beings cannot escape their destiny.
Some people criticise them for travelling in motor cars,
living in palatial residences and wearing costly, beautiful clothes, but what can they say when they see the
samadhi shrines of the great *tyagi* saints being adorned
with silver and worshipped by devotees?

Knowledge is of two types, pure and impure. The
awareness that, "I am a gardener," "I am a potter," "I
am forty years old" or "I have a wife and children"
is impure knowledge. To understand that "I am
Shiva; I pervade this entire universe" is pure knowledge.
With impure knowledge, man remains a limited being
whereas, after gaining pure knowledge, he becomes
Shiva. The *Shiva Sutras* say, ' शुद्धविद्योदयात्चक्रेशत्वसिद्धिः । '
"As soon as a seeker attains pure knowledge, he becomes
a Siddha." Try to attain knowledge of the Self;
discover the answer to the enquiry "Who am I?" In
doing so, your environment or circumstances will not
be an obstacle for you. Hanuman's attitude of a
servant to Rama did not prevent him from realizing, "I
am Rama."

The world is a drama. In a drama there are many
characters each played by a different actor. A skilled
actor can bring out the character exactly as portrayed
without forgetting who he really is. Similarly, while
playing your part in this world, you must constantly

be aware of your true nature. This true knowledge
is the only source of happiness. Man experiences
pleasure or pain according to his awareness. If he
constantly remembers, "I am Shiva," he will be in bliss.
Sanjay, for example, was just a charioteer, but compared
to the king he was much happier. Such is the power
of knowledge of the Truth. This awareness is called
pure knowledge. This knowledge brings you liberation.

Thoughts such as "I am the body" or "This is mine"
belong to the ordinary mortal. The scriptures do not
advocate contemplation on such thoughts, nor have the
saints and seers uttered such statements; nonetheless,
man spends his entire life immersed only in such
thoughts. The teaching of the Vedas, seers and saints
is *aham brahmasmi*—"I am the Absolute." It is surprising
that no one believes in this; no one has any respect for
this idea. On the contrary, everyone believes in that
which is false. Such is life in this world. Man
remembers only the experiences of his mundane, day-
to-day life. According to Vedanta, the world does not
exist and yet, one experiences it. This is a matter of
great wonder. All this confusion arises out of man's
ignorance of his real nature. If someone does not
address a doctor by his proper title, he feels insulted
because he firmly believes in his identity as a doctor
and he constantly wants to be reminded and to remind
others of his status. If someone is referred to by a
wrong name, he takes the matter to court because he
identifies himself only with a particular name. This
type of thinking or belief is ignorance, or impure knowledge. It brings about only mundane results, not
liberation.

Wednesday, March 17, 1965

Today Shri Rasik Kadakia came to the ashram accompanied by some friends. While talking with him, Baba gave a beautiful discourse on *japa*.

THE IMPORTANCE OF JAPA IN SADHANA

Rasik: *A learned* acharya *who gives discourses has said that* japa *does not have an important place in* sadhana.
Baba: Those who do not consider *japa* to be important in *sadhana* are ignorant. Whatever the chosen method, the aim of *sadhana* is to make the mind one-pointed and *japa* is a simple and easy method. Although *japa* loses its significance after liberation is attained, it carries great importance during the period of *sadhana*. Whether or not you do *japa*, it is automatically going on within you. Man is alive by virtue of this *japa*. When he realizes this *japa*, he becomes liberated. In *Sadachar*, Shankaracharya says,

सर्वत्र प्राणिनां देहे जपो भवति सर्वदा ।
हंसः सोऽहमिति ज्ञात्वा सर्वबन्धैः प्रमुच्यते ॥

"Within every being the japa of *so'ham* is constantly vibrating. When this *japa* is realized, man attains liberation."

One must actually do *japa* in order to understand its importance. What can one who does not understand *japa* himself tell others about it? Only those who have attained *nirvikalpa samadhi* by means of *japa sadhana* can make a judgment in this matter. If you were to attain *nirvikalpa* meditation, you would understand this for yourself. The vibration of letters is called *japa*. It is the theory of *Spanda Shastra* that the first thought wave, or vibration, arises in that state in which the mind is *nirvikalpa* (thought-free) and *nirmaya* (comple-

tely still). *Spanda* is that *savikalpa* state (with thought;
the mind recognises a distinction between subject and
object, knower and known, etc.) through which the
mind passes before it enters *nirvikalpa samadhi.*

A verse in the *Upanishads* says, एकोऽहं बहुस्याम्
"I am One; let me become many." Here "I" signifies
the *nirvikalpa* state and "many" signifies vibrations.
The *"ham"* of *"aham"* has created this entire universe.
This vibration is its root cause.

The scriptures describe God as both with and
without attributes. The *Shiva Sutras* say, "आदौ
भगवान् शब्दराशिः" । "Before the creation, God existed
in the form of letters." The *Bhagavad Gita* says, 'यज्ञानां
जपयज्ञोऽस्मि' । "Among the various types of *yajnas*
(ritualistic sacrifices), I am *japayajna.*" Namdev says,
'नामा म्हणे नाम चैतन्य निज धाम' "The name is my own
abode, full of consciousness." Great beings such as
Prahlad, Dhruva and Vasishtha crossed over this ocean
of birth and death through the constant remembrance
of God's name. Saint Tulsidas says:

शुक सनकादिक सिद्ध मुनि जोगी, नामप्रसाद ब्रह्मसुख भोगी ।
चहुँयुग चहुँश्रुति नामप्रभाऊ कलि बिशेष नहिं आन उपाऊ ॥

Shuka, Sanaka and other Siddhas, sages and yogis
attained the bliss of Brahman by singing God's holy
name. According to all four Vedas, remembrance of
God's name is the most effective means of *sadhana* in
all four *yugas.* In the present Kaliyuga, there is no
better path than the name of God.

The *sadhana* of repeating God's name is advocated
by all the sects of Hinduism and by Christianity and
Sufism as well. All seekers vouch for it regardless of
whether they are *jnanis, bhaktas* or yogis. The *Yoga
Sutras* say, 'तज्जपस्तदर्थभावनम्' "One should repeat the
mantra and contemplate its meaning."

In the words of Tukaram Maharaj, the taste of God's name is so delectable that it can cause even a *jnani's* mouth to water.   Mahatma Laldas says:

ऐसो रामनाम रसखान,
मुरख जाको मरम न जाने,
पीवत चतुर सुजान।
रामरस मीठो ऐसो मीठो नाहिं और कोई॥

"Fools do not understand how sweet and nectarean the name of Rama is.   The intelligent and the wise drink this nectar.   Its sweetness is beyond compare." The following verse is from Saint Dadu:

राम रस मीठा रे, कोई पीवे साधु सुजान।
सदा रस पीवें प्रेम सौं, सो अविनाशी पान॥
सिद्ध साधक जोगी जती, सती सबै सुख देबु।
पीवत अंत न आवई, ऐसा अलख अमेबु॥
इहि रस राते नामदेव, पीपा अरु रैदास।
पीवत कबीरा ना थक्या, अजहूँ प्रेम पियास॥
यहु रस मीठा जिन पिया, सो रस ही मांहिं समाई।
मीठा मीठे मिली रह्या, दादू अनत न जाई॥

"Sweet is the name of Ram and rare
Are the wise and the holy who taste its nectar.
Drinking its love, they glide into eternity.
It is the resting place of the enlightened.
Of the seeker and the yogi, of the faithful wife
and the one who controls his senses.
Beyond vision and imagination is its perennial flow.
It is this nectar that kept Namdev,
Pipa and Raidas intoxicated day and night.
Never tiring, Kabir was always athirst for more
of its love.
Whoever has drunk this sweet nectar has drowned
In it, sweetness mingled with sweetness.
Ah, how can Dadu describe it!"

Many saints have sung the glories of *japa*. How can anyone say that the repetition of God's name is of secondary importance?

Sri Adi Shankaracharya, in his commentary on the *Vishnu Sahasranam*, writes that if any error is made in following the scriptural injunctions and rites during the performance of a *yajna* (ritualistic sacrifice), it remains incomplete. In order to complete it, he advises chanting God's name three times by chanting *om*. Such is the power of God's name. *Japa sadhana* is very important and most auspicious under all conditions, at all times and for all people.

One further point is that the practice of *japa sadhana* is very simple and straightforward and has no special requirements. In *dhyana* yoga, or meditation, for example, a proper place and observance of certain rules are essential requirements. In *jnana* yoga, a Guru and books are needed. In *japa sadhana*, nothing extraneous is required. It can be practised at any place and time without any prior preparation. It can be practised by everyone—children, the elderly, the virtuous and sinners. Both the one who chants God's name and the one who hears it derive the same bliss.

Ratilal: *How can this bliss be obtained? I chant the* Vishnu Sahasranam, *but I don't derive any joy from it.*

Baba: Chant with one-pointed faith and you will begin to experience the joy in it. The nature of God is nectarean; it is natural to feel an attraction toward Him.

Ratilal: *Perhaps I don't understand the meaning of the chant and, therefore, I do not experience joy in it.*

Baba: Even if you do not understand it, continue to chant it. You will certainly attain the fruit just as surely as you would be burned by stepping, even unknowingly, on hot coals.

In the study of Vedanta, fifteen steps must be

ascended one by one in order to obtain knowledge.
Yoga has eight stages. But the remembrance of God's
name is always one and the same right from the beginning until the end.

That which is beyond words is achieved through
words. The *ajapa* state is achieved by doing *japa*. The
name of God signifies the *nirvikalpa* state. To obtain
that state, take refuge in God's name. Tukaram Maharaj
says, " मुखीं नाम हातीं मोक्ष " । "If you have God's name
on your tongue, realization will be in your palm." The
essence of this entire discussion is contained in that one
sentence.

Rasik: *The acharya to whom I referred claims that he
speaks from his own experience.*

Baba: Everyone's experience is different. Which of
them can be considered true? If you were approached
by two people who had had opposite experiences, how
would you decide whose was true? And if both of these
experiences were contrary to the scriptures, would you
accept the scriptures or these experiences as true? To
assert the truth of anything, three types of evidence are
required: (1) scriptural statement, (2) the Guru's
words and (3) personal experience. Where these three
coincide, that alone is truth.

GIVE UP ATTACHMENT TO THE MIND

Madhubhai: *How can the mind be quieted?*

Baba: The mind is like the wind—sometimes steady,
sometimes agitated. To say "My mind is agitated" is
like saying "My horse is sick." What is the relationship
between you and the horse? Your feeling of my-ness
for the horse is what causes you to worry and feel sorrowful. A farmer develops attachment for a bull saying,
"This is my bull." When the bull dies, he starts
crying. He could have said without crying, "The bull

is dead. Bury it in the pit." You can maintain a similar detachment towards your own mind.

Madhubhai: *How can the stream of thoughts be stopped?*

Baba: Stop paying attention to what the mind is doing. Give up identifying with the mind as your mind. Vedanta asserts that the less you identify with the mind, the quieter it becomes. Give up the company of the mind. The resident of a house can stay in it with an attitude of either "the house is mine" or "the house is not mine."

I will give you another example. There were two families living in neighbouring houses. A girl from one house became engaged to a boy from the other house. Once, when the boy fell sick, the girl became very concerned. After a few days, the boy recovered from his illness. Later on, a quarrel arose between the two families and the engagement was broken. The girl married someone else. Two years later, the boy to whom she was first engaged died. This time, however, she did not feel sorrowful at all because she no longer had the feeling that the boy belonged to her.

Observe from where the waves of thoughts arise and where they subside. Watch the pulsations of the mind; see where they go. You can either flow with them or stand apart from them. Understand that the one who watches the mind is different from the mind. Attachment or identification with the mind is only ignorance. The best way to destroy this ignorance is to give up saying "my mind."

The truth is that the mind is the means by which you enjoy the painful or pleasant fruits of your past actions. It is for this reason that God has created this entity called the mind. Sometimes the mind is happy, sometimes sorrowful. Just as we immediately feel happy if someone praises us and angry if someone criti-cises us, our virtuous and bad actions also immediately affect our minds.

The mind is not different from Chiti; it is Con-sciousness in a subtle form. It is Chiti alone which takes the form of the mind, *chitta* (subconscious mind) and speech. In the *Bhagavad Gita* the Lord says, 'इन्द्रियाणां मनश्चास्मि' "Among all the senses, I am the mind." (10-22) By doing *japa* ceaselessly, the mind assumes the form of God; it is not destroyed. God dwells within you in your mind. What can you do to that which is the dwelling place of God Himself? Because the mind is the abode of God, the name of Rama fills it with peace. If God Himself is Arjuna's charioteer, how can that chariot be stopped? Now, you tell me, should we try to con-trol the mind or should we install God within it and transmute it into the form of God?

Madhubhai: *A swami used to advise concentration on the sound of "Sri ram, jaya ram."*

Baba: This is also a means of *sadhana*. When the name finally dissolves into silence, the seeker experiences the *nirvikalpa* state.

Thursday, March 18, 1965

Mr. Anthony Brook, a friend of Gita Obel, arrived at five o'clock this evening after spending two months at Pondicherry. He has also visited Ramanashram. His grand-father was king of the State of Sarawak in Malaysia, and Anthony fought against the British, who ultimately captur-ed the state. He has now become a pacifist engaging himself in the work of world peace. In the evening when all the devotees gathered together, he had a very interesting dis-cussion with Baba.

ON THE SPIRITUAL AWAKENING OF THE WORLD

Anthony: *I feel that the spiritual awakening of the world will accelerate tremendously in the coming three years. God is manifesting Himself in order to hasten this awakening. The consciousness of the world is being awakened, seemingly by the descent of Consciousness from above. Do you agree with me?*

Baba: Just as space is all-pervading, similarly, Chitshakti is also all-pervading. It is not that She dwells in one place and not in another, or that She exists to a greater extent in one place than another. Furthermore, whenever the world needs a saviour, there is a great being ready to perform that function. Therefore, it is not that someone particularly descends from above. The Lord says in the *Bhagavad Gita*:

यदा यदा हि धर्मस्य ग्लानिर्भवति भारत ।
अभ्युत्थानमधर्मस्य तदात्मानं सृजाम्यहम् ॥ ४-७ ॥

"O Bharata! Whenever righteousness is in peril and unrighteousness takes a strong hold, I incarnate myself into this world." (4-7)

Anthony: *I feel that God has incarnated in several places in order to bring about a spiritual awakening.*

Baba: You have this perception according to your own thoughts and ideas because an awakening is taking place within your own mind. Your consciousness is expanding each day and so you are seeing God everywhere.

Anthony: *Yes, what you say is true. In 1951, I experienced everything as God for seven days.*

Baba: The final state is attained when this experience becomes firmly established.

Anthony: *I pray that you will help me become established in that state through the grace of your Shakti.*

Baba: It is already becoming firm.

Friday, March 19, 1965

Anthony planned to return home today so when Baba seated himself on his *asana*, several devotees gathered around.

Baba: Did you have a good meditation last night?

Anthony: *I couldn't sit continuously so it was not real meditation, but I did experience a kind of joy arising from within.*

Baba: Everyone meditates for this experience of joy. The real attainment is to experience this joy without having to sit for meditation.

Anthony: *The Buddhists say we must become desireless, but desirelessness creates a state of void. I do not have any other desires except a desire for liberation that is so intense that I can't get rid of it despite my best efforts. Is this kind of desire an obstacle to spiritual progress?*

Baba: According to Vedanta, one who has such a desire is said to be in a divine state. An intense longing for liberation coupled with renunciation of all worldly desires is also a *sadhana*. Besides, isn't the striving for desirelessness also a type of desire?

RELIGIOUS SECTS

Anthony: *Babaji, on my way back to Malaysia, I will visit several countries where I plan to continue meeting with saints and leaders and members of various institutions. What would you like me to tell these people? Do you have any message for them? In this atomic age when disharmony prevails everywhere, I want to make an effort to establish peace in the world by conveying to everyone that we are all one.*

Baba: Wherever you go, tell people to live with self-control and to develop love for one another. Spread the

message of universal brotherhood. Universal brotherhood is true religion. Our ashram emblem says, *paraspara devo bhava*—"See God in each other."

Inner peace is lacking in the lives of Westerners.
In the name of God, they have established narrow
sects and, in order to increase their membership, they
have offered people various tempting inducements. Any
religion which attracts members with the help of such
enticements cannot have much truth in it. Even wars
have been waged in the name of religion. Isn't it
uncivilised for men to kill each other? Even in the
jungle, tigers do not prey on one another. In the olden
days, those who engaged in such atrocities were called
rakshasas (demons). I call such people modern
rakshasas. Look what ultimately became of Stalin.
Even his dead body was dug up and thrown away like
trash. His photos and everything else that might
serve as a reminder of him were destroyed. The state
of those who follow religious sects is somewhat similar.
It is outrageous for these religious sectarians to lure
the poor and ignorant by feeding and clothing them,
educating and nursing them, and converting them to
their own religion. Yet such persons consider themselves to be civilised, cultured, and progressive when,
in fact, they are worse than the wild beasts of the jungle.
The fact is that everyone wants to spread his own religion to the greatest possible extent.

There was once a prostitute who became rich
trading on her youth and beauty. As she approached
old age, however, she decided to devote the remainder
of her life to gaining some knowledge of religion and
thereby obtain peace. She decided to give away all
her wealth in charity. Hearing of this, leaders from
many different religions and sects went running to
advise her. The woman tried to learn from all of

them, but after hearing so many contradictory discourses, she became confused and could not decide
which of the many religions was true.

A poet from Karnataka has written that there is
only one heaven and one hell for all the religions, not
separate ones catering to Hindus, Muslims, Jains,
Buddhists and Christians. Then how did so many
religions and sects come into existence in this world?

God is beyond religion. Therefore, teach people
to live a life of self-control with a feeling of universal
brotherhood. This is my message.

Present this evening were Dr. Pratap Shroff, his sister
Malti, and an elderly seeker who often comes for *satsang*.

Seeker: *Can one achieve the attributeless Brahman
through the worship of God with form?*

Baba: It is the attributeless which manifests as a form
with attributes. Tukaram Maharaj writes from his
own experience, "सगुणी ध्याता निर्गुणी गेलो ।" "While
meditating on God's name and form, I reached the
attributeless Absolute."

Seeker: *Is this world true or false?*

Baba: The world is real for some and unreal for others.
Because the world exists only on the basis of the triad
of knower, known and knowledge, it is unreal for a
person who is asleep. If even one of these three
factors is absent, the world will cease to be. The
Vivartavada of Vedanta is meant to explain that the
world is unreal.

Seeker: *Yes, but in the example of the snake and the
rope, the rope does exist. How can you say that the
rope is unreal?*

Baba: The Supreme Brahman (symbolised by the rope
in the analogy) is also true. The world appears to
exist because of That. The snake also exists in the
rope. Where was the snake in the beginning? In the

rope. Where was it seen? In the rope. Where did it vanish? Into the rope. The snake is a form of the rope. Before its manifestation, this world existed in Brahman; it remains Brahman when it appears, or manifests; and it merges back into Brahman at the time of dissolution. Therefore, a *jnani* sees this world as a form of Brahman, who is its material cause.

Seeker: *Then why do we have experiences of pleasure and pain?*

Baba: Pleasure and pain will certainly be experienced as long as we remain individual souls.

Seeker: *Can we again meet the Self-realized saints after they give up their bodies?*

Baba: After they have completely merged with the all-pervasive Brahman, how can they meet you? However, saints who have transcended their bodies can certainly meet you.

Seeker: *Despite an intense desire to do* sadhana, *I can't do it. My surroundings are not conducive to spiritual practice. What should I do?*

Baba: Let the surroundings remain as they are. Without thinking about them, continue your efforts.

Seeker: *This way, when will I reach the final state?*

Baba: Why do you want a promise as to when and at what time you will attain the goal? What does it matter if it comes to you after two or ten more births? Since you have already lived millions of lives without attaining anything, why should you worry if there are ten or twelve more lives? Don't become disheartened. Efforts in this direction never go to waste. Everything will take place according to your destiny.

Seeker: *Can't destiny be changed?*

Baba: Destiny is our own creation. For a wise man, undergoing one's destiny or changing it are both one and the same. Nevertheless, destiny can be changed by very intense efforts as sage Markandeya demonstrated.

Seeker: *Despite my best efforts, my mind keeps pursuing me.*

Baba: This is a state of the mind. It is so because you are engrossed in the world. You should live peacefully in your old age like a true *sannyasi*. The four *ashramas* (stages of life) described in our scriptures have great significance. They were conceived after profound contemplation. Give up your attachment to your children and worldly objects; they can never give your mind happiness. More than anything else, the mind is the greatest cause of pain. For this reason, the scriptures advise man to give up his life as a householder after a specified time and to enter into the *vanaprastha ashrama* (retirement to the forest for spiritual practices) followed by the *sannyasa ashrama*.

Eat whatever you receive and sleep wherever a place is available to you. Sing the glories of God constantly. In this way, you will at least attain a better birth next time.

Seeker: *Can we get a birth according to our own wishes?*

Baba: You get a birth according to your desires; birth is according to the desire that is most powerful.

Seeker: *Do yogis have a desire for any particular type of birth?*

Baba: The only desire of yogis or seekers is to attain liberation. They yearn for the *nirvikalpa* bliss, not for another birth and again becoming entangled in the snares of this world.

Seeker: *But if everyone were to have such a desire, the world would come to an end.*

Baba: That's God's problem; why should you worry about it? Rid your mind of all thoughts. Entrust the burden of this world to God. It is His job to keep it going.

Someone once asked Swami Ram Tirth, "Can we become the Supreme Brahman?" He replied, "I have already become the Supreme Brahman." The question was then raised, "Can you do anything you wish?" He replied, "Yes, I can do anything."

"Can you create another world?"

"Yes, certainly I can, but please tell me where it is to be created. Show me a place where no creation yet exists, and then I can certainly create a new world there. But, right from the sky down to the sea and the earth, God has already created the world."

Malti: *With what material has God created this world?*
Baba: God does not require any material to create the world. He has created it out of His own Self. The world that requires some other material for creation is a human being's creation, for example, a house, a garden, a road or a car.

God created this world by His will alone. He thought, "I am One; let me become many," and the world came into being. This power also exists in man although in a smaller proportion. Man's creation is dependent upon action whereas God's creation does not require any action. The *Bhagavad Gita* says, ' मद्भावा मानसा जाता येषां लोक इमाः प्रजाः ।' (10-6) "The seven great sages of old and the four Manus are of My nature and born of My mind, and from them are born all these creatures in the world." (10-6)

Tuesday, March 23, 1965

Miss Mina Sarpotdar, a lecturer in Ancient Hindu Culture at Siddhartha College, has been staying at the ashram for the past five days. Her family members are devotees of Sri Rangavadhut of Nareshwar, who was brought up by Mina's grandfather in Godhra. This morning Mina had the following discussion with Baba:

THE TRUE NATURE OF DEVOTION AND MEDITATION

Mina: *Baba, I want to have* bhakti *(devotion)*.
Baba: Do you know what the real nature of *bhakti* is? Read Narada's *Bhaktisutras* thoroughly at least three times if you want to understand the real meaning of *bhakti*. Narada says: यज्ज्ञात्वा मत्तो भवति स्तब्धो भवति आत्मारामो भवति । "One who has *bhakti* is intoxicated with bliss. He is peaceful, knowing that he has achieved his goal. He has no desire for sensual pleasures; hence, he becomes the Supreme Brahman."

Knowledge (*jnana*) devotion (*bhakti*) and yoga are, in essence, the same. To see God everywhere is *bhakti*. To become steady in meditation without any mental vibration is also *bhakti*.
Mina: *I sit for meditation, but I can't enter into* sama-dhi. *I remain fully aware of my surroundings and know, for example, if someone arrives, if someone is talking—whatever is happening around me.*
Baba: You may become fully immersed in meditation, but the knower within you remains ever present. The Self is the knower; it is omniscient. It will naturally know everything. It knows not only what is happening here in the vicinity, but also what is happening in Delhi or Mathura. This power of knowing will not vanish because it is not a faculty of the gross body; it belongs to the knower who dwells within the body.

It is the mind that attains *samadhi,* not the knower of the mind. When the mind becomes steady, when it becomes peaceful even in the midst of activity, that is meditation. To sit behind a closed door controlling the senses alone is *jada,* or inert, *samadhi.*

Sunday, April 4, 1965

This morning some devotees gathered in the *satsang* hall. B. C. Dalal asked Baba a question.

Dalal: *Since the mind can never be without thoughts, then what thoughts are best?*
Baba: Think of the Self. Truly speaking, the only real existence is the *nirvikalpa* state. Thinking of the Self is a means to drive away all other thoughts. It is like removing one thorn with another thorn and afterwards throwing both of them away.

You do experience the *nirvikalpa* state or a state devoid of thoughts when you are overcome with anger or struck with wonder. Suddenly, for a fraction of a second, the waves of the mind are absolutely still.

Monday, April 5, 1965

In the evening, a woman presented Baba with a book by a famous poet. Baba accepted the book and then spoke about two different kinds of poets.

DIVINELY INSPIRED POETS AND ORDINARY POETS

Baba: There are two types of poets. Some are inspired by God. Others create through their own effort. A divinely inspired poet is one who becomes a poet by the blessing or grace of God. His language emerges as a natural impulse from within and is, therefore, pregnant with meaning. It uplifts the mind of the reader. His work becomes immortal as, for example, *Jnaneshwari,* the *abhangas* (devotional poems) of Tukaram and *Dasbodh* by Samarth Ramdas.

The other type of poet turns and twists the words,

somehow making them fit into a particular metrical form. Such poems are easily forgotten; the words never touch our hearts.

Tuesday, April 13, 1965

This morning Yogacharya Hansraj Yadav came from the Santa Cruz Yoga Institute. Under instructions from the Government of India, he is preparing a systematic report on the condition of all the yoga centres in India. He brought an official questionnaire with him, which he used as the basis of his discussion with Baba about the ashram.

THE RELIGION OF YOGA

Yadav: *Who was the founder of your institution?*
Baba: Bhagawan Patanjali. Our knowledge has been handed down to us according to tradition.
Yadav: *Which religion or philosophy do you teach or follow?*
Baba: Yoga is an aspect of religion. We do not need any other religion. The purpose of Sankhya philosophy is to obtain the knowledge of the Supreme Self. *Bhakti* arises from an intense desire to attain God. Meditation is an effort in that direction. Therefore, yoga includes all the religious paths.
Yadav: *How is the financial aspect of this institution managed?*
Baba: A yogi does not expect any wealth. He lives according to his destiny. Yoga is complete in itself; it is powerful and independent. It can fulfill whatever is required on its own.
Yadav: *Are there any specific sources of income for your institution?*

Baba: Yes, we have many—the hearts of the devotees. Our wealth is the faith of the devotees.

Yadav: *How much money have you been able to collect to date in order to further your work?*

Baba: My business is not to collect money. I work here without any selfish interest. When man seeks inner happiness and peace, the question of money does not arise.

Yadav: *How much does each student pay per month?*

Baba: There is no system here of soliciting or demanding anything; we have not made yoga a business.

Yadav: *How many persons do you employ here?*

Baba: In yoga there is no such thing as paid employment. The people here offer their services with selfless devotion to Yogeshwar, the Lord of Yoga.

Yadav: *What are the necessary qualifications for being admitted to your institution?*

Baba: An intense desire for yoga *sadhana*. Since every man is an inseparable part of God, it is his birthright to practise yoga and that is his basic qualification.

Yadav: *Can yoga be taught to all or only to a select few?*

Baba: It can be taught to everyone. In a way, all the creatures in this world are yogis because they all observe some discipline in their daily lives. They sit in a particular posture and that is *asana*. They concentrate on their work and that is *dhyana,* or meditation. So, knowingly or unknowingly, every individual is qualified to practise yoga.

Yadav: *Should the science of yoga be kept secret?*

Baba: What is the necessity of keeping it secret? If yoga is taught openly, everyone will benefit, everyone will become inspired. What in yoga needs to be concealed? In books such as Patanjali's *Yogasutras* and *Hathayoga Pradeepika,* yoga has been clearly explained. Only one who wants to be accorded unjustified importance will speak of concealing it.

Yadav: *Do you feel that the traditional methods of yogic practice need to be changed in any way?*

Baba: The saints and seers who originally conceived the science of yoga were neither ignorant nor imperfect. Whatever they have expounded is perfect. To change their teachings would amount to considering them imperfect and such consideration is sheer foolishness.

Yadav: *Would you like to suggest any improvements in the manner in which yoga is being taught at present?*

Baba: He who wants to teach yoga must himself attain the final stage, the experience of *nirvikalpa samadhi*. After he has obtained the fruit of yogic *sadhana,* he should then transform the hearts of others by his own Shakti, giving them the experience of peace and bliss. Dry or fruitless yoga is of no use.

Yadav: *Do you know of any book or individual who has made an innovative or basic contribution in the field of yoga?*

Baba: There are the lives of many yogis of the past and, in modern times, there are our experiences. What more is necessary? *Jnaneshwari* is an excellent book on yoga. Patanjali's *Yogadarshan* is a complete book with no scope for enlargement or improvement.

Yadav: *Are you doing any research on yoga?*

Baba: There is no need for any new research on yoga because the science of yoga is perfect as it has been handed down to us.

Yadav: *What are you doing in order to spread your work?*

Baba: Our work does not require publicity in newspapers because the changes in seekers who have obtained inner peace automatically spread the fame of our work.

Yadav: *Do you have any suggestions as to how the government should spend its resources on propagating* *yoga so that it will be beneficial to the nation?*

Baba: Cultivating a feeling of universal brotherhood is for the real welfare of the people. Without this nothing else can really benefit them. Peoples' welfare certainly cannot be achieved simply with the help of money.

Yadav: *Do you agree with the viewpoint that yoga should be included in the regular school curriculum as a part of physical education?*

Baba: Yoga is not physical education; it is a spiritual subject. Nevertheless, the study of yoga certainly improves one's physical well being.

Yadav: *Do you agree that yoga is a method of curing diseases?*

Baba: It is a great mistake to associate yoga with disease. There is an independent science called Ayurveda for the treatment of disease.

Yadav: *How many sick people are treated here through yoga?*

Baba: We do not do anything particularly for healing diseases; however, the purification of the *nadis* in yoga automatically cures any disease a seeker may have.

Yadav: *How many patients have been cured here so far?*

Baba: We have not kept any statistical data. Nonetheless, many people have benefited. Bhagawan Nityananda cured innumerable patients. For him it was a very simple matter.

Yadav: *What medicines do you use for patients?*

Baba: Yoga itself is the perfect medicine. The physical rejuvenation brought about by yoga creates the internal medicine.

Yadav: *What diseases can be cured by yoga?*

Baba: The worst disease—birth and death—is completely cured by yoga.

Yadav: *By what means do you teach yoga here?*

Baba: We do not require any means other than the practice of yoga.

Yadav: *How many assistants do you have to help you in your work?*

Baba: A yogi is absolutely independent. He does not require anyone's help.

Yadav: *Are yoga classes conducted regularly?*

Baba: The practice of yoga goes on here constantly and systematically; therefore, no formal classes are necessary.

Yadav: *Are there any classes to explain the philosophy of yoga?*

Baba: Whenever the necessity arises, this subject is explained, but no special classes are held for this.

Yadav: *How much time is required for the study of yoga at your institution?*

Baba: Yoga has to be practised regularly until one reaches perfection.

Yadav: *How many students are here?*

Baba: This question applies to ordinary schools, not an ashram. We are not concerned about numbers so we do not count how many seekers have joined the institution, nor do we maintain any register for this purpose.

Yadav: *What are the age limits for gaining admission as a student? Are classes segregated according to age groups?*

Baba: We do not have any age limitations here. Children and the elderly, men and women, all can practise yoga. The time at which a person arrives here is the proper time for him or her to begin the practice of yoga and everyone is in the same class. We do not segregate seekers into different classes.

Yadav: *By what method do you judge who has made progress in yogic* sadhana *and who is lagging behind?*

Baba: A yogi is able to judge this for himself. A Guru who is not hungry for disciples can judge their progress by himself.   We do not have any instruments to measure the progress of yoga students, nor do we hold any examinations for them.

Yadav: *Can the students of your institution help in propagating the knowledge of yoga?*

Baba: Any seeker who has himself reached perfection in yoga will certainly be able to impart his knowledge to others.

Saturday, April 17, 1965

During the summer, the ashram is especially crowded with devotees. Tomorrow is the Sunday holiday and many devotees have come today to spend the weekend. Since Baba's room could not accommodate everyone for *satsang*, people moved to the ashram lobby. Baba came and sat in their midst. Among the devotees were B. C. Dalal, Virendrakumar Jain and Amrita Bharati, a Sanskrit professor and poetess. The discussion began on the simple nature of Dr. Brahma Prakash, a director of the Atomic Energy Commission and a devotee. Baba then spoke of the similar nature of Professor Bhagwat of Ruia College and described his first meeting with him.

Baba: About eight or nine years ago, Professor Bhagwat came for Nityananda Baba's *darshan*.   He was actually a professor of philosophy, but he was also very knowledgeable in chemistry.   He could tell the composition of a sample of earth or ore just by holding it in his hand. He felt, however, that his abilities were not sufficiently appreciated in India and that he was not receiving the necessary financial assistance to use his talents effectively. Therefore, he was thinking of emigrating to Russia, hoping that he would receive a better salary and adequate facilities for his chemistry experiments.

Before making his final decision to go, however, he came to Ganeshpuri to seek the advice of Nityananda Baba, but Baba would not give him an answer. Professor Bhagwat then became confused and did not know what course to take. When he again began to ask Baba, someone advised him to seek an answer to his problem from Swami Muktananda so he came to the Gavdevi ashram (now Gurudev Siddha Peeth).

In those days, the ashram consisted of only three rooms. The compound walls were not even built. When Professor Bhagwat arrived, I was sitting alone on a stone wall.

THE LAW OF DESTINY

Bhagwat: *I have been told that a certain swami lives here. Is this his place?*
Baba: Yes, it is.
Bhagwat: *Is he here?*
Baba: Yes.
Bhagwat: *I want to see him.*
Baba: What is his name?
Bhagwat: *Swami Muktananda*
Baba: Everyone calls me by that name.

Professor Bhagwat was completely surprised. He couldn't believe that he had been speaking to Swami Muktananda, but I reassured him and he sat down and narrated his story from beginning to end.
Baba: What kind of work are you doing now?
Bhagwat: *Sir, I am a professor of philosophy.*
Baba: Have you studied this subject merely to teach it to students, or have you studied it for your own benefit as well?
Bhagwat: *For my benefit also.*
Baba: You may be aware of the law of destiny as ex-

plained in our philosophy.   Do you accept it?

Bhagwat: *Certainly I do.*

Baba: Then can you tell me how your difficulties that cannot be overcome in India will be resolved in Russia? Don't you know that everyone's destiny follows him? It cannot be changed.   You may live anywhere;   you may go to Russia, or you may remain in India, but you will only get that which is written in your destiny. Therefore, the duty of a wise man is to remain content wherever he is.

Professor Bhagwat was at last satisfied; his mind became peaceful.   He gave up the idea of going to Russia.   He knew how to make brass out of copper and other metals.   He had a great desire to make gold out of these metals, but that technique is kept secret and is written in a code that can only be deciphered by one who has rececived the grace of God.   Our seers and saints had knowledge not only of the Self, but also about Ayurveda, chemistry and botany.   I myself know about the qualities of mercury.   When it is melted and slowly rubbed into the palm, it spreads throughout the entire body and imparts such tremendous strength that one can even climb mountains without getting tired.   Afterwards, the mercury can be removed from the system. But ultimately, such knowledge is of no use.   This body may be protected and maintained even for thousands of years, but at last a day will come when you will have to leave it.

AFTER MERGING WITH BRAHMAN, NO TRACE OF A SIDDHA'S INDIVIDUALITY REMAINS EVEN IN SUBTLE FORM

Virendrakumar: *Baba, Tukaram Maharaj is said to have ascended to Vaikuntha in his gross body. How is that possible?*

Baba: His devotees may have seen him depart in that form, but where the body is of no use, what could be the point of retaining it? If one can see without eyes, why should one have eyes at all? In the state of complete liberation neither the gross nor the subtle body is of any use. For a great soul to remain even in the subtle body is a state of imperfection, let alone in the gross body.

Virendrakumar: *Some Siddhas and great beings give* darshan *even after they have departed from the gross body. How is that possible?*

Baba: It does not mean that they exist in the subtle body. The subtle body is also a kind of bondage. If the gross body can be compared to iron handcuffs, the subtle body can be compared to gold handcuffs, but they are both still bindings. If anyone were to say that Nityananda Baba still exists here in a subtle body, it would indicate imperfection in his Siddhahood. You tell me, is the space inside a pot greater, or is the total space greater? Is a drop greater, or is the ocean greater? Why should you want to limit the limitless?

Chaitanya (Consciousness) has great powers. It can assume any form it chooses. All the forms in the world are His so it is a very simple matter for Him to assume the form of Rama, Krishna or any Siddha or great being. Whatever you see in this world is Consciousness and it can appear before a devotee in any form according to his faith.

Virendrakumar: *Some people claim that a certain sannyasi is an incarnation of some other saint. Is that true?*

Baba: According to the *Bhagavat Purana,* there have been only ten incarnations. Whenever a Siddha or a great being comes to this earth for any special purpose, he returns as soon as his work is completed. Some individuals attain Siddhahood after practising auster-

ities over many lifetimes. As soon as they have
exhausted their *prarabdha karma* (*karma* that must
bear fruit in their current lifetime), they drop their
bodies. They do not have to be incarnated again and
again, nor is there any possibility of their being
reincarnated.

THE COSMOS CREATED BY GOD CANNOT BE CHANGED

Virendrakumar: *Is it true that after achieving oneness
with the Universal Self, who is even beyond the mind,
we will be capable of effecting changes in the gross
world?*

Baba: Perhaps such possibilities are discussed, but has
anyone ever demonstrated this? Are there any examples of such feats related in the scriptures? On the
other hand, we have many examples of individuals
attaining Siddhahood that we can see for ourselves. The
first is only wishful thinking while the second is a
reality. To ensnare devotees and disciples by making
false promises for the future is to capitalise on their
hopes while to give them a direct, immediate experience
is an actual proof in the present.

This cosmos, which has been created by God's will,
cannot be changed in any way. No one can transgress
the limits set by God. God created everything systematically. Without God's direct order, no one can
interfere in His creation. Even a judge must proceed
according to the law. The same principle applies to
saints. Jnaneshwar was a Siddha yogi with such extraordinary powers that he made a buffalo recite the
Vedas and a brick wall move. He had the power of
infusing consciousness into inert or lifeless objects.
Even so, he did not attempt to make any changes in this
cosmos created by God.

Amrita Bharati: *Everyone has really enjoyed today's question and answer session.*
Baba: If one question is answered, another one will arise. There is no end to it. What is the use of asking so many questions.
Amrita Bharati: *If the questions and answers give us joy, why shouldn't we ask questions?*
Baba: Because that joy which is dependent on any outside source is artificial. The bliss that arises independently of anything else is the only true bliss.

Sunday, May 2, 1965

Many devotees have come to the ashram over the three-day holiday. Rasik Kadakia and some friends were among them and today they had an interesting *satsang* with Baba.

Rasik: *Which* sadhana *must be practised to attain God?*
Baba: You may do any *sadhana* that you choose, but it must be a complete one. The *sadhana* of the Siddhas is complete; therefore, it is advisable to follow the path trodden by them. Yoga, *jnana* and *bhakti* are all complete *sadhanas* created by our seers, who showed these paths to others only after practising them themselves and attaining perfection.

Give up insisting that only one particular type of *sadhana* is correct. Follow whichever path you like best and your *sadhana* will then be very easy. It is not necessary to follow all the paths simultaneously. In fact, to do so would only increase the likelihood of mental confusion. If you can make the mind thought-free, you will attain the Truth. This thought-free state can be achieved by any of the paths. The ultimate aim of all paths of *sadhana* is the same so follow any one path. Each path includes the other types of *sadhana* to some extent. For example, in *japa,* or constant remembrance of God, yoga and *jnana* (knowledge) are included. The posture which you adopt becomes an *asana,* which is a part of yoga. What is *japa?* To know how to practise it and what its aims and objectives are is *jnana.* Therefore, *japa,* the repetition of God's name, automatically includes yoga and *jnana.* The vision of oneness obtained through *bhakti,* the mature, subtle *prajna* (understanding) attained through the study of Vedanta, and the *nirvikalpa* state achieved by the practice of yoga are all one and the same. When you achieve perfection in any one type of *sadhana,* you will have reached the final perfection.

Rasik: *What should one think of while doing* japa?

Baba: Concentrate your mind on either aspect of God, with form or without form, according to your preference. Even if you think of God as having from and attributes, you will ultimately reach the formless, attributeless Brahman.

The means and the end of *japa* are the same whereas in other paths they are separate. In yoga, the practice of the eight steps is the means leading to the goal of *nirvikalpa samadhi.* In Vedanta, the means is contemplation on the Self leading to attainment of the *turiya* state. In *japa sadhana,* the aim is to attain the *ajapa* state in which *japa* takes place automatically without any effort or attention.

THE MANTRA RECEIVED FROM THE GURU

Rasik: *Which mantra should be used for* japa?

Baba: It should be a Siddha mantra, a mantra which Siddhas have used for *japa.* It is best to take a mantra from one who has himself done *japa* with it. Such a mantra is alive or conscious and, therefore, yields better results.

Before doing *japa* of any mantra, one must have a thorough knowledge of it. Such knowledge can be obtained only by taking refuge in a being who knows and has directly experienced that mantra. Without knowledge of the mantra, one cannot appreciate its value.

A Guru once gave the mantra *sri rama* to his devoted disciple, telling him to keep it secret. The disciple was very pleased and started doing *japa*. The next day he went to bathe in the Ganges where he came across several other people loudly chanting the same mantra, *sri rama*. Immediately a doubt arose: "If so many people already know this mantra, what is the need for secrecy? Why did my Guru attach so much importance to this mantra?" Even after pondering this matter for a long time, the disciple could not resolve his doubt. At last, he went back to his Guru and explained his doubt. The Guru told him, "I shall reply to your question later. First, I want you to do something for me." The Guru then handed him a clear, sparkling bead telling him to ascertain its worth in the bazaar. He ordered, "Go and only ask its price; don't sell it." The obedient disciple immediately went to the bazaar. First, he asked a vegetable vendor the price of the bead. The vendor replied, "I'll give you two eggplants in exchange for this glass bead." Next, he went to a goldsmith who said, "This is a topaz. I'll pay you Rs. 100 for it." Now the disciple's curiosity was aroused so he stopped next at a diamond dealer. The dealer exclaimed, "This is a precious gem. It is the biggest diamond I have ever seen. I'll pay you Rs. 100,000 for it." Finally, the disciple went to the largest diamond dealer in the area, who examined the bead with awe. He said, "O brother, this gem is invaluable! Even if the entire wealth of the country were paid for it, it would not be enough. I would advise you not to sell it." The disciple, being intelligent, immediately understood why his Guru had sent him to find out what the value of the gem was. His doubt cleared up. He returned and fell at the Guru's feet, begging his forgiveness for having raised a doubt about the mantra.

So you see, he who does not know the worth of something cannot appreciate its real value. Even if you already know the mantra that the Guru gives you, it is always more powerful when it is received directly from him.

Mantra *japa* must be done with total faith and love. Repeat it with a concentrated mind and lose yourself in it. A mantra is the sound form of God and has tremendous power. Look how much power there is in ordinary words. On August 15, 1947, Lord Mountbatten declared, "From today onward, India is a free nation." These words brought about a complete transformation in India. Insulting words immediately create anger in our minds. The sages did not create bad or insulting words, they cannot be found in the scriptures, nor does anyone perform any recitation or repetition of them. Even so, you can see what a powerful effect they have. If even trivial words have such power, then you can imagine the infinite power in God's name. Forget about yourselves and merge with the mantra.

You may choose any path; you may adopt any means of *sadhana,* but the one basic requirement is that you must completely lose yourself in it. A saint has said:

खुदी को न मिटाओ तब तक खुदा नहीं मिलता ।
मिटाओ अपनी हस्ती को जो कुछ मरतबा चाहता ॥

"You cannot attain God as long as you have not given up the notion of 'I' and 'mine.' One who aspires to a higher state must first give up his own identity."

Radha became so engrossed in Sri Krishna that, as a poet describes it:

कृष्ण कृष्ण करत राधा कृष्ण बन गई ।
पूछत सखियन से प्यारी राधा कहाँ गई ॥

"By constantly repeating 'Krishna, Krishna,' Radha herself became Krishna and began asking her friends, 'Where has Radha gone?'"

Follow whichever path you prefer, but become one with it. Then you may stay anywhere or you may go anywhere. All external circumstances will appear the same to you. You will see God everywhere and eventually you will experience that you yourself are God.

Faith has tremendous power. The Muslims obtained Pakistan only because of their faith. Always contemplate "I am the Supreme Brahman" while following the path you like—*bhakti,* meditation, *japa* or *jnana*—and you are bound to attain the final goal, the Supreme Self. In the *Bhagavad Gita,* the Lord says, 'ममैवांशो जीवलोके जीवभूतः सनातनः।" "An eternal part of me lives as creatures of the world." In order to return to our origin, we have to retrace the path by which we came. We have lost our way in the jungle of such thoughts and ideas as "I am so and so, my name is such and such, I belong to such and such a family." We have to turn back and retrace the same steps that led us astray. Our name, family, lineage, home—none of these is different from the Supreme Self. Give up the wrong path of limited thinking—I am so and so—and return to the correct path, *aham brahmasmi,* "I am the Absolute." This is the essence of all the scriptures.

Monday, May 3, 1965

SEE THE WORLD AS A FORM OF BRAHMAN

Rasik: *A learned professor is currently in Bombay giving discourses to large audiences. He does not believe in idol worship. He teaches that when you see a beautiful idol, you should only observe it without allowing any thoughts about it to arise in the mind.*

Baba: By this, he means that one should not contemplate its name or form, doesn't he?

Rasik: *Yes, the mind should be emptied.*

Baba: Instead of having any thoughts about the world, it would be better to perceive it as a form of Brahman. It is the formless that has assumed form. Instead of breaking the idol into pieces to discover that it is made of clay, it would be better to see the clay in the form of the idol. Instead of separating every single thread from a cloth to discover that it is cotton, it would be better to see cotton in the texture, colour and appearance of the cloth.

You should have the vision of the goldsmith, not that of his customer. For the customer, a ring, bangle and necklace are all different. He evaluates them according to their design and craftmanship whereas the goldsmith sees them only as different forms of gold. He sees only how much gold they contain. Similarly, the world can be perceived in two different ways. One viewpoint corresponds to that of the customer, the other to that of the goldsmith. Even after gold has been transformed into a bangle or a ring, it still remains gold. In the same way, Brahman pervades every form in this world.

The vision of a scholar differs from that of a realized being who has experienced the Universal Self. You should learn to have the vision of the realized being.

See the Supreme Brahman everywhere and try to accept
both pleasure and pain with equanimity.

Thursday, May 13, 1965

Today Draupadi asked some questions at *satsang*.

RICHES AND POVERTY

Draupadi: *Babaji, an Indian swami recently visited
America where people asked him, "You give big
lectures here, but what is the condition of your own
country? How does your philosophy help your poor
people?" Swamiji replied, "It makes them wiser."*
Baba: If I had been in his place, I would have replied,
"Our philosophy enables a man to experience riches
even amid poverty." It is said:

कंगाल को मालोमाल, दरिद्र को निहाल,
रंक को भूपाल, शाह को शाहनशाह बनाती है ।
पापों की हननी, ज्ञान वैराग्य की जननी,
मूर्ख को पण्डित, पण्डित को अखण्डित बनाती है ।

"Knowledge makes a pauper rich, a beggar a king,
and a king an emperor. It destroys all sins. It
creates dispassion. It makes the ignorant learned, and
it makes the learned unconquerable."

Draupadi: *But philosophy is not noticeable among the
poor. Vivekananda once said, "First give them enough
to eat and drink, and then talk to them about
philosophy."*
Baba: Learn to fully observe and study all aspects of any
given situation. Study Vedanta completely. Then you
will understand the Truth.

Who says that philosophy is nonexistent in the

lives of the poor people of our country? In fact, many
of our philosophers have lived like ascetics. After
seeing this ashram, you may feel that philosophy can
spring up only where there is wealth, but that is not
so. Saint Kabir was an ordinary weaver. Swami
Narasimha of Pandharpur used to wear only a loincloth.
He would cover himself with an old, torn blanket and
sleep in any available place. He would eat only when
offered food. Nonetheless, his inner experience was
"I am the Lord of this universe." Another saint,
Bapumai, used to wear a ragged loincloth. He would
save any alms received during the day and in the
evening throw the entire amount into the Chandrabhaga
River. Wasn't this an indication of his wealth?
Ramakrishna Paramahansa was also poor, and what
wealth did Vivekananda have? There was never
enough food in the house to feed his family. What
about Ramana Maharshi? Even Nityananda Baba lived
in poverty. There was wealth around him only after
he settled down in Ganeshpuri.

Speak to those who are offering their services in
this ashram. Many of them come from poor families,
but ask them about their present state of mind. Ask
them if they suffer from even a slight feeling of poverty.
Our philosophy can be realized even amid material
poverty.

Sunday, May 23, 1965

THE MIND

Kadakia: *Babaji, can the mind be known by the mind?*
Baba: Just as the sun is seen by its own light and it also
illuminates the world, the mind can be known by the

mind.   The mind perceives others and can also perceive itself.

Kadakia: *Can the mind be known with the help of yoga?*

Baba: Yes, just as a singer who sings with a concentrated mind immediately knows when the rhythm or melody is off, one who meditates or chants with a concentrated mind remains aware of his own mind and notices its every activity.

Why are you chasing the mind? What do you hope to achieve by controlling the mind?   Let it do whatever it wants to do.   Consider what your aim is.   You want to achieve God, don't you? Then obtain knowledge about God.   After that, you will understand that you have nothing to do with the mind.   Give up thinking about the mind for now.

Kadakia: *Many devotees sincerely do* sadhana *and have exalted experiences.   Then why are their minds still so full of thoughts, both good and bad, and why do they still have so much doubt and confusion?*

Baba: An ordinary man's mind is constantly immersed in the affairs of this world.   Often he is not even aware of his mind.   The awareness of the mind arises in the company of saints.   The thoughts were there before, but as the mind becomes quiet, the thoughts become more noticeable.   Before becoming completely quiet, the mind appears to be more agitated.

Kadakia: *How can the ego be eliminated?*

Baba: There is only one remedy for all such diseases: seek refuge in God.   This entire universe came into being through the expansion of the universal "I." The entire universe is a form of God.   There is this difference between our "I" and the "I" of Brahman: if anyone insults us, our anger is aroused whereas the vibration of the universal "I" created this entire universe.

Make an effort to achieve contentment and peace of mind. This is possible with practice. Your mind can attain satisfaction and contentment because these qualities already exist in it. Contentment destroys ego.

Kadakia: *Why does a man become disturbed in adversity despite his faith and devotion?*

Baba: This happens because he expects something in return for his devotion. Have devotion without any expectations.

Wednesday, May 26, 1965

Bhimsen Chadha, a devotee of Baba, and his sister Mrs. Kailash Pratap have come from Delhi to spend a few days in the ashram. This morning they had *satsang* with Baba.

THE GITA EXPOUNDS A SYNTHESIS OF PATHS

Bhimsen: *In some places the* Bhagavad Gita *advises a seeker to become a yogi and in other places to become a* bhakta. *Which is the true path, yoga or* bhakti *(devotion)?*

Baba: If we do not understand the real meaning of the scriptures, they can act like a boomerang. You have understood just the opposite of the intended meaning and thus your thinking is misdirected. Learn to synthesise the scriptural verses into a unified whole and then you will be able to understand each one in its proper perspective.

Bhimsen: *Even the power to do this is obtained by the grace of God, isn't it?*

Baba: One must also learn to think and discriminate for oneself. Krishna has expounded both *bhakti* and yoga in the *Gita,* but to whom were the teachings given? To the same person or to different people? They were given only to Arjuna. This indicates that the same seeker has to incorporate both of these paths. Each *sadhana* automatically includes the other *sadhanas.* Yoga, *bhakti* and *jnana* are not different from one another. It is incorrect to conclude that the *Gita* gives different teachings in different chapters. Some say the *Gita* prescribes *karma* yoga, some say it advises the practice of *raja* yoga, some say it advocates *jnana* yoga while others say it teaches the path of *bhakti.* The truth is that we have to synthesise all of these paths to progress in *sadhana* and attain God.

Kailash: *My mind does not turn toward spirituality. Should I consider this to be God's will? Can we seek God only if He desires it?*

Baba: If you want to follow this line of reasoning, then why not apply it in other fields as well? For example, why did you put so much effort into building your house? You should have sat with folded hands saying, "If God so wishes, He will build a house for me." On the contrary, you took so much trouble to draw up the plans, carefully considering each step that had to be taken. You decided to buy land from the government and to take a loan from a bank. You planned how to build the house with the minimum expense while ensuring the maximum possible return in terms of rent and also to make it useful for you in your old age and for your children later on. In this way, you thought out every detail very carefully before building the house. Isn't that so? Just as you plan ahead in your mundane affairs, you must give some thought to your spiritual life. Contemplate on who you are, from where you have come, where you will go after death and what the source of true happiness is. Also consider who God is and

how you can attain Him. Contemplate these points.
Why don't you determine to obtain an experience of
God-realization and make a wholehearted effort in that
direction?

Bhimsen: *Should we consider all saints as the same or
different?*

Baba: All saints are the same. Despite being in different
times and in different places, they all do the same work
just as one collector goes and another takes his place
and also does the same work. Even different collectors
in different places do the same work. It is the same
with saints.

Friday, May 28, 1965

D. M. Parulekar is a lawyer famous throughout Maharashtra for his expertise in land revenue law. During the
time of Bhagawan Nityananda, he often came to Ganeshpuri and on many occasions he also had *satsang* with Muktananda Baba. Today he has taken time out from his busy
schedule to come to the ashram.

THE GREATNESS OF NAMA JAPA (REPETITION OF THE LORD'S NAME)

Parulekar: *Baba, from time to time the thoughts you
express are very original and I wish to collect them and
keep them with me.*

Baba: Thoughts are like waves arising on the surface
of the sea. Many ripples arise each moment. Which
of these are you going to collect?

Parulekar: *This is true, but permit me to gather those
thought waves that create joy and inspire the mind so
that they can be preserved.*

Baba: I have no objection to it.

Parulekar: *Tukaram Maharaj says, "O Vithoba, your name is the essence, the final essence; your name is the real essence." Many other saints have also sung in a similar way about the greatness of God's name. Why is remembrance of God's name considered to be the very essence of God?*

Baba: You can see the play of the Lord of this universe in God's name; you can see the play of Brahman. The name is the complete and pure form of God.

Parulekar: *How can one realize this?*

Baba: This can be understood when you no longer have to make any effort to do *japa* of God's name, when *japa* starts going on automatically in your heart.

Parulekar: *How can one know when* japa *is arising automatically in the heart?*

Baba: The inhalation and exhalation that result from the functioning of *prana* and *apana* in the body is the naturally occuring internal *japa*. This is the *so'ham japa*. That Supreme Self, which pervades every minute atom in this universe, sports in every body as Consciousness in the form of *so'ham*. Tukaram Maharaj says, काया ही पंढरी, आत्मा हा विठ्ठल, नांदतो केवल पांडुरंग ' । "This body is Pandhari, Vitthal is my Self, all this is the play of Panduranga." However, man thinks God is somewhere outside himself, but this is a great illusion. God is within and very close to him. Sundardas says:

भ्रमत भ्रमत कहुँ भ्रम को न आवै अंत ।
चिरकाल बीत्यो पै हव रूपकुं न लह्यो है ।
तैसे ही सुन्दर यह भ्रम करि भूल्यो आप ।
भ्रम के गयेतें एक आत्मा सदाई है ॥

"It is with deep frustration that I say my confusion has not come to an end. Such a long time has elapsed and yet I have still not seen my own Self. O Sundar,

forget that you are confused. Once that feeling of confusion goes, only the Self will remain."

The musk deer searches everywhere for the precious
musk, that is actually within its own navel. It
wanders here and there vainly seeking that which it
already possesses and ultimately dies of exhaustion. Man,
too, because of his own ignorance, has forgotten the
Self dwelling within him. There is no difference
between him and the musk deer.

Parulekar: *What is the cause of man's confusion?*

Baba: This confusion or misapprehension is caused by
the three *gunas* of *prakriti*. The *Bhagavad Gita* says:

सत्त्वं रजस्तम इति गुणाः प्रकृतिसंभवाः ।
निबध्नन्ति महाबाहो देहे देहिनमव्ययम् ॥ १४-५ ॥

"O Arjuna, the three *gunas,* or qualities— *sattva,*
rajas and *tamas*—born of *prakriti*, bind the immortal
Self to this perishable gross body in which It dwells."
(14-5)

Parulekar: *How can this confusion be eliminated?*

Baba: By transcending the three *gunas*.

Parulekar: *How can that be done?*

Baba: It is for this purpose that the saints have given us
the simple means of chanting the name of God. They
have said, "This mantra *hare rama* is very easy; repeat
it constantly." Without devotion to God, life is a waste.
Jnaneshwar Maharaj says:

गलित शिर हे कलेवर रे । उद्कंविण सरिता भयंकर रे ।
रविशशिविण अम्बर तसें । हरिविण जिणे असार रे ।

"Without the head, a body becomes a corpse.
A river is a terrible chasm without water.
Life without Hari is worthless
Like the sky without the sun and moon."

The *Bhagavad Gita* says:

अनन्यचेताः सततं यो मां स्मरति नित्यशः ।
तस्याहं सुलभः पार्थ नित्ययुक्तस्य योगिनः ॥ ८-१४ ॥

"O Arjuna, I am easily attainable by that steadfast
yogi who ceaselessly remembers me with a one-pointed
mind." (8-14)

In the present times when life is so full of hustle
and bustle, only the seeker who keeps firm faith in God
and constantly remembers Him can attain God-realization. Saint Tulsidas says, बिनु हरिभजन न भव तरिए, यह
सिद्धान्त अपेल । "Without singing God's name, you cannot swim across the ocean of this world. There can be
no doubt about this."

The remembrance of God's name that occurs
naturally with each inhalation and exhalation is the
best. Kabir says, राम नाम रट्ते रहो, जब लगि घट में प्राण । "As
long as *prana* is dwelling in this pot (the gross body),
continue to chant the name of Rama." As long as
chaitanya is dwelling within this body, let your remembrance of God's name be like a steady stream of oil
flowing from one vessel to another. The saints have
always advised seekers to chant God's name with each
incoming breath and each outgoing breath. If you
breathe out without chanting God's name, that breath
has gone to waste. But remember one thing: if you
repeat His name mechanically without any love or
devotion in your heart, its spiritual value is zero. In
fact, the love in the devotee's heart is considered to be
more important than the actual chanting of God's name.
Saint Tulsidas says, नाम सप्रेम जपत अनयासा । भगत होहिं
मुद मंगल बासा ॥ "The devotee who repeats God's
name naturally and with love enjoys happiness and also
sanctifies his dwelling place."

Parulekar: *Are there different types of* nama japa?
Baba: Yes, there are three main types. The first is

verbal or *vaikhari japa,* which is done by chanting with
the tongue in a low voice. The second type is *upanshu
japa,* which is done with the movement of the tongue
and lips, but the sound is inaudible. The third is
manasa japa, or mental *japa,* which is subtle and done
only in the mind. Even more subtle and superior to that
is the *ajapa japa* that goes on constantly within you day
and night. It is said:

येकांती मौन्य धरून बैसे ।
सावध पहाता कैसें भासे ।
सोहं सोहं ऐसे शब्द होती ।

"Sit quietly in seclusion without any thoughts.
Watch attentively. Then what do you discover? You
discover the following words: *so'ham, so'ham* (I am
That, I am That)."

Parulekar: *Why are there these different types of* japa?
Baba: Because of the varying degrees of worthiness of
different seekers. Each one is given the type of *japa*
that he is capable of doing. Seekers differ in their
worthiness and they are advised accordingly to observe
the *sadhana* or spiritual discipline that suits them.
Parulekar: *Yes, I understand, but I still have one doubt.
If the name is a form of God, why is it necessary to
receive it from a Guru? Isn't it possible to attain God
by repeating any mantra that one selects for himself?*
Baba: A mantra that has not been imparted by a Guru
lacks the power to grant God-realization. A mantra
received from the Guru is called a mantra with seed. It
has been sown with the seed of Shakti, which has the
power to carry one to God-realization.
Parulekar: *By what means does the Guru impart the
mantra?*
Baba: The Sadguru has realized the Self; he is an
embodiment of the Supreme Self. He enters into the

disciple through his ears in the form of the mantra and infuses divine energy into his body. A mantra given by the Guru is charged with divine energy and takes the seeker along the path to God-realization.

Parulekar: *But in the modern world, how can a seeker find a real Sadguru? Many sincere seekers have had bitter experiences at the hands of impostors posing under the guise of saints and sannyasis. As a result, many people are hesitant to accept anyone as a Guru. The mind, however, cannot rest in peace until a Guru is found. In such circumstances, how can a real Guru be recognised?*

Baba: One obtains a Guru as a result of merits earned in previous lives and also by pursuing *sadhana* sincerely in this lifetime. One must continue his *sadhana* and attend *satsang* with saints. By persisting in such practices, one will certainly be able to recognise a real Guru for oneself.

Parulekar: *What are the signs of a true Guru?*

Baba: A true Guru is beyond any signs. No one is fit to become a Guru until he has totally merged himself with the Supreme Self. A true Guru is beyond any attributes or signs. The only sign is his being established in the *nirvikalpa* state.

Parulekar: *Please tell me something more about the Guru.*

Baba: The Guru is like a pot maker. Just as a potter shapes the clay, the Guru lays the foundation for his disciple's spiritual life in a systematic way. The Guru is the doctor who cures the disease of transmigration from birth to death and death to birth. He uproots all the undesirable characteristics from his disciple such as the six inner enemies (lust, anger, pride, jealousy, ignorance and greed), all kinds of sorrows, agitations and also physical illnesses. Not only this, but he also nourishes the disciple with the nectar of love, consolidates his faith and devotion, and strengthens his knowledge. Just as a skillful boatman easily ferries his passengers across a river, a Sadguru takes his disciple safely across this sea of painful transmigratory existence and sets him on the opposite bank of supreme bliss.

Saturday, May 29, 1965

Dr. Jivanlal Amin, a professor of Ancient Indian Culture at a college in Khambat, has come today after hearing about the glories of Baba and the ashram while in Pondicherry. He is a sincere seeker with a keen interest in spirituality and he asked Baba many questions.

HAVE FAITH IN THE INNER SELF

Amin: *It is my personal experience that a seeker does not feel satisfied until his sadhana is properly guided by a Guru. What should he do until he meets a true and able spiritual teacher? How can he make progress on his own in sadhana?*

Baba: Even though the individual soul is a part of the Universal Soul, he considers himself to be limited. This is his ignorance. Since the individual soul is not different from God, he has the capacity to know everything, to cognise everything, so until he receives guidance from a Guru, he must surrender himself completely to his own inner Self and concentrate his mind on God.

He must keep faith in the inner Self because It possesses divine Shakti. Consider, for example, the dream state. This state is neither true nor false. Since it rests in the Self, it cannot be said to be false.

A simple, straightforward old man named Mudanna lives and works in the ashram. He had a vision in a dream which revealed that Bhagawan Nityananda was going to leave his body within two days and that's what happened. Everyone has the power to know and understand the truth. An individual may not be aware of this inner power, but this Shakti is ever present, lying dormant in his Self.

Tukaram Maharaj received mantra initiation in a dream. The *antaratma* (inner Self) exists in every human being. The great Vedantic statement *aham brahmasmi*—"I am the Absolute" is true. If a dream turns out to be false, it is due to some limitation of the mind superimposed on the Self.

Amin: *What attitude should one have toward whatever is seen or heard during meditation?*

Baba: It is just a mental play; it is like watching a movie. You should use these experiences to cultivate the attitude of being a witness of the mind.

Amin: *I have heard that many seekers meet their Guru in his bodily form and receive instructions despite being miles away from him. Is this possible?*

Baba: Such experiences are necessary as long as a disciple has not completely merged with his Guru. A seeker will get such experiences from time to time according to his needs.

Amin: *How can sadhana be made easy?*

Baba: Whichever *sadhana* you do will be easy if it is according to your liking. The aim of every kind of *sadhana* is the same, but for *sadhana* to become simple and effortless, it must come directly from the Guru. A man who used to teach yoga once came here. He was suffering from a severe headache despite having tried many remedies to alleviate it. I told him to stop doing *japa*. He followed my advice and his trouble soon

vanished. He had not understood that the headache
was caused by the vibration of the mantra in his head.

Many obstacles may arise like this in a self-prescribed *sadhana* because of limitations in your understanding. It is most improper for such imperfect
seekers to become gurus. It is harmful for both the
guru and the disciple. How can such a guru understand others when he doesn't even understand himself?
Only he who knows himself can also know others.

Friday, June 4, 1965

In today's discussion, Baba explained the secret of
mantra to Kailash Pratap.

THE SECRET OF MANTRA

Kailash: *Which mantra should I use for japa, the one
I am already using or the one you have given me?*
Baba: Which mantra are you now using?
Kailash: *A swami gave me his Guru's name as a mantra.*
Baba: The term 'Guru mantra' does not mean the
mantra of the Guru's name, but the mantra that is
received from the Guru. The Guru gives that mantra
to others by which he himself has achieved liberation.
This is called the Guru mantra. I give the mantra
that enabled me to become Shiva to others. I would
not give my Guru's name as a mantra such as *om namo
nityananda,* nor would I ever advise anyone to meditate
on my form. I tell everyone to meditate on his own
inner Self.

Just as one king can easily meet another king or
one rich man can make friends with another rich man,
you can attain Shiva by becoming like Shiva yourself.

This means that you will attain God when you realize "I am God." The four great statements of Vedanta proclaim the same vision.

You should remember That which is our root cause. Remembrance of this root cause is the real mantra. The mantra is that which enables you to realize your own true nature. Only that mantra is called a Siddha mantra or *chaitanya* mantra that unites the seeker with the deity of the mantra. The mantra, repeater of the mantra and the mantra deity are all one. The *Shivasutra Vimarshini* says, पृथङ्मन्त्रः पृथङ्मन्त्री न सिध्यति कदाचन । "If the mantra and the seeker who repeats it remain separate, it will never bear any fruit." This is the secret of mantra. The *Mahanirvana Tantra* says:

मंत्रार्थं मंत्रचैतन्यं यो न जानाति साधकः ।
शतलक्षं प्रजपतोऽपि तस्य मंत्रो न सिध्यति ॥

"The seeker who does not know the meaning of the mantra and does not understand that it is conscious will not attain any result even after repeating it a million times."

Saturday, June 5, 1965

A group of devotees who come to the ashram regularly on Saturday was sitting with Baba in the *satsang* hall. Barrister Nain was also present.

Nain: *Baba, what is the special feature of Kundalini Yoga?*
Baba: The yoga in which all yogas are automatically included is called Kundalini Yoga, *mahayoga* or Siddha Yoga. It can be obtained only by the grace of a

Siddha Guru; thus, it is called Siddha Yoga. Its special feature is that it enables one to reach the Supreme Self quickly and easily whereas to perfect the eight stages set forth in Patanjali's *Yoga Sutras* takes a very long time.

Nain: *In order to obtain perfection in this yoga, is it necessary to be a* sthitaprajna *(one who is established in steady wisdom unaffected by the pairs of opposites)?*

Baba: No, it is not necessary to be a *sthitaprajna* right from the beginning, but after taking up this path, a seeker acquires these qualities naturally.

Tuesday, June 8, 1965

Anthony Brook arrived at 8:30 this morning for a ten-day stay. Around 10 A.M. Baba met the devotees who had gathered in the *satsang* hall. Anthony asked Baba some questions.

TRANSCEND THE PAIRS OF OPPOSITES

Anthony: *It seems that divine Consciousness is about to descend upon earth. What would you say about this?*

Baba: When cunning and cruelty become dominant in the world, divine Consciousness has to make itself felt; God has to assume a form in order to manifest on earth. For example, the Lord had to appear on earth in the form of Rama to vanquish the cruel *rakshasa* Ravana; he had to come as Krishna to destroy the evil Kansa. Man turns toward God when life becomes unbearable for him. He remembers God after undergoing extreme misery, poverty and hardship.

Anthony: *When will such an incarnation come? I personally feel that the time is not too far away. Do you*

*also feel that a time will come when misery and upheaval
will cease to exist in this world?*
Baba: Yes, certainly such a time will come. The life of
the world is like a wheel. The pairs of opposites always
exist within it. Pleasure and pain, wealth and poverty,
love and hatred, day and night keep rotating like the
spokes of a wheel. After one, its opposite is sure to
follow. Thus, after misery, happiness will certainly
return to this world.

There was once a great saint who had a peculiar
habit. Whenever his devotees would talk about their
pleasure or pain, the saint would reply, "This, too, will
not last." If someone said to him, "My wife has run
away, my sons do not obey me, I have no money, and
I am undergoing very bad times," he would always
respond, "This, too, will not last." If anyone were to
say, "Maharaj, I am very happy. Due to God's grace,
I have acquired two lakh rupees," he would also tell
him, "This, too, will not last."

A reading of the *Puranas* gives one the feeling that
a time did exist when everybody was happy. Today
it appears as if nothing but misery and sorrow prevail
everywhere, but it is this very misery and pain that
compel God to come to the earth. If you read the life
stories of saints and great beings, you will notice that it
was only after undergoing tremendous suffering that
they turned towards God and ultimately attained Him.

Knowing this, a wise, discriminating man must go
beyond the opposites of pleasure and pain, and understand the truth. This world is a play of God; it is His
own sport. God makes use of people like Ravana as
His reason for incarnating on earth. The world proceeds
according to the will of God. Understanding this, a
wise, intelligent man of discrimination will consider
it to be all the same whether he dies from an atom bomb

explosion, a gunshot, a disease or the natural deteriora-
tion of a body that has reached the end of its life span.
He never sees disharmony anywhere in the world.

Wednesday, June 9, 1965

Anthony came to the *satsang* hall at seven this morning. Shortly thereafter, Baba arrived and their discussion
resumed.

PENETRATE TO THE ROOT CAUSE OF THOUGHTS

Anthony: *This morning while sitting in the veranda of
your meditation room, my body became perfectly still
and I felt as if my mind had become absolutely peaceful.*
Baba: This is precisely the experience of the awakening
of Kundalini. To have a peaceful mind is an exalted
experience. It is not necessary to have only certain
types of experiences due to the awakening of Kundalini.
A variety of experiences may occur. Steadiness of mind,
peace and bliss are some of the most significant experiences.
Anthony: *But at other times when I sit for meditation,
my mind keeps wandering here and there. What should
I do to keep it under control?*
Baba: An excellent method is to watch where the mind
goes. Discover who watches the mind and remain steady
in Him.

Clouds in the sky keep assuming different shapes
and sizes, and then disperse. Where do they go? No
one knows. They are born in the sky and dissolve
back into the sky. Waves in the sea arise on the surface
of the water and again subside. In the same way,
thoughts come up and vanish again. Try to discover

from where these thoughts arise; understand their origin. The source from which they originate is the Self. This Self has no connection with the mind. It only functions as the witness. The Self is uninvolved and untainted. Just as the sea and the sky remain unaffected despite the waves or clouds arising within them, similarly, our inner Self always remains unaffected despite the thoughts in the mind.

Therefore, maintain witness consciousness; establish yourself in Him who is the witness of all thoughts. When you become steady in Him, the desire to cling to your thoughts will cease and you will understand that all this is a play of the inner Self. That witness state is the abode of God, the source of the light of Truth.

Vedanta describes the four states of the individual soul: the waking, dream, deep sleep and *turiya* states. Upon attaining the fourth state, *turiya,* pleasure and pain lose their effect and the world appears to be only a dream. Then you experience "I am the Absolute." Just as man experiences his body from head to toe as "I am this," God experiences this entire universe as "I am this; this is my body." After God-realization you, too, will feel "I am not only this body, but I am this entire world." Then you will be unaware of either pleasure or pain anywhere in this world.

THE FUNCTION OF SAINTS

If the son of a rich man were to start feeling impoverished and if he were to complain to you, "I am very poor," you would naturally explain to him, "Your belief is wrong. You are the son of a wealthy man. You have plenty of money. How can you be poor?" The function of a saint in relation to ordinary men is similar. Saints are here to explain to man, "You

are not an individual soul; you are Shiva." In other
words, they are here to make man aware of his real
nature, to dissolve his individuality and to merge it
into the totality just as a drop merges into the ocean.

Anthony: *Your words are absolutely true. Man clings
to his individuality so tenaciously that he will not give
it up for any price. God is always ready with out-
stretched arms to embrace him.*

Baba: Yes, that is so. I shall tell you about Gurudev
Bhagawan Nityananda. It would be very difficult to find
another great *avadhut* like him in this world. He was
a great being, a great Siddha. His main work was to
make man transcend his *jivahood* (individuality) and
become established in the awareness of his Shivahood.
Thousands of people used to come to him, but I hardly
saw one among them who prayed to attain Shivahood.
On the other hand, I saw many, nay, innumerable people asking for such mundane things as sons, money,
business or employment, or to be cured from disease.

This reminds me of a story. There was a shepherd
named Ramzan who used to take his sheep to graze in
the jungle every day. While tending them, he would
eat whatever he could cook for himself. One day the
king of that area was hunting in the jungle and lost
his way. While wandering about he came across Ramzan. The king was hungry so he asked Ramzan for
some food. Even though the food that Ramzan served
him was not properly cooked, it tasted delicious to the
famished king and he was very pleased with Ramzan.
Before departing, the king gave him a note and told
him "Whenever you are in need of anything, come to
me."

Ramzan's son was to be married, so a few days
later he went to the city to sell some sheep and then
he went to see the king. The king welcomed him

warmly and served him a meal of several delicious dishes. Then the king reminded him, "You can ask for anything you want." Ramzan liked to chew tobacco so he asked for some lime to mix with it. All that the wretched fellow asked for was lime! He was not even aware of the king's infinite wealth and power. Similarly, very few people knew about the divine power of Gurudev.

Anthony: *Can man be turned toward God by seeing miracles performed?*

Baba: This world is full of the miracles of God: the sun and moon rise and set at fixed times; the seasons come in rotation; birds fly in the sky and fish live in water; from a small drop of semen, a beautiful, adult human body consisting of bones, muscles, flesh and blood is formed. Aren't these miracles? When such great wonders already exist, the display of some trivial miracle is like holding a candle before the sun. I don't mean to say that miracles are false. The mind can acquire almost limitless power through concentration. To perform miracles is not something great. But what is the purpose of such things? It is more likely that worldly-minded people would follow a wrong path because of such miracles. It is not the function of saints to perform miracles.

THE SOURCE OF TRUE HAPPINESS

Anthony: *Last night while meditating, I felt something happening behind my mouth and nose, and there was also a loud noise.*

Baba: This was caused by your *prana* moving along the *sushumna*. Listen, it sounded like this, didn't it? (Baba demonstrated the *kriya*.)

Anthony: *Yes, it was exactly like that.*

Baba: This *kriya* clears the *sushumna* channel, enabling the *prana* to travel toward the *sahasrara*. Opening the disciple's *sushumna* is the Guru's main function. This is the true miracle, not those worthless magic shows that are put on merely to entertain others. Whatever is to be gained is gained through the *sushumna*. True happiness is experienced when the *prana* dwells in the *sushumna*. That is Chitshakti, the elixir of life. It is because of this Chitshakti that the body is alive, beautiful and attractive. If you were to cut away a piece of the body's flesh and put it aside, it would soon start stinking. The body becomes ugly when this Chitshakti leaves it at the time of death. Even the dead person's near and dear ones are anxious to remove his corpse from the house. This is the quality and effect of that Shakti. It is verily the omnipresent God dwelling inside and outside us.

This wonderful Shakti dwells in the *sushumna*. It is this power that sees through the eyes, smells through the nose and hears through the ears. It is with this Shakti that man performs all his activities and work in this world.

According to the *Yoga Shastra*, the body contains 72,000 *nadis* (subtle nerve channels). Just as a tree is kept alive by water and supported by the earth, the body is supported and given life (*chaitanya*) by the *prana shakti*, which keeps moving through these *nadis*. This verily is Kundalini Shakti, which is the *pranic* energy as well as the knowing faculty. It pervades every inch of the body down to the smallest cell; it energises the entire body. Just as a king's power extends throughout his kingdom even though he himself remains seated on the throne, Kundalini Shakti pervades the entire body in the form of *prana*.

This Kundalini, this Chitshakti, is either turned outward or turned inward. When turned outward, She causes man to perform worldly activities; when She turns inward, She turns man toward God.

When a seeker's Shakti is awakened by the grace of the Guru, She makes him indrawn and gives him the experience of knowledge and bliss. As She travels up the *sushumna* toward the *sahasrara,* the seeker has various kinds of experiences. There was a time when I did not believe in the existence of *swargaloka* (heaven) and *chandraloka* (region of the moon). I considered happiness as heaven and suffering as hell, but when I actually saw *chandraloka* and Siddhaloka in meditation, I had to admit that, just as this earth exists, other worlds also exist in this universe. A seeker may experience flowers being showered on his head. At that time, the golden lotus that falls from Siddhaloka may also be seen, indicating that the seeker has become a Siddha.

After attaining that state, one certainly experiences happiness in pleasurable experiences, but one also experiences happiness in painful and adverse circumstances. No desire for attaining anything remains. Even so, wealth and *riddhi-siddhis* come to a Siddha on their own. Just as ordinary people go to a saint and he becomes their support, *riddhi-siddhis* go to a saint and beg him for powers. The *siddhis* are ever at the command of the Siddhas to fulfill their work.

The main goal of human life is to become merged in the *sahasrara.* Then one understands that this world will always remain the same as it is now. The Guru's main function is to enable a seeker to achieve this state. No one can ever snatch away this wealth bestowed by the Guru. You may have all the pleasures of worldly life, but if you do not have this spiritual wealth, you are poor and miserable.

THE GREATNESS OF MAN

Anthony: *How can one come to understand that man is great?*

Baba: Everyone sees his own reflection in the world. A virtuous man sees virtue everywhere while a wicked man sees vice everywhere. Hence, if man considers himself to be God, he will certainly have an experience of God. Once you have realized God, you will easily understand that the *jivatma,* or the individual soul, is the same as *vishwatma,* or the Universal Soul.

Man again and again remembers his essential nature. It is for this reason that he constantly desires to be happier and greater than others. It is God who is searching for God, but the individual does not know this truth. Because his true state is Godhood, he experiences *shivoham*—"I am Shiva," *so'ham*—"I am That" or *analhaq*—"I am God" in meditation. All realized beings proclaim the same truth that your true identity is "I am the Absolute."

A Sufi saint says, "When I had some understanding, I realized I am not this body; I am that light which has expanded in the form of this universe."

Therefore, you must always maintain the understanding, "I belong to Him; He is mine; I am He and He exists in everyone." It is that God principle alone that exists everywhere in this world, pervading everything equally. Nowhere is It bigger or smaller, more or less, better or worse. It is That which exists in brooks and rivers, in the sky and the mountains, in stones and grass, in birds and animals, and also in human beings. It can take innumerable different forms. We call this principle Parabrahman.

Just as a tree grows out of a seed, this world evolves out of Parabrahman. Just as the tree is in the seed in a subtle form, the world is in Parabrahman and His qualities are seen in the world. The nature of Parabrahman is *satchidananda* (existence, consciousness and bliss) ; therefore, this world also manifests these three qualities. Every individual has this divine essence.

The principle परस्पर देवो भव —"See God in each other" states the same truth. Everyone should behave toward others keeping this fully in mind. If this were imbibed by everyone, there would be no more wars, unrest or chaos. Just as a father has a feeling of my-ness toward his sons and grandsons, God has a feeling of my-ness toward this world. For Him, all are equal. And just as a father does not like his sons to fight among themselves, God does not like us to fight among ourselves. God is pained by wars; therefore, we must resolve our differences and live together peacefully in this world.

Anthony: *Can God experience pain?*

Baba: This is only a manner of speaking. From the viewpoint of the individual, it can be expressed in this way. Pain, hardship and sorrow cannot even come near the state of Godhood.

Anthony: *How can one develop the attitude of seeing God in others?*

Baba: This can be achieved by expanding and developing your inner Shakti because everything is within you. Man is great, but out of ignorance, he considers himself small. He wastes a lot of valuable time in pursuing many useless sense pleasures. He does not understand that human life is a very precious gift. If man were to sincerely try, he could attain a state in which he could have whatever he wished.

Anthony: *If a great leader were to start spreading the message "See God in each other," would it achieve the same result?*

Baba: Yes. In a way, we are already practising this.
For example, when we meet someone, we greet him
with folded hands saying *"namo narayan," "salam-
alaiqum,"* or we shake hands and say, "Good Morning."
What is the meaning behind these greetings? When
you visit someone's home, he rises and welcomes you,
and honours you by offering water, tea and snacks. To
some extent, this is a practical application of the motto
"See God in each other," but we do not perceive it as
such. If you propagate this message, it would certainly
be implemented by some and an appreciation for it
would be nurtured in others.

Thursday, June 10, 1965

THE FOUR STATES OF THE INDIVIDUAL SOUL

Anthony: *Last night I slept soundly. I was not even
aware of falling asleep. When I woke up in the morning, I felt that I had just gone to sleep and awakened
again. Was it all right for me to have slept, or should
I have controlled sleep and sat for meditation?*
Baba: What did you experience in sleep?
Anthony: *I was not aware of anything and I had no
experience except a feeling of happiness and contentment. In the morning I felt quite refreshed.*
Baba: From this, it is clear that true happiness is where
there are no activities and that is right within you.
Happiness lies in detachment, not in involvement. To
explain it, I'll give you an example.

A businessman spends his entire day attending to
his business and making money. By evening, he is
exhausted and returns home. He finishes his dinner,
removes his expensive clothes and gets ready for bed.

At that time, if his secretary comes to discuss even a transaction involving two lakhs rupees, the business-man would say, "I am not prepared to listen to any-thing now." Without even talking to his wife and children, he falls fast asleep. When he gets up in the morning, he feels refreshed. Then he calls his secre-tary and happily resumes his business. What does this example illustrate? It illustrates that happiness is in that state in which there are no activities or thoughts regarding his wife, children, business, costly clothes, ornaments or money; that is, in a state of detachment. A patient asks a doctor for a medicine to put him to sleep because, without sleep, he feels unwell. The first question a doctor asks a patient is whether or not he slept well the previous night. This indicates that there is great happiness in sleep, which is a state free from worries and thoughts.

To understand this, one must have knowledge of the four states of the individual soul—waking, dream, deep sleep and *turiya*. In the waking state, the individual soul enjoys the external world with the help of the nineteen instruments: the five organs of actions; the five organs of knowledge; the five *pranas;* and the four aspects of the *antahkarana* (inner psychic instrument), which are mind, intellect, subconscious mind and ego. The individual soul who enjoys the waking state is the size of the gross body. His colour is red; his dwelling place is in the eyes. In meditation, he is seen in the form of a red light. The *Mandukya Upanishad* refers to the individual soul in this state as *vaishvanara.*

In the dream state, the individual soul experiences the subtle world with a subtle body the size of a thumb. His colour is white and his dwelling place is in the heart. In meditation, he is seen as a thumb-size white light. The individual soul in this state is known as *taijasa.*

In the deep sleep state, the individual soul experiences happiness in the causal body, which is the size of a fingertip. His colour is black and he dwells between the eyebrows. In meditation, he is seen in the form of a small black light. The individual soul in this state is known as *prajna.*

After these, the last, or "fourth state," is called *turiya.* In this state supreme bliss is experienced. It is seen in meditation as a small blue dot, which is the supracausal body. Its dwelling place is the *sahasrara.* In meditation, yogis see it as a shining Blue Pearl, which appears and disappears. Sometimes it is also seen with the eyes open. In fact, what is within is seen outside. This Blue Pearl is verily Parabrahman as well as Kundalini. The Self is realized within this Blue Pearl. It is your true form.

These four bodies of the individual soul are seen in the form of lights during meditation. Bhartrihari says, धन्यानां गिरिकन्दरे निवसतां ज्योतिः परं ध्यायतां । "Blessed are those who meditate in mountain caves and see these lights." As you go from one body into the next, from one state into the next, your happiness keeps increasing. Compared to the waking and dream states, there is more happiness in deep sleep, and the bliss experienced in the *turiya* state is greater still; it cannot be described in words. This is absolutely true. Everyone can experience it and today you had such an experience. Isn't that so?

The fulfillment of human life lies in obtaining this bliss. In its absence, birds and beasts are superior to man. How beautiful the peacock is! The chakor drinks only the nectar of moonlight, and it is difficult to find anything comparable to the sweet, melodious tune of the cuckoo. The elephant has the strength of a hundred men. Man looks attractive and vibrant only after obtaining inner bliss. Gurudev Nityananda used to wear only a loincloth and his complexion was black; even so, his devotees found him so attractive that they would gaze at him for hours and still their hunger for the sight of him could not be satisfied. What attracted them was the inner bliss that radiated from him in all directions.

Many people ask me, "Can we also achieve that state? Would it be possible for us to do *sadhana?*" I tell them, "It is easier to become God than to become a doctor or an engineer because, to become a doctor, you have to fill yourself with everything from outside whereas God is already within you. You have to attain what is already attained. Then knowledge becomes complete and perfect. After obtaining That, nothing else remains to be obtained. Ask any doctor, "Have you mastered all the knowledge available in your field?" He will reply, "I still have a lot more to learn. There is no end to it." On the other hand, after knowing God, nothing else remains to be known.

Friday, June 11, 1965

This morning at nine o'clock, the devotees gathered in the hall for *satsang* with Baba.

Anthony: *Babaji, will such a time come when the medium of language will become unnecessary and people will be able to communicate automatically through the mind?*
Baba: In ancient times it was so and such a time can also come again. There is a place in the heart where you

can obtain knowledge of all the objects in this world. By being in that place, one can see all other countries and all other worlds while sitting here.

GIVE UP THE TEMPTATION FOR SIDDHIS

Anthony: *Can we also know about the pleasure and pain of others?*

Baba: Yes, we can know that, too. The mind has such power. An unusual story about a painter appeared in a publication called *Imprint*. While painting on the second floor of a building, he fell and remained unconscious for two or three days. When he regained consciousness, he had acquired the power to know everything about others. He spoke out everything about whoever came before him. This incident demonstrates that the mind does possess such powers.

But I ask you, what do you gain from knowing about the pleasure and pain of others? True happiness and bliss are beyond such *siddhis*. One who wants to reach Delhi quickly will not stop off at any of the small intervening stations *en route,* but will go directly to Delhi. Similarly, the seeker whose aim is God-realization will be indifferent to trivial *siddhis*.

It is not difficult to know the thoughts of others or to perform magic. Magic can be done by mental concentration; it is the creation of the mind. It has no connection with your *sadhana* for liberation because God is beyond the realm of the mind. God has created this entire universe by the will power of His mind. Therefore, since man is a part of the very same God, what can be beyond the capabilities of his mind? Actually, it is like creating a world of the mind within the outer world.

An intelligent seeker views this world itself as an obstacle to his progress so what is the use of creating another magical world of wonders within this world? Both of these worlds are limited and perishable. God is eternal, changeless and uninvolved in any worldly activities. Matsyendranath taught his disciple Gorakh-nath:

गुपत होकर परगट होवे, जावे मथुरा काशी ।
चलता है पानी के ऊपर, मुख बोले सो होवे ।
सो ही कच्चा बे कच्चा बे, नहीं गुरू का बच्चा ॥

"A man may learn to vanish and reappear, he may travel in an instant to places of pilgrimage like Mathura and Kashi, he may walk on water, whatever he says may come true, still he is not a perfect being; he cannot be called the Guru's son."

A man may display any number of wonderful phenom-ena; he may make the impossible possible; even so, if he has not merged with Brahman, he is still imperfect.

It is easy to learn how to perform magic, but it requires a lot of effort to attain the *nirvikalpa* state. There will be no real peace until the mind is free of all thoughts. One who wants to achieve permanent peace must give up the desire for insignificant *siddhis* and go far beyond them. He has to achieve the kind of high *siddhi* by which Prahlad made the Lord manifest in the form of Narsimha (the man-lion, Vishnu in His fourth incarnation) and by which the *gopis* made Him dance within the compounds of their houses.

If you attach importance to the outer world, it will constantly be reflected in your mind where it will create agitations. By giving importance to the world, your mind acquires the qualities of the world. So drive away all thoughts from the mind. Make it void.

At half past three in the afternoon, the devotees again assembled in the hall. Also present were Professor Jivanji Amin from Cambay and Virendrakumar Jain.

Amin: *While pursuing meditation, how long does it take for a seeker's desires to be completely destroyed?*

Baba: It takes time for desires to be completely eradicated. Sometimes during meditation, desires become even stronger and one may see hell or a naked man or woman.

Amin: *Yes, I asked this question because I see such things.*

Baba: This is a good sign. It indicates that your *sadhana* is progressing very well. Sometimes your sexual desire may become intense. This happens because the impressions and desires of many past lives lying dormant in the *sushumna* gain strength and are activated. After this, you will see lights of red, white, black and blue, and then you will see the Blue Pearl. You will have the *darshan* of gods, goddesses and Gurudev. Such phenomena are seen in the *tandra* state, which is between waking and deep sleep. In this state, you feel as if you are asleep, but internal *kriyas* are taking place.

The *sadhana* of *shaktipat* belongs to the *siddhamarg* (the path of the Siddhas.) The seeker's Shakti is awakened by the grace of a Siddha. After that, *sadhana* progresses automatically and the seeker has many experiences. This is not a topic for discussion, discourse or philosophy. It can be understood only through personal experience. You can be sure that anyone who poses as a Guru and tries to guide others without knowing anything about this is not a realized being.

रक्त श्वेत नील का नहीं ज्ञान । तहाँ मूर्ख-पंडित एक समान ॥

"Without knowledge of the red, white, black and blue lights (seen in meditation), the illiterate and the learned are equal."

Amin: *I am no longer getting the same kind of medita-*

tion as when I first came here.
Baba: That state will return slowly. Early in your *sadhana*, you may have an experience of *samadhi*, the *nirvikalpa* state, or realization of Truth. Later on, as you continue your *sadhana*, this state recurs at the appropriate time and eventually remains steadily and permanently with you.

THE STATE OF JIVANMUKTI

Virendrakumar: *What is the state known as* jivanmukti?
Baba: That man who performs all his activities while knowing in his heart of hearts that all the world is like a dream is called a *jivanmukta*. The poet-saint Sundardas expresses this in verse form, ऊपर तौ व्यवहार करै सब, भितर स्वप्न समान जु भासै। "Outwardly, he performs his worldly activities; Inwardly, it is all a dream to him." Such beings are free from the restrictions of rules and regulations. Rituals, rites, injunctions and prohibitions are meant for those who are living in ignorance. They are similar to the codes of law that are intended to regulate the activities of the common people. But the man who has realized the Truth transcends all such limitations. It is said, "Codes (of conduct) can howl like jackals in the forest only till the mighty lion of Vedanta starts to roar."

For those who have not realized the Truth, scriptural injunctions and prohibitions are necessary. After realization, they become superfluous. The remainder of a *jivanmukta's* (realized being's) life unfolds according to his destiny. It is said in *Vichar Sagar*:

भ्रमण करत ज्यों पवन तें, सूखो पीपरपात।
शेष कर्म प्रारब्ध तें, क्रिया करत दरसात॥

"A dry leaf is blown along with wind, going wherever the wind carries it. A *jivanmukta* acts in this world in the same way."

This means that the actions of a *jivanmukta* are like roasted seeds, which do not sprout or bear fruit. He is seen to be acting in the world, but he does not have to undergo the fruits of his actions.

The scriptures do not mention anything about the *jivanmukta's* way of life. We perceive and know the world by name, form and the qualities of objects whereas the *jivanmukta* perceives it according to its reality. A saint named Shukadevji once lived in Icchalkunjeri, a town in Karnataka. One day the tribal jungle dwellers fed him fish and gave him toddy (wine) to drink. As a result of this incident, the townspeople became very critical of him. Finally, a *jnani* admonished them saying, "Saints are beyond all these things. Put some shit in front of him and see what he does with it." The townspeople did as he suggested and the saint ate the shit as well! So a *jivanmukta* may live in any way, he may eat and drink anything, but his mind is always steady and indifferent.

The *jivanmuktas'* ways of living are varied. One may live in poverty and act like a simpleton while another may live like a king with pomp and show. The *Vicher Sagar* says:

कबहुँक चढ़ि रथ बाजिगज, बाग बगीचे देखि ।
नग्नपाद पुनि एकले, फिर आवत तिहिं लेखि ॥
विविध वेश, शय्याशयन, उत्तम भोगन भोग ।
कबहुँक अनशन गिरिगुहा, रजनि शिला संयोग ॥
करि प्रणाम पूजन करत, कहुँ जन लाख-हज़ार ।
उभय लोक तें भ्रष्ट लखि, कहत कर्मी धिक्कार ॥

"Some move about in chariots or on elephants and stroll in gardens; some lack even footwear and wander barefoot. Some wear different clothes, sleep in beautiful beds and enjoy the best of everything in the world while others wander with empty stomachs in mountains and caves and sleep on stones. Thousands of devotees flock to them and worship them while some worldly people consider them degraded and condemn them."

There was a *raja* yogi saint named Amritrai who lived like a king. He sat on a silver swing and slept on a silk mattress in a canopied bed. He ate rich food from silver plates and had women to serve him. But he used to preach to others, "Why do you want to gather wealth? Why do you need a bungalow to live in? Why do you crave rich and tasty food? It is better to beg for food. It is better to live in a hut and wear rags!"

Upon hearing this, one *sadhu* got enraged. He challenged Amritrai saying, "Why are you entangled in all this? If you really believe what you say, come along with me. We will go on foot and beg for our food, eating whatever we get." Amritrai immediately agreed to go with him and they set out on a pilgrimage.

The next day as they were passing through a jungle, the *sadhu* told Amritrai to sit under a tree while he went to fetch some water. Nearby, a king had set up his camp. When it was time for the king to have his meal, he ordered his servants to go out and find a saint and invite him for lunch. The servants came across Amritrai and brought him to the king. The king seated him on a silk mattress, supported him with pillows and served him delicious food on a sliver plate while the queen sat beside him and fanned him. At this point, the *sadhu* arrived on the scene in search of Amritrai. He was stunned to again find him surrounded by luxury and he prostrated at his feet.

The moral of this story is that no one can escape his destiny. The inner state of a *jivanmukta*, however, is unchanging in all situations and circumstances. He

who sees everything as Brahman cannot be bound by
any *karma,* nor can his actions be limited by such factors
as time and place.

Saturday, June 12, 1965

REPAYING ONE'S DEBT TO THE GURU

Anthony: *Baba, you have given me so much and you
want to give me more, but how can I become worthy of
receiving your grace?*
Baba: The debt you incur by receiving something from
the Guru can be repaid only by achieving oneness with
the Guru. The scriptures say that the devotee and the
Lord, the disciple and the Guru, the means and the
object of *sadhana* are inseparable; they are one. When
the disciple is completely merged with the Guru, the
devotee with the Lord, or the means of *sadhana* with its
object, then Truth is attained. Then one feels, "O
Lord! You are me and I am You. It is You who
pervades everywhere." After this, the disciple's sense of
separate existence, or his idea of I-ness and my-ness,
vanishes. As long as I-ness and my-ness remain,
there is a separate existence. As long as a drop identifies with its drop-ness, it remains a drop, but when it
identifies with and merges into the ocean, it becomes
the ocean itself. When a person experiences, "I am
everywhere," then the sun, the moon and the stars rise
and set within him. Ram Tirth says:

वायु बहती फर फर मुझमें मुझमें मुझमें ।
नदी बहती झर झर मुझमें मुझमें मुझमें ॥

"The wind is blowing within me, within me, within
me; The river is flowing within me, within me, within
me."

Sundardas says:

ज्यूँ बन एक अनेक भये द्रुम, नाम अनंतनि, जाति हु न्यारी ।
वापि तडाग रु कूप, नदी सब, है जल एक सु देखु निहारी ॥
पांवक एक, प्रकाश बहुविधि, दीप चिराग मसाल हु बारी ।
सुन्दर ब्रह्म विलास अखंडित मेद-अमेद कि बुद्धि सु टारी ॥

"Although there are trees of different varieties and names, the forest is one; although there are lakes, wells and rivers, water is always the same; although there are different sources of light such as a candle flame and a lamp, the light is the same. O Sundar! Get rid of the idea of differences. It is Brahman alone who is manifesting as the play of this world."

This is the Truth. After realizing this, one feels that one is the Lord of the entire world. Whatever is seen in the world is the Self. The *Upanishads* proclaim, "Thou art That." The world has emerged from the Supreme Self.

Anthony: *Has the human body also come out of the Self?*

Baba: Yes, you will understand this when you know what the body is. Man's body is formed from the semen of his father. Semen is formed from food. Thus the body is said to consist of food. अन्नाद् भूतानि जायन्ते । जातान्यन्नेन वर्धन्ते । "Beings are born out of food; those who are born grow by food; and into food they merge." (*Taittiriya Upanishad*) Food comes out of the earth. Food is earth so the body is also earth. The body, which consists of food, comes out of the earth, grows on the earth and, in the end, it is either buried in the earth or its burnt ashes return to the earth.

Earth has emerged from water. To understand this, fill a glass with water and leave it undisturbed. After a while, you will find that some particles of earth have settled to the bottom. Water is the cause and earth

is the effect. Water, in turn, has emerged from fire.
The summer heat forms clouds that produce rain.
Also, when it is hot, we perspire. Fire has taken birth
from air. The damp clothes we hang outside are dried
by the element of fire in the air. Where there is space,
there is air. Wherever there is space in the body, there
is also air. This is everyone's experience. This space
is ether. Air emerges from ether and ether arises from
the Self. तस्माद्वा एतस्मादात्मन आकाशः संभूतः "Ether was
born from the Self." (*Tattiriya Upanishad*)

The Self is the root cause of everything. The
sequence is from the Self to ether, air, fire, water, earth,
food and then the gross body. The same steps are
retraced and everything returns to the Self. Therefore,
the entire world is full of consciousness. He is a
realized being who understands, "I pervade the entire
world in the form of consciousness."

The world appears to you according to your own
outlook. Sundardas says:

द्वैत करि देखै जब, द्वैत ही दिखाई देत ।
एक करि देखै तब, उहै एक अंग है ।
सूरजकूँ देखै जब सूरज प्रकाशि रह्यो ।
किरनकूँ देखै तो किरन नाना रंग है ॥

"If you are given to differentiating, duality is what
    you will see,
But if you look at it as a unity, all This is only One.
When you look at the sun, it is one whole blaze,
But if you look at its rays, their colours are so
    many."

If you have the outlook that the world is Brahman,
you will see Brahman everywhere. This entire world
of objects, mundane activities, science and politics—
everything is full of Consciousness. Nothing but Con-

sciousness exists.   This entire world is Its play.
Sundardas says:

देखत ब्रह्म सुनै पुनि ब्रह्महि, बोलत है वही ब्रह्महि बानी ।
भूमिहू नीरहू तेजहू वायुहु, व्योमहु ब्रह्म जहाँ लग प्रानी ।
आहिहु अंतहु मध्यहु ब्रह्माहि, है सब ब्रह्म यहै पति ठानी ।
सुन्दर ञेय रु ञानहु ब्रह्महि, आपहु ब्रह्महि जानत ञानी ॥

"The one who sees is Brahman, the one who hears
is Brahman, the speech coming from the tongue is
Brahman.   The earth, water, fire, air, · ether and all
creatures are Brahman.   The beginning, the middle
and the end are all Brahman.   Understand without a
doubt that everything is Brahman.   O Sundar, the
jnani understands that the knower, known and knowledge are all verily Brahman."

If you maintain this vision of the world, you will see
Swami Muktananda everywhere.   You yourself will
also become That.   True religion is to understand
things as they are in reality and non-religion is to understand the opposite.   If man understands that he himself is the all-pervading Supreme Brahman, that truly
is religion; but if he feels, "I am so and so and this is
mine," then that is non-religion.   To make distinctions
between one man and another is also contrary to
religion.   A seeker who maintains a divisive attitude
achieves nothing in this world or in the next world.
मृत्योः स मृत्युमाप्नोति । य इह नानेव पश्यति ।   "One who sees
many in this world goes from death to death." (*Kathopanishad*)

Anthony: *It is true that one must attain unity with the
Guru, but isn't is also true that one must keep a respect-
ful distance from him?*

Baba: Cut through the separateness and attain oneness,
but, at the same time, worship the Guru as if he were
separate.   You should have a feeling of oneness in your

heart, but outwardly you have to maintain some distance. You should not, for example, go and sit on the Guru's chair just because you feel that you are one with him. You must have the humility and modesty of a disciple in your daily behaviour. With respect to the gross body, you should behave as his servant while, at the same time, understanding that your Self is not different from the Guru. This is true worship of the Guru.

BESTOWING GRACE ON A MULTITUDE OF PEOPLE

Anthony: *Can grace be bestowed on many people gathered together?*
Baba: Yes, certainly, but all cannot receive grace that way. Not everyone is worthy of receiving it. Just as a student must first pass his high school examinations before he can enter college, similarly, a person must be worthy before he is able to receive grace.
Anthony: *Since the last world war, the entire world has been filled with sorrow and pain. Will this pain purify the world and bring about a transformation?*
Baba: For the world to be purified and transformed, God Himself must will it. Only God possesses the power to influence the mind of the people and bring about a mass transformation. Such work is dependent on God's will and is carried out by an incarnation of God.

Saturday, June 13, 1965

The devotees gathered in the ashram courtyard at 10 o'clock this morning.

Anthony: *How can one understand that God is manifest everywhere in the world?*

Baba: This cannot be understood until you have achieved Self-realization. Until then, you must have faith in the words of the scriptures. You will understand the truth for yourself at the proper time. For example, when a six-year-old boy asks his father, "How do you grow a moustache?" his father will reply, "When you are sixteen years old, you will find out for yourself." Similarly, when you achieve God-realization, your understanding will be, "This entire world is my play." As long as your mind is turned outward, absorbed in the activities of the world, you will not be able to comprehend this secret.

Anthony: *Baba, when will an era of righteousness dawn in this world?*

Baba: We can speak of one era with respect to the individual and another with respect to the world as a whole. With respect to the individual, a period of righteousness has begun when a person turns toward God. Nothing can be said about such an era with regard to the world as a whole.

After realizing the Truth, such questions will not arise at all. Our present question-and-answer session is taking place only in a dream. Whatever you are saying now is in that dream. After the true awakening and divine realization, you will have no more questions.

THE WAKING AND DREAM STATES ARE BOTH FALSE

Anthony: *Can the Truth be understood only after Brahman has awakened from His dream?*

Baba: Brahman is always awake. It is you who are dreaming so it is you who must wake up. In this connection, listen to a story about Ashtavakra and King Janaka.

King Janaka once dreamed that another king had

attacked his kingdom, defeated him and banished him from his former domain. After this happened, he wandered unknown and uncared for, with nothing to eat or drink. Nearing the point of starvation, he went into a corn field and began to eat an ear of corn. The farmer, seeing the trespasser, went running up to him and started beating him. As soon as the farmer struck him with his wooden stick, King Janaka awoke. He immediately saw that he was lying on his usual soft, scented bed with a retinue of servants fanning him. He again closed his eyes and saw the same scene—the corn, the farmer and the stick. Thus, he was seeing two entirely different scenes, one with his eyes closed and another with his eyes open. The king was perplexed by these two contradictory appearances and started wondering which of the two was true. Was the dream true or was the waking state true? The king could not decide for himself so he assembled all the learned scholars, sages and saints of his kingdom and asked them, "Is this true or is that true?" but nobody could answer him. The king got annoyed. Considering them to be wise and learned, he had supported them for such a long time and yet none among them could answer his question. Finally, he put all of them under arrest.

One of the imprisoned scholars had a son who was about sixteen or seventeen years old. The son was ugly and everyone called him Ashtavakra because his body was bent in eight places. He was a great *jnani*. Hearing of his father's predicament, he went to the king's court to get him released. When Ashtavakra arrived, everyone started laughing at him. Standing in the centre of the court, Ashtavakra also started laughing heartily. The king asked him, "Why are you laughing? We have a reason to laugh, but I don't see any reason for your laughter. Can you answer my question?" Ashtavakra replied, "First, you tell me the reason for your laughter then I shall tell you the reason for mine." The king said, "I laughed because a crooked, lame fellow like you has come to answer the question that has baffled even great learned scholars. Now, tell me, why did you laugh?" Ashtavakra said, "I have heard that King Janaka is a great *jnani,* but now I find that you are a *jnani* not of the Self but only of the flesh. You do not see the Self; you see only the gross body. That is why I laughed." Hearing this, the king and his entire court became silent.

Ashtavakra then told the king, "I have come here to answer your question on behalf of my father. Ask me the question." The king related the whole story and asked him which was true, this or that. Ashtavakra replied, "Just as this is false, that is also false. Like the dream, the waking state is also unreal. The state in which we are dwelling appears to be true while it lasts; however, when we enter the next state, the one we have just left appears to have been false. In the waking state, the dream state appears to be false while in the dream state, the waking state does not exist. The waking state is also just a long dream. Come out of the waking and dream states and enter into the *turiya* state. Only then will you understand what the Truth is."

Tuesday, June 15, 1965

Today's *satsang* started at about 10 o'clock in the morning.

Anthony: *Baba, can you tell me how many and what kinds of previous births I have had?*
Baba: I could tell you about your past lives, but you

would think it was purely my imagination. How could you determine whether what I told you was true or false? What proof would you have? Give up such futile enquiries. What is gained by knowing about your previous lives? On the contrary, sometimes such knowledge is painful. Instead of knowing about your past five, ten or fifteen lives, attain realization and recognise yourself as the Supreme Self. Then you yourself will be able to know about all your previous lives. Sometime during meditation, you may see your past lives like a movie. I once saw in meditation that I had been a king in one of my past lives.

Wednesday, June 16, 1965

THE IMPORTANCE OF CELIBACY IN SADHANA

Anthony: *Is the world an obstacle on the path to Self-realization?*

Baba: This world was created by God. How can it be contrary to Him? If the relationship between husband and wife is proper, it will not become an obstacle to one's *sadhana,* but deviation from one's *dharma* (duty) is harmful. Attachment is the obstacle for a seeker, not the world.

Anthony: *If a man wants to realize God, can he still marry?*

Baba: One who really wants to attain God does not need anything of this world. Why should one who wants to drink nectar drink from brooks or rivers? We have created the institution of marriage to provide love, happiness and bliss, but when bliss manifests independently from within, what is the necessity of seeking it outside?

Anthony: *What about the responsibilities of a man who is already married?*

Baba: Marriage is not opposed to God-realization. After marriage, the husband and wife have responsibilities toward each other and toward the children, but you must not think that the entire burden is to be carried by you alone. God, who has created this world, looks after all beings. Everyone must live out his own destiny. However, this does not mean that you should give everyone up. In short, you should not think that there is no one besides you to take care of others. So many women in this world have lost their husbands, so many men have lost their wives, many fathers have no sons and many sons have no fathers. So many infants lose their mothers soon after birth. Nonetheless, they all go on living. Everyone's life goes according to his destiny.

Anthony: *Is it true that a celibate progresses faster on the path to realization?*

Baba: A celibate can concentrate better and he also develops greater powers of comprehension. For this reason, the scriptures advise students to observe celibacy during the period of their education.

Anthony: *I would like to bring my family here, but they are independent. I can't compel them.*

Baba: Quite true. Spirituality is not for everyone. Very few tread the path of *sadhana*. In the *Bhagavad Gita* Lord Krishna tells Arjuna, मनुष्याणां सहस्रेषु कश्चिद्यतति सिद्धये । "Only one man in a thousand will make the effort to realize the Self." In those days, one such man in a thousand may have been available, but in the present times such a man can scarcely be found ever among ten thousand. Not everyone can tread the path to Self-realization. It is essential that the person be worthy of it.

Anthony: *America and England have made valuable contributions to the material progress of the world. Will they be able to make any contributions in the field of spirituality?*

Baba: They will be able to accomplish something in the field of spirituality only after turning away from materialism.

Anthony: *My daughter has a keen interest in the material world.*

Baba: It sometimes happens that a person with a keen interest in the material world turns toward spirituality and develops an equally keen interest in and love for God.

Anthony: *One of my friends in England has asked for your blessings. What shall I tell him?*

Baba: Tell him to remain intoxicated in devotion to God. No harm can befall the man who makes friends with God. The *Bhagavad Gita* says:

यत्र योगेश्वरः कृष्णो यत्र पार्थो धनुर्धरः ।
तत्र श्रीर्विजयो भूतिर्ध्रुवा नीतिर्मतिर्मम । १८.७८ ॥

"Wherever Lord Krishna, the Lord of yoga, and Arjuna the wielder of the bow, are, I know that prosperity, victory, glory and righteousness abide there."

Friday, June 18, 1965

Anthony again had *satsang* with Baba this evening.

Anthony: *Would you explain the importance of Guru Purnima?*

Baba: One's own feeling is more important than the particular day, time or object. In the daily life of Indian culture, certain days such as the full moon day, the new moon day, certain weekdays and days of the lunar cycle are associated with God. Among these are Guru Purnima, Sharad Purnima, Shravani Purnima, Vatasavitri and Holi. In India, you will see that even trees such as the pipal, banyan, ashoka and tulsi are worshipped as gods and goddesses. Wherever you go in India, you will find many temples. Such is our Indian culture. All this may appear meaningless to you, but this religion was not established by fools. It is the great Truth that we have inherited from our ancient, all-knowing saints and seers. This religion was established after deep contemplation. By living this religion, man sees God everywhere. God is omnipresent. He exists in rivers, seas, mountains, trees, leaves—in everything. Therefore, we worship all these things. This idea eventually takes a man from the outer world toward his own inner world; it makes his mind indrawn and gives him a clear experience that God dwells within him as well.

Saturday, June 19, 1965

Since Anthony planned to leave today, *satsang* took place early in the morning.

Anthony: *Doesn't God ever get tired of creating such a vast universe?*
Baba: God never gets tired. From your viewpoint, the universe appears immense, but for God it is like a game. He creates this entire universe in a fraction of a second. We are so entangled in the mundane world that we cannot comprehened this. After the final realization, you too will feel that the universe is quite small.

TWO TYPES OF DIVINE INCARNATIONS

Anthony: *Who would be considered an incarnation of God?*

Baba: He who comes to this earth to perform some special work that cannot be carried out by any ordinary mortal is called an incarnation. There are no obstacles in his work and even if obstacles do arise, he overcomes them successfully because his Shakti can never be defeated. He doesn't have to beg for help or depend upon anyone else to fulfill his mission. He has the capacity "to do, to undo or to do otherwise." Some wicked beings may try to harass him, but they can never defeat him. An incarnation has the power to rule over all. No one can rule over him.

There are two types of incarnations. The first are special incarnations of God such as Rama, Krishna and Narsimha (the man-lion, Vishnu in His fourth incarnation). The second are called messengers of God. Lord Vyasa and Shankaracharya are said to have been God's messengers.

At one time, Buddhism became widespread in India. It was Shankaracharya who counteracted its influence and reestablished the Hindu religion from Kanyakumari to the Himalayas with no help or support but that of his *yogadanda* (yoga stick). Even while the great Sufi saint Mansur Mastana was being hanged, he kept proclaiming to the very end, *analhaq*—"I am God." Shamsher Tabrez was condemned by his enemies, who decided to remove his skin, but he himself stripped the skin off his body and threw it at them. Such great beings have achieved oneness with God and are never defeated at the hands of this world. No sorrow can touch them as they are always intoxicated with supreme bliss. Jnaneshwar endured harassment by so many people, but he did not yield. When the bullet was fired at Gandhiji, he did not cry, "O God, save me! I am dying!" The last words he uttered were, "O Rama."

Mirabai drank poison without any harm. Prahlad, a staunch devotee of God, saw God everywhere: in fire, in the sea and even in poison. His father made many attempts to kill him, but they all failed. God Himself had to manifest for such a sincere devotee. If a devotee of God possesses so much power, you can imagine how much power must reside in an incarnation of God Himself.

Anthony: *Some incarnations of the Lord such as Sri Rama, Sri Krishna and Buddha were kings. Can God's messengers also be kings?*

Baba: Saints and yogis are considered to be kings. For this reason they are called *raja* yogis. The king wields his external power while the yogi uses his divine inner power. The king sits on a lion-shaped throne while the yogi sits on a lion skin because the lion is recognised as the king of beasts. The lion is not a cruel beast; it never preys on anyone without a reason.

Anthony: *Can animals subsequently obtain human birth?*

Baba: If a man performs cruel actions, his next birth will be as an animal, but the Self remains the same. The Self never changes. By observing the behaviour of some animals, we can easily conclude that they were human beings in their previous life. Those animals who live with and enjoy the company of human beings obtain a human birth in their next life. Some animals seem to be more intelligent than humans. The Queen of Jhansi's horse was able to recognise her enemy immediately. Such animals are very close to being human. Either they have been human beings in their previous life, or they are going to have a human body in their next birth.

THE SELF HAS NO BIRTH

Anthony: *What is the Self? What are Its attributes? How is it born?*

Baba: The Self is the Self. There is nothing similar to it in this world that I could point to for the sake of comparison. The Self is never born and never dies. When man does not even understand such a simple matter as how and when the body contracts disease, then how can he understand such a great mystery as the Self? The Self is all pervading. It is without birth and death. It is only from our perspective that It appears to be born and to die. The relationship between the Self and the body can be compared to that between the body and the clothes worn on it. You may change your clothes, but your body remains as it is; it does not change. Similarly, the Self remains as It is; it is only the body that changes. This means that it is the body that is born and the body that dies.

The subject you want to discuss is extremely profound. This science is even more abstruse than that of atomic energy or aeronautics. In order to understand it, you must study Vedanta. After such study, you will consider your initial questions to be like those asked by children.

According to the Vedantic philosophy of non-dualism, the Self is only one, even though there are many bodies. Although we see as many suns as the number of mirrors we place in the sun, the sun remains only one and unaffected by its reflections. We cannot destroy it by breaking the mirrors. The sun remains as it is. This is known as the principle of *bimba prati-bimba*—original object and its reflection. You may think you are seeing many Selves, but the truth is that the Self is only one. The Self is as It is. It never undergoes any change.

By what power does this body function? From where does this power come? Who experiences pleasure and pain? After pondering these questions, you will understand that the Self is beyond the body, mind, intellect and even the subconscious mind. The body is gross; it is inert. It derives consciousness from the Self and then it perceives objects through the sense organs. It sees with the eyes, hears with the ears and speaks with the tongue. Although the Self pervades the entire body, it is not attached to it. It remains ever pure and Godlike. It neither takes birth nor does It die.

Anthony: *Can one understand this through meditation?*
Baba: Along with meditation, you must practise contemplation. You must combine meditation and knowledge, then it becomes easier to understand the Truth.

Wednesday, June 30, 1965

Today a Parsi woman named Daulat Dalal came to the ashram to invite Baba to the annual function of a yoga school she attends.

Daulat: *Since our Guru became a* paramahansa *two years ago, he is not able to leave the ashram. All the ashram's teaching work is done by Mataji.*
Baba: Who told you that a *paramahansa* cannot go out anywhere? The scriptures say that a *paramahansa* is beyond rules and regulations as to what he should and should not do. There is nothing that he must or must not do.

What kind of *sadhana* are you doing?
Daulat: *I am practising concentration on* chidakasha (*the space of Consciousness*).

Baba: How?

Daulat: *Our Guru has initiated us and taught us* chida-kasha dharana *(concentration on* chidakasha*). We concentrate our minds on the tip of the nose and take our meditation from the* ajna chakra *to the* sahasrara. *From there, we take the meditation through the* sushumna *to the* muladhara, *passing through the* anahat, manipur *and other* chakras *on the way. We also call this practice* kriya yoga.

Baba: Initiation is a divine act by which the disciple's deficiencies and imperfections are removed and he is taken to perfection. Imperfection means ignorance, or limitation. Perfection means Godhood, or knowledge. Just as a patient's blood is automatically purified when the doctor administers an injection, similarly, the Guru makes the Shakti flow through the disciple, initiating a spontaneous process of purification. The body contracts disease through indiscriminate conduct and regains health through proper conduct. An impure disciple becomes pure by the touch of the Guru. True kriya yoga is that in which *kriyas* take place spontaneously without any special effort.

Saturday, July 3, 1965

A young seeker named Mohan who is from a new ashram near Bombay has been staying here for the past few days. His guru has initiated him into *brahmacharya* and given him saffron clothes. Currently he is interested in investigating other ashrams for himself.

A TRUE DISCIPLE CAN RECOGNISE A TRUE GURU

Mohan: *How can one recognise a true Guru?*

Baba: If you possess true discipleship, you will be able to recognise a true Guru. How many years have you been staying at the ashram?

Mohan: *Two and a half years.*

Baba: How much have you changed during that time?

Mohan: *How can I judge for myself how much I have changed?*

Baba: Recognise him to be a Guru by staying in whose company, even for a short while, you notice some change or transformation in yourself. Know him to be a Guru who can change you by taking you to a new and higher state from the one in which you first went to him. Do not think that your inner state has changed just because you are wearing these saffron clothes. Your life changes when you take to true discipleship. Nothing happens just by dressing like a *sannyasi*.

What did you do for two and a half years in the ashram?

Mohan: *I studied Vedanta. I read books on Vedanta such as* Atmabodh, Vivekachudamani *and others.*

Baba: Can you explain the Vedantic teachings to me? Which *sadhana* is indicated in Vedanta for Self-realization?

Mohan: *How can I explain it just like that? Kindly tell me.*

Baba: There is no means for attaining the Self because Vedanta says that the Self is always with you. We have to liberate that which is already liberated; we have to attain that which is already attained.

Sunday, July 11, 1965

Yesterday Dr. Brahma Prakash and his wife came to the ashram. Dr. Brahma Prakash is a director of the Bhabha Atomic Research Centre at Trombay.

KNOWLEDGE OF THE TRUTH RESOLVES ALL DOUBTS

Brahma Prakash: *Swamiji, please explain to me when, how and by whom this world was created.*

Baba: God created this world. He willed, 'एकोऽहं बहुस्याम् "I am one; let Me become many," and the world came into existence. He is both the efficient and material cause of this world. Just as a spider spins its web from the secretion of its own saliva and later withdraws it back into itself, this world has emerged from God and will ultimately merge back into God.

Don't ponder over when, how and for what reason this world came into being. Try to get liberated from it. I shall give you an analogy. Once, two men with a desire to eat mangoes entered a mango orchard. According to the rules of the place, no one was allowed to stay in the orchard after 12 noon. One of the men immediately climbed up a tree and ate as many mangoes as he could. The other man started looking around the orchard, analysing the different kinds of mangoes growing there: their breed, shape, place of origin, the age of the trees and so on. He became so involved in his enquiry that soon the allotted time came to an end and he had to leave the orchard without having eaten even one mango. Recognise God and attain Him before your time is up. Then all your questions will be automatically answered. Become God yourself and then you will feel that this entire world is your own.

Brahma Prakash: *How can one recognise God?*

Baba: There are four different means of gaining knowledge of a particular subject. They are: (1) direct perception, (2) inference, (3) scriptural statements and (4) statements of reliable people. To accept the statement of an expert in a certain subject about which we ourselves are ignorant is trustworthy evidence. For example, I would accept completely any statement you make about atomic energy because I believe that you know the subject thoroughly. Similarly, you should accept whatever I say with regard to spirituality because that is my area of expertise.

At the moment of birth, you did not know who your mother or your father was. As you grew up and gained understanding, you came to know from the statements of your parents and others that a particular person was your mother and a particular person was your father. You accepted what you were told; you simply had to believe it. Similarly, you should accept the statements of Mother Shruti (the scriptures) and all the saints that your true Father is the Supreme Self.

मानव ! तुझे नहीं याद क्या ? तू ब्रह्म का ही अंश है ।
कुल-गोत्र तेरा ब्रह्म है, सद् ब्रह्म तेरा वंश है ॥

"O man! Don't you remember? You are a part of Brahman. Your family and ancestors are Brahman. Your descendants will also be Brahman." You must believe in the words of Mother Shruti. Only the Mother can tell you who your true Father is.

You can also know about God by direct experience, but you will first have to spend a few years doing *sadhana,* just as one has to spend several years of systematic study to become a scientist or a doctor. If you invite me to see your laboratory, I will certainly come and see everything directly for myself. Likewise, I am inviting you to come to my laboratory (the ashram). Like you, I am an expert in my subject and I shall give you a direct experience of it.

According to Vedantic teachings, the world was never created; it exists only because of our delusion. Just as in darkness a rope may appear to be a snake, the mind superimposes the world on Parabrahman (the

Supreme Reality). The world appears to be real before acquiring true knowledge. After gaining true
understanding, it is seen as false. When the roaming
mind becomes still, the Truth can be understood. The
world exists for the ignorant because it is visible to the
gross eyes, but when the subtle eyes of a *jnani* are
opened, the gross world vanishes for him. How then
can he answer any questions with regard to that world?

Once a man was sleeping on a chair beside Swami
Ram Tirth. The man saw a tiger with two horns in a
dream and he woke up screaming with terror. He asked
Swamiji, "Where did the tiger with two horns go?" Of
course, Swamiji had not seen the tiger so what reply
could he give? If two people are on the same level, then
a real discussion can take place between them; otherwise,
their dialogue is like the conversation between persons
listening to two different radio stations. If one were
to ask the other, "Which *raga* (tune) is this?" the
other one would reply, "What *raga* are you talking
about? I'm listening to the news."

Take another example. The experience of a crow
is opposite to that of an owl. The crow sees the sun
while the owl does not. What then can they say to each
other about the sun? If they try to say anything, they
will only start quarrelling. It is better if they don't
open a discussion at all. If the owl became a crow, or
if the crow became an owl, then they could have a
meaningful discussion.

Every man experiences the three states of waking,
dream and deep sleep. There is a higher fourth state
beyond these three known as *turiya*. It is the state of
Self-realization. After entering that state, this world
appears like a dream. Try to achieve the *turiya* state
by realizing the Self. Then all your questions will be
answered.

Friday, September 3, 1965

Rasik Kadakia arrived this morning with some friends.

Rasik: *Can yogis take on the destiny of others?*
Baba: Yes, yogis possess such power; but, in general, they would not do so because it is not in harmony with the laws of destiny. The one who performs an action must undergo its consequences. If one person is guilty, does the judge give the punishment to someone else?

Sunday, September 26, 1965

Recently Ram Chadda has been reading the English translation of *Jnaneshwari* (Jnaneshwar Maharaj's commentary on the *Bhagavad Gita*). At 8.30 this morning, he approached Baba with the book. Many other devotees were also present.

THE GREATNESS OF JNANESHWAR MAHARAJ

Chadda: *Babaji, I am amazed by Jnaneshwar Maharaj's ability to write a wonderful book like* Jnaneshwari *at the young age of fifteen.*
Baba: I, too, used to wonder how a young boy could expound such profound knowledge. From a literary standpoint, the language and poetry excels even that of Sanskrit works. It is a very beautiful book.

Omniscience is a state and Jnaneshwar Maharaj was omniscient. I'll tell you how I came to believe this. One of the *Shivasutras* says "Knowledge is bondage." The *Shivasutras* is a book about Kashmir Shaivism. Seven or eight hundred years ago, the *Shivasutras* was available only in the form of a handwritten manuscript. In those days there was no possibility of its being printed and Jnaneshwar never went to Kashmir. It was not possible for a 15-year-old boy to make such a journey. Nevertheless, it is obvious from the books written by him that he knew about the *Shivasutras*. For example, he says in *Amritanubhava*:

आणि ज्ञान बन्धु ऐसें । शिवसूत्राचेनि मिसे ।
म्हणितले असे । सदाशिवें ॥

"Lord Shiva says in His *Shivasutras* that knowledge is bondage." How could Jnaneshwar have come to know about this *sutra*? This indicates that he was omniscient. He also writes about *shaktipat* in the sixth chapter of *Jnaneshwari*.

Jnaneshwar was a supremely powerful yogi. His teachings uplifted even Changdev, who was by far his elder. Changdev had an amazing control over tigers and snakes, but don't we see this even in the circus today? Jnaneshwar, on the other hand, had the power to infuse life into inert objects. He made a wall move. His greatness was such that even old people addressed him as Guru Maharaj. He took live *samadhi*.

Jnaneshwar's *Changdev Pasashthi* contains the highest philosophy. While writing *Jnaneshwari*, he had to contain himself within the framework of the original verses of the *Bhagavad Gita,* but he had no such restrictions while writing *Pasashthi,* in which his writing is even more profound than Vedanta.

Friday, January 7, 1966

At today's satsang, Hariyantlal Sonawala, his wife, Pushpa, Suryakant Jhaveri and Vasuben Mapara were present.

DO NOT RENOUNCE FAMILY LIFE: RENOUNCE THE IDEA OF "I" AND "MINE"

Haryantlal: *Babaji, please give some advice to those of us who lead a family life so that we may progress in spirituality while at the same time attending to our family responsibilities.*

Baba: What is worldly life?   Man and wife, children, home and business do not constitute worldly life.   The worldly life consists of ideas of "I" and "mine" and "you" and "yours."   That is the world. As long as there are vibrations of the world in the mind, pleasure and pain, which arise as a reaction to these vibrations, will persist. So learn to forget the world.   The world exists only because of the mind.   Mentally give it up.   There is happiness only in mental renunciation.   This is proved by our own direct experience.   At night you put aside all your costly belongings such as expensive clothes, the latest wrist watch imported from Germany and ornaments.   You give them up and then go to sleep.   At that time, you forget all those things.   Not only that, you forget about your business too.   Only after doing so can you fall into a deep sleep where you experience peace and happiness.   When you wake up, you feel refreshed.   This common experience proves that man finds happiness not in thinking about the world, but in forgetting it.   Achieve such a thought-free state of mind in the waking state too.   Practise detachment; that is where true happiness lies.

To attain God, it is not necessary to outwardly give up anything.   Even if you want to renounce, you will not be able to unless it is your destiny.   You cannot escape from your destiny by running away from it, nor can you get something not destined by asking for it. Therefore, let the world remain as it is.   Just try to forget it and go within.   Sit quietly and meditate; reflect on

the Self; try to become God yourself. See the God who
dwells within you; know and understand Him. Learn
to properly use the objects, situations and events of
this world.

I would advise you to set aside some time each day
for contemplation of God just as you reserve some time
for eating, drinking, sleeping, going to clubs, dramas
and movies. If you practise this regularly, after a while
you will experience that its pleasant effect remains with
you throughout the day. The remembrance of God's
name is so powerful that it enables man himself to
become God. This does not happen in worldly life.
No one becomes an engineer or a doctor simply by
remembering the name of an engineer or a doctor!

Try to cultivate faith and an attitude of surrender
to God. Insure yourself with God so that when the
need arises, He will be there to protect you. Insurance
policies are taken out for financial protection against
unforeseen accidents and damage. A wealthy man once
insured himself for a huge sum. When someone
threatened to murder him, his insurance company made
prompt arrangements for his protection. Therefore,
keep in mind the Lord's words, 'सर्वधर्मान् परित्यज्य मामेकं
शरणं व्रज'   "Give up all other *dharmas* and seek refuge
in Me alone." Insure yourself with God and He will
say, 'अहं त्वां सर्व पापेभ्यो मोक्षयिष्यामि मा शुचः'। "Grieve not;
I shall liberate you from all sins and defects."

Wednesday, January 12, 1966

Today Dr. Vora, a friend of Pratap Yande, and some
other devotees were sitting with Baba.

A SEEKER'S EXPERIENCES DURING MEDITATION ARE HIS OWN

Dr. Vora: *I don't have any experiences during meditation. Won't you give me some?*

Baba: Many people tell me the same thing. Put aside the thought of experiences; sit quitely for meditation.

A seeker's experiences are his own. Saints and sages are only an apparent cause. You experience your own Self; I don't give experiences to anyone. The light is within you; it is neither in Vaikuntha nor in heaven. You will see it right within yourself. Whatever is in God is also in you. God pervades your body just as the seven elements do. You can certainly experience this, but you must make a devoted effort. That which you want to realise is within you. I can see that. If you cannot, what can I do about it? I can only show you the path; you have to walk on it and do *sadhana*. Whether you have experiences or not is a matter of your own good fortune. See, this woman started having experiences as soon as she arrived here. One more point: What is an experience? A seeker must know the exact meaning of experience because many times it so happens that a seeker has experiences but does not recognise them as such.

Sunday, February 6, 1966

Yesterday, a Frenchman named Manuel Densil came to the ashram with Ram Chadda. During today's *satsang*, he asked Baba some questions.

Manuel: *Is it true that beings living in other worlds have progressed further than beings in this world?*

Baba: Yes. It is true that beings in Siddhaloka and Indra-loka have many *riddhis* and *siddhis*. They have the power to curse and to bless. Compared to man, those beings are stronger, more energetic and more brilliant. They enjoy eternal youth without any disease, misery or disappointment; but as soon as their merits are exhausted, they have to come back to this earth.

Remember, though, that compared to the infinite universal Being, all other worlds are limited and imperfect. Whatever can be measured is considered to be ultimately limited. Just as India, America and England are limited in size, these other worlds also have boundaries, or limits. In the end, they are limited and it is said, यद् अल्पं तद् मर्त्यम् । "Whatever is limited is perishable."

Manuel: *What is your opinion about flying saucers?*

Baba: Have you seen them?

Manuel: *A pit created by the descent of one can be seen in Mexico.*

Baba: The aircraft of other worlds are mantra aircrafts. They do not need any gasoline, engines or pilots, but are operated by the mind. This means that they are mental instruments.

Manuel: *Yes, I remember having read something like that somewhere.*

Baba: Before you read any book, try to find out about the background of its author. The writings of our saints and sages don't contain even a trace of fiction. They had no reason to write anything false. They had no desires or ambitions and lived simple lives full of *tapasya*. In modern times, books are written to earn money and fame or for propaganda; it was not so in those days. Therefore, the saints and sages had no reason to write anything false. Due to the power of their *tapasya*, true knowledge was awakened in them.

They wrote with the help of supramental powers. Their writings are not based on dry research, poetic imagination or bookish learning. The sages came to know of the existence of Chandraloka and Suryaloka (the realms of the moon and the sun). Not only that, but they had a direct experience of these realms during meditation. It was only then that they accepted their existence and told others about them.

Sometimes we also have the experience of seeing something in a dream that later comes true. There is a place within us by reaching which nothing remains unknown. The scriptures are based on knowledge obtained from this source.

Manuel: *Is it true that there are some great beings in the Himalayas who are not visible, but who sometimes come down and move in society?*

Baba: Such great beings are not only in the Himalayas, but also at other Siddha *peethas*, such as Sri Shailam, Tibet and Girnar. They can take up a subtle body and go wherever they want. Their bodies can move about anywhere without any difficulty because they cannot be obstructed by any object, nor can they be burnt by fire. They do not have the limitations of modern airplanes.

Manuel: *Is it true that beings from the planet Venus come here?*

Baba: Venus is a world of Siddhas. The beings living there have the power to come here. If you do spiritual *sadhana*, you will also be able to see them during the higher stages of meditation.

Manuel: *Perhaps you have also come here from some such world.*

Baba: No, I belong to this very world.

Manuel: *Are there men in the Himalayas known as abominable snowmen?*

Baba: Have you seen them?

Manuel: *No, but there are frequent reports of their large footprints, which are visible in the snow.*

Baba: This is only an inference. There are Siddha yogis in the Himalayas who are taller than us. In our *Puranas*, it is mentioned that *yakshas* (demi-gods) whose height exceeds ours live in the Himalayas.

Manuel: *Is it true that man is constantly evolving?*

Baba: Yes, this evolution has been going on for ages. The true evolution of a man is his inner, or spiritual, progress. The inner awakening can occur at any time. Man is always worthy of aspiring to be liberated.

Manuel: *I am not talking about spiritual evolution. I am referring to the theory of evolution proposed by Darwin, according to which man has evolved from the ape.*

Baba: His theory is based entirely on inference, isn't it? The truth of any statement can be proved in one of two ways, either by seeing it directly through experimentation and research or by experiencing it during the higher stages of meditation.

Manuel: *Can I also have experiences like other seekers?*

Baba: If you become like those people who have experiences, then you can also have experiences. They have intense devotion, faith and an earnest desire to know God. If you want to experience the cold of the Himalayas, you must go there; you cannot know it by sitting here. In the same way, if you want to have experiences, you must become worthy by preparing a fertile ground for them.

Manuel: *There is a seeker who initially had many experiences during meditation, but now he has none.*

Baba: It is not that a seeker must have experiences continuously. If you have them constantly, it is just like witnessing a drama or a movie.

Manuel: *A friend of mine, who is a doctor, went to see Anandamayi Ma and he had some wonderful experiences.*
Baba: Saints and great beings are not interested in performing magic. The power dwelling within them automatically influences a seeker, enabling him to start having some inner experiences. Such experiences are not within our control, but depend on the inner Shakti. This Shakti is independent and works according to Her own wishes.

Sunday, February 13, 1966

This morning, all the devotees were gathered in the *satsang* hall. Ram Chadda asked Baba a question.

WHO IS THE GURU?

Chadda: *Baba, tell us something about the Guru. Who can be called a Guru?*
Baba: Only he who has merged himself completely in God can become a Guru. The Guru has achieved total unity with God; therefore, the Guru is also called Parabrahman (the Supreme Self).

Many ornaments are made of gold, but the gold in all of them is the same. Similarly, all the various objects in this world have emerged from the same God. It is because different qualities are superimposed upon pure Consciousness that diversity is seen, just as the walls of a room create the illusion that the space inside the room is different from the space outside the room. In reality, space is all one. If you remove the walls, you will find that the inside space and the outside space are one and the same. Similarly, the Self is not different from God. The Guru is one who has given up all external attributes and has merged with God. The

Guru is one who has the power to bestow grace on his disciples. He alone is considered fit to guide others. You can call him a Guru, a saint or God: all are the same. The scriptures say that Self, Guru and God are one; hence, worship them as such.

ईश्वरो गुरुरात्मेति मूर्तिभेदविभागिने ।
व्योमवद् व्याप्तदेहाय तस्मै श्रीगुरवे नमः ॥

"Although he is as all-pervasive as space, he assumes the threefold division of God, Guru and Self. I bow to such a Guru."

The Guru is he who has the ability to show others what he himself has seen. Since nothing in this world is different from God, then why not accept the Guru as God? He is not like God—he is God Himself.

Sunday, February 20, 1966

Barrister Raman Vyas, the brother of Pandit Hariprasad Vyas of Secunderabad, came today. He asked Baba some questions.

THE NATURE OF HAPPINESS

Raman: *What is the happiness of Self-realization like? Is it like the happiness we experience through the senses or is it different from that?*

Baba: Happiness is of two kinds: permanent and temporary, or transient. The happiness you derive from sensual enjoyments is transient whereas the happiness experienced within yourself is permanent. It should not be called happiness; it should be called supreme bliss.

We have two kinds of instruments: the outer instruments and the inner instrument. The outer instruments, or sense organs, are directed toward objects in the outer world. It is the inner instrument that gives you an experience of exalted inner bliss.

Raman: *Does one also obtain material pleasures after receiving the grace of God?*

Baba: Material pleasures are dependent on one's destiny. By receiving God's grace, you obtain God Himself. After attaining God, getting material pleasures or losing them are both the same. One person may become completely detached from the material world while another seems to get deeply involved in it. For example, after realization, King Gopichand left his palace and went to live in a cemetery whereas Shikhadhvaja returned to his kingdom.

One gets the results of one's *karmas* from previous lives, but a wise man will say that it was all given to him by God.

Sunday, March 6, 1966

As is usual on Sunday, many people were gathered in the *satsang* hall. Ram Chadda recently attended the discourses of Arthur Osborne in Bombay and he spoke to Baba about them.

Chadda: *Baba, in all his discourses, Osborne repeats the same instruction, which is to contemplate the question "Who am I?" Many people in the audience told him that they found this very difficult and asked him how it could be done. In reply, Osborne told them to drive all worldly thoughts away from their minds, to make their minds vacant and then it would be possible to contemplate "Who am I?" He was then asked how the thoughts could be driven away, but he was unable to answer this question.*

SEE THE WORLD AS A FORM OF THE SELF

Baba: If he were to tell me to practise this, I would ask him, "Have you yourself driven the thoughts from your mind and then contemplated 'Who am I'?" If he replied, "Yes," I would then ask him a second question: "You have come here and you are talking to us. Are you performing these activities while thinking about the world or without thinking about it?" He would certainly reply, "While thinking about the world." That means that when one is immersed in the Self, thoughts about the world cannot remain and when one is engaged in thoughts about the world, the experience of the Self cannot remain. Therefore, you would sometimes be in that state (immersed in the Self) and sometimes in this state (thinking about the world). What is the use of achieving such an unstable state? The state of true Self-realization always remains the same.

The truth is that we do not have to eliminate all thoughts; we have to make them assume the form of the Self. We have to see this world as a form of the Self. Nothing is different from the Self.

Monday, March 7, 1966

An experiment of *kayakalpa* (rejuvenation) is being conducted in the ashram. Vaidya Shri Antarkar has been here for seven days supervising it. Today his brother, who is a professor of philosophy at Ruparel College and a seeker, also came with him.

THE NEED FOR SADHANA

Professor: *Many thought waves arise in my mind, but during meditation, I drive away all extraneous*

*thoughts and concentrate on only one thought such as
a sound, an idol of God or the letters of a mantra and
become one with it. But this does not satisfy me
because my aim is to drive away all thoughts while in
this practice one thought wave remains constant.*

Baba: Because there are waves in the mind, there is
meditation. If there were no waves, how could there
be any meditation? Meditation is practised until the
Truth is realized, until knowledge of the Truth is
obtained. *Sadhana* is done according to one's own
worth because perhaps only one among millions is so
worthy that, without doing any *sadhana*, he is able to
obtain knowledge immediately upon receiving the
Guru's teaching, "Thou art That." Therefore, as long
as thought waves arise in the mind, as long as the mind
engages itself in thoughts, *sadhana* has to be practised.
Until knowledge of the Truth is attained, the various
triads will remain, namely, the meditator, meditation
and the object of meditation; the seer, seen and seeing;
the knower, known and knowledge; the seeker, *sadhana*
and the goal. In fact, the person who meditates, the
object on which he meditates and meditation are all
one and the same, but for one who cannot grasp this
subtle truth, various types of *sadhana* are prescribed.

Professor: *Yes, but one does experience peace through
meditation.*

Baba: Do meditate, but at the same time keep in mind
that whether or not waves arise in the mind, they do
not bring about any change in the Self, which is never
affected by anything. The Self can never be bound
by anyone. What difference does it make to your Self
whether the mind becomes agitated or remains quiet?
Does it make any difference in the state of your Self
whether a gale wind is blowing, carrying everything
with it, or whether the air is calm and all objects

remain steady?

These thought waves can be compared to the
phenomenon of flowers and fruit appearing on trees
in the proper season and dropping off when the season
passes.   Know and recognise the Self as separate from
the thought waves.   Agitation or quietude are only
mental states; the Self has no connection with them.
Professor: *Sankhya philosophy says that it is* prakriti
that is liberated, not the purusha.
Baba: That which is dirty needs to be washed, not that
which is already clean.   The Self is always pure.   How
can it be contaminated or impure?   As long as one
does not understand this truth, one has to practise
sadhana.

                                    Sunday, March 20, 1966

     Today G. N. Vaidya, Yogendrabhai, Bhaskar Desai and
Pratap Yande were present for *satsang.*

SACRED ASH CANNOT EXIST IN THE ABODE OF GOD

Vaidya: *Last night, I went to see a* sannyasi *at Gwalior
Palace.   He materialises sacred ash from his hand and
his devotees consider it to be prasad from God.*
Baba: It is worth analysing from where this sacred ash
comes.   *Chidakash* is absolutely pure and objectless.   It
is the dwelling place of the Supreme Self, or God; it is
where the light of the Self shines.   Where the pure Self
alone exists, there is no room for sacred ash.   Ashes are
an impurity whereas *chidakash,* the abode of God, is
without any taint or impurity so how can ashes exist
there?   One thing is certain: the ashes do not come
from the abode of God.

Moreover, ashes represent the earth element of the five great elements. They can be seen, smelled, tasted and touched. These qualities of *prakriti* are found in the world created from the five elements. The sacred ash, therefore, belongs to this very world. Hence, there is a vast difference between such magic and the abode of God.

Monday, May 2, 1966

Mr. Korgaonkar, a friend of Pratap Yande, came today. He asked Baba some questions.

SHAMBHAVI SHAKTI (THE SHAKTI OF SHAMBHU)

Korgaonkar: *Which Shakti is transmitted in* shaktipat?
Baba: The science of *shaktipat* has come down from time immemorial. It is also known as *shambhavi vidya.* Discussions of it can be found in such books as *Trik Siddhant* and the *Agama Shastra.* According to Shaivism, the absolutely pure and spotless state is Shiva, in whom Shakti dwells. This Shakti pervades the whole universe, performing innumerable wonders. The description of this Shakti is awe inspiring.

Shakti is inseparable from Shiva. She cannot be divided into portions, nor can she be multiplied. She is infinite and omnipresent. Her wonderful power enables her to remain as water in water and as fire in fire. She is not concealed; She is manifest. She dwells in man in the form of *prana.* She dwells in the *muladhara chakra* in the form of a coiled serpent called Kundalini. When this Kundalini is awakened by *shaktipat* from the Guru, man experiences this Shakti. Until then, he cannot understand anything about Her.

Korgaonkar: *Why does Jnaneshwar Maharaj refer to this world as 'my play'?*

Baba: Because that is his actual experience. When one experiences this entire world as one's own expanse and play, that is the true state of Self-realization.

SAINTS ALSO ABIDE BY THE LAWS OF GOD

Korgaonkar: *Why was it necessary for Jnaneshwar to take live samadhi?*

Baba: Great beings always abide by God's laws. They practise what they preach. Once even Mr. Nehru waited in line to obtain a ration card in accordance with the laws made by his goverment. The laws of God are also applicable to his messengers; therefore, all the Siddhas act in conformance with these laws.

Jnaneshwar convinced the great yogi Changdev that he should give up his desire for a long life so how could he himself harbour such a desire? Changdev was a great yogi and had earned a life span thousands of years long through kayakalpa. Jnaneshwar advised him not to lengthen his life with stolen time and gave him knowledge of the Truth. So why would Jnaneshwar have tried to lengthen his own life? Life and death are equal for one who has realized the Truth. He has no desire to prolong his life. Such beings always act according to God's will. The changes they bring about are also in accordance with God's will. They never act contrary to the scriptures and they understand religion in its real sense. One who has one-sided knowledge cannot be called a yogi or a Siddha.

Yogis who have attained a high state have knowledge of all three periods of time: past, present and future. They have foreknowledge of their time of death. This is called the knowledge of time. Jnaneshwar Maharaj wrote some verses that indicate his knowledge of this subject. Such yogis withdraw into samadhi a day or two before their impending death and give up their *pranas* at the appointed time. Some Siddhas live till the end of the cycle, but what is the purpose of such a long life?

THREE TYPES OF SIDDHAS

Korgaonkar: *Who can be called a Siddha?*
Baba: Siddhas are mainly of three types: (1) *janma* Siddhas are those who are born as Siddhas, (2) *kripa* Siddhas are those who obtain Siddhahood through grace, and (3) *sadhana* Siddhas are those who become Siddhas as a result of their own *sadhana.*

Those who have practised *sadhana* in many previous lifetimes and complete it in this life without the help of a Guru are called *janma* Siddhas. In their former life, such individuals were not able to completely give up their identification with *jivahood* (individuality) and hence, could not entirely realize their Shivahood. In this life, they take up *sadhana* on their own without a Guru and become Siddhas. It is certain, however, that they must have had a Guru in their previous life. They resume *sadhana* in this life from whatever point they left it in their past life. They manifest *siddhis* at a very early age, for example, whatever they say comes true and they are able to foretell events. Sai Baba of Shirdi and Nityananda Baba were Siddhas of this type. *Siddhis* reside in such great beings right from their birth, but they are not even aware of them. Their *siddhis* work for them in a natural way without any effort on their part. In spite of having great powers, they act according to the will of God. Such *janma* Siddhas complete their *sadhana* without any effort on their part. Shakti Herself ensures that they complete it. Those saints who attained perfection

after receiving mantra initiation in a dream also belong
to the class of *janma* Siddhas.

Those who attain Siddhahood as a result of an
inner awakening by the grace of a Siddha Guru are
known as *kripa* Siddhas. Later, they have the same
powers as *janma* Siddhas including the ability to bestow
grace on others. One who becomes a Siddha by
receiving a mantra from a Guru also belongs to this
class of Siddhas.

Those who become Siddhas after practising yoga
and doing *sadhana* are known as *sadhana* Siddhas.

A *janma* Siddha has had a Guru in his past life
and his *sadhana* proceeds automatically in this life. A
kripa Siddha receives the Guru's grace and attains liberation without any strenuous effort.

They are known as Siddha incarnations who come
to this earth from Siddhaloka with a message from **God**
or who come to fulfill a special mission. They may
remain here till the end of the cycle. They are unaffected by pleasure or pain and they have infinite
powers, but they cannot be called incarnations of God.

Wednesday, May 11, 1966

The Banavalikar family has been staying at the holiday
camp in Ganeshpuri for the past three or four days. They
are devotees of Shree Ramadevi. Every evening they come
for *satsang* with Baba. One of them, Sulochanaben, has
a keen interest in *sadhana*.

KNOWLEDGE OF THE SELF AND THE MANTRA GIVEN BY THE GURU

Sulochana: *Baba, should one contemplate knowledge
of the Self, or should one repeat the mantra given by*

the Guru?

Baba: Knowledge of the Self is superior to all, but it is not so easy to obtain. You have to see That which cannot be seen; you have to catch That which has no form; you have to touch That which cannot be felt. Even the sages are wonderstruck by this Self. The *Bhagavad Gita* says:

आश्चर्यवत्पश्यति कश्चिदेनमाश्चर्यवद्वदति तथैव चान्यः ।
आश्चर्यवच्चैनमन्यः शृणोति श्रुत्वाप्येनं वेद न चैव कश्चित् ॥ २-२९ ॥

"Some see the Self as a great wonder, some speak of the Self as a great wonder, some hear about the Self as a great wonder and yet, even after hearing about Him, no one knows Him." (2-29)

In the *Kathopanishad,* Yamaraja, the Lord of Death, says:

श्रवणायापि बहुभिर्यो न लभ्यः शृण्वन्तोऽपि बहवो यं न विद्युः ।
आश्चर्यो वक्ता कुशलोऽस्य लब्धा आश्चर्यो ज्ञाता कुशलानुशिष्टः ॥

"Many never even hear about the Self; though hearing about it, many do not understand it. Wonderful is he who imparts this knowledge of the Self and wonderful is he who attains the Self. He who comprehends this transcendental divine Self is indeed supremely wise."

If you were to see a man who has realized the knowledge of the Self, you would certainly be wonderstruck. Such is this knowledge of the Self.

That mantra by which the Guru was able to attain oneness with the Supreme Self is given or taught by him to others. By repeating this mantra, a seeker spontaneously begins to experience the *so'ham* mantra within himself. Then the knowledge of the Self, "I am That," starts manifesting from within. After that, contemplation of the Self is no longer necessary.

DESTINY CANNOT AFFECT ONE'S WORSHIP OF GOD

Sulochana: *Is it true that one can worship God only if it is one's destiny?*

Baba: Destiny is related to the experiences of life in the world, not to the worship of God. Man has to undergo painful and pleasurable experiences in relation to his body and life in the world according to his destiny. As far as the worship of God is concerned, he is absolutely free; it is entirely within his own control. Saint Dayarnava says:

ऐका दयार्णव-कृत प्रार्थना भोग प्रारब्ध योगे जाणा ।
पुरुषार्थी साधिजे भगवद्भजना ये खूण मनामाजी धरिजे ॥

"Listen to this request of Dayarnava. You will undergo your destined life experiences, but make every effort to worship God. Understand that the worship of God is within your power."

Let your destiny remain as it is; you can neither add anything to it, nor subtract anything from it. Continue to worship God, paying no attention to destiny. One attains God while living out his destined experiences. Even great saints cannot escape their destiny.

Sunday, May 15, 1966

Today Shri Shivjibhai, a Jain, came with a friend from Bombay. He asked Baba some questions about his *sadhana.*

Shivaji: *I have done a lot of* sadhana *and yogic practices. As a result, I had various experiences and also attained* siddhis. *At one time when I sat for meditation, Shakti would be transmitted from me to another.*

*He would get up as if asleep and answer my questions.
This all came to a halt six years ago. Now my* sadhana
*does not bear fruit, nor do I have any experiences. I
have sought the advice of many saints and sages regarding this lapse in my* sadhana, *but each one has a different explanation. Very few of our Jain sadhus have
practised yoga; very few have any knowledge of it.
They are mostly ritualists. I did meet one Jain* muni
*who knows about Kundalini Yoga. He told me that
the* kriya *in which the head touches the ground during
meditation is harmful. According to him, I lost all
my powers because of that* kriya. *He taught me an*
asana *which I practised for three months, but without
any benefit. My state has remained the same.*

Baba: Sometimes during meditation, the head touches
the ground. This is one of the yogic *kriyas.* What
ever was happening to you was all right; nothing was
wrong. In yogic practice, many such *kriyas* occur
during the purification of the *nadis.* There is no
reason to have any fears or doubts about them. You
must allow whatever is happening naturally to happen.
Do not try to obstruct it.

THE DIVINE SHAKTI IS COMPASSIONATE

Shivji: *Another Jain* sadhu *told me, "Chakreshwari,
the deity of your lineage, is angry with you; hence, your*
sadhana *has come to a halt."*

Baba: How could that have happened? Even our
earthly mother, who has given us birth, tolerates all our
faults and offences so how could Shakti, the Divine
Mother of the universe, get angry? The study and
practice of yoga is not a reprehensible activity. It is
the means by which you are trying to obtain the Mother
Herself. Would this incur her wrath? The Mother
is extremely forgiving. Chakreshwari is Kundalini

Shakti Herself.   She is that Shakti who opens all the
chakras.   Do you consider the Shakti that you worship
and experience during yoga practice to be different
from Chakreshwari?   Shakti is only one everywhere.
For Christians, Parsis, Hindus, Muslims, Buddhists and
Jains, there is only one Shakti.   People give this
Shakti different names such as Sita, Radha and Mary,
but ultimately all are one.   If your Shakti is different
from that of other sects and religions, then is your
Shakti true and theirs false?   Do you think that the
others will go to hell?

Moreover, if you seek someone's advice about your
sadhana and that person misguides you and your
sadhana is disrupted, do you think that Goddess Chakreshwari will be angry with you?   On the contrary, why wouldn't she be angry with the one who
misled you?   Your story is analogous to the following
one: A man sold some land on which a cobra goddess
lived and the new owner removed her abode and dis-
posed of it.   Later on, the cow of the original owner
died and people started saying that the cobra goddess
was angry with him.   Is such a conclusion justified?
The offence was committed by one man so why would
another man be punished for it?   Wouldn't the cobra
goddess be angry with the man who removed her abode?

God is never angry. The Divine Shakti is extremely
compassionate.   Putana tried to poison Lord Krishna,
but he still granted her liberation.

PAST LIVES ARE REVEALED IN MEDITATION

Shivji: *Shri Rajachandra says that to know your past
lives, you must regress yourself back into the past.   If
you are forty years old now, you must contemplate on
what you were like at age thirty-nine, then at thirty-
eight and so on, continuing back to your past life.   Is*

it possible to know about one's past life using this method?

Baba: This is called *layachintan* (contemplation in retrospect), but what is the need for practice when one's previous life is revealed automatically in meditation? All the impressions of former lives are stored in the *sushumna*. After awakening of the Kundalini, the door of the *sushumna* is opened and many seekers receive knowledge of their past lives spontaneously in meditation without any special effort.

Shivji: *Is it necessary to know about one's past life? Of what use is such knowledge?*

Baba: Knowing about your past life is like knowing about past history; it is like knowing the succession of Indian kings from Babar to Aurangzeb. There is no advantage in knowing your past. On the other hand, you will derive benefit from performing some meritorious actions in the present. By improving your present life, you will gain something; by only trying to delve into the past and the future, you will remain where you are. Think only of the present and make good use of the time and opportunity available to you. Make some effort to attain God.

Shivji: *There are two Jain sects. One sect, called Dehravasis, believes in idol worship; the other sect, called Sthanakvasis (to which I belong), does not believe in idols. What then should be the support for my meditation?*

Baba: Shakti Herself is the support. When you practise yoga, you have some experiences and *kriyas*. On what are they based? The support for all of them is Shakti. Why do you need any other support for your meditation?

Gita and Mark Obel arrived from South Africa five or six days ago. Today when everyone was assembled in the *satsang* hall, Gita asked a question about her *sadhana*.

THE OUTLOOK OF THE GOPIS

Gita: *Babaji, when I go into meditation, I see light. Sometimes I feel that I am that light and that the light is my Self.*

Baba: What you are now experiencing is only a glimpse of the Self. The Self is much greater than that. Are we able to see our entire body? We can see our arms and legs, but not our back. Similarly, you are seeing only a fraction of the Self.

I'll give you another example. If you put a bowl of water in the sun, you will see the sunlight reflected in it, won't you? In a small bowl, you will see a small light; in a big bowl, a big light. This reflected light is only a small fraction of the sun's widespread radiance. Similarly, the Self, or God, pervades everywhere. He appears to be limited in varying degrees due to the modifying factors of mind, intellect, ego and sub-conscious mind in which He is reflected.

What is the object of your meditation? The one on whom you are meditating is within you. If the Self is sought outside of oneself, it is like the sun going out in search of heat or the moon in search of coolness. Sundardas says:

ज्यूँ रवि कूं रवि ढूंढत है कहुं, तत्त मिलै तन शीत गमाऊँ ।
ज्यूँ शशि कूं शशि चाहत है पुनि, शीतल है करि तत्त बुझाऊँ ॥
उयूँ सनिपात भये नर टेरत है घर में अपने घर जाऊँ ।
त्यूँ यह सुन्दर भूलि स्वरूपहि, ब्रह्म कहे कब ब्रह्महि पाऊँ ॥

"Just as if the sun were searching for the sun to warm his body, or the moon were searching for the moon to cool her body, or a man safe inside his own house were frightened and wanted to seek shelter in his house, similarly, O Sundar, Brahman has forgotten His own nature and says, 'Let me try to find out what Brahman is like'."

The *gopis* had become so completely united with Krishna that they entirely forgot themselves. They saw nothing in this world as different from Krishna. In this connection, I'll tell you a story about Krishna and Uddhava. Krishna imparted knowledge to Uddhava, enabling him to understand the inner lights, meditation and so forth. Krishna knew, however, that Uddhava had not properly grasped his teachings. A teacher has unique ways of teaching a person who does not understand. Krishna gave Uddhava a test. He told him to go to the *gopis* and give them knowledge. Uddhava was very pleased and he went at once to Braj, where the *gopis* were living. He announced his arrival by exclaiming, "Gopal ki Jai !" He saw the *gopis* embracing all kinds of objects such as trees, cows and water, saying, "O Krishna, O Krishna." Uddhava concluded that the poor *gopis* were ignorant. He asked them, "What are you doing?" The *gopis* replied, "What you are trying to attain through meditation we see everywhere." Realizing the truth of their statement, Uddhava lost all his pride.

If we have the outlook of the *gopis,* we need not practise any *sadhana;* lacking that outlook, any amount of meditation or any number of experiences are futile.

Sunday, June 26, 1966

Barrister Nain was among the devotees gathered in the *satsang* hall today. He commented that the ashram saplings and creepers grow very quickly and even small trees yield large, delicious fruit.

NECTAREAN CHAITANYA

Baba: The trees and creepers imbibe *chetan* Shakti from the all-pervading Chaitanya (Consciousness). Our clothes prevent this *chetan* Shakti from entering our bodies. I keep most of my body uncovered so that the Shakti can enter me easily. This is why my skin shines. This nectarean and radiant Consciousness is combined with air. Wherever the air enters, this Consciousness also penetrates. Where the vapour from boiling water diffuses in the atmosphere, you can see bright vibrations. Consciousness is something like that. If you watch the sun's rays entering a room through a skylight, you see movement in the sunbeam. Consciousness is something like that. These chairs, stones, clay, etc., are inert forms of that Consciousness which pervades every place and every object. That Consciousness is the ultimate Truth, which is seen after practising meditation for a long time.

Nain: *Baba, I recently read that as a man reduces his food intake and gradually loses weight, his mental power is enhanced.*

Baba: The mind should be sentenced to solitary confinement to increase its power. If the mind constantly runs after sense objects, it becomes unstable, but if it remains quiet and concentrated, it becomes more powerful. Let me tell you about an incident that happened this morning. While I was walking through the garden, it immediately struck me that a coconut had been stolen from the coconut tree. Everyone must have thought that Baba knows about everything, but that is not so. Such things arise automatically in a concentrated mind. There is, however, no special advantage in being able to know everything in this way. The coconut cannot be recovered just by knowing that it has been stolen.

Monday, June 27, 1966

Today L. R. Patel, who works with Amar Construction Company, came for Baba's *darshan*. He has come to the ashram before with Sri Ranchod Bapu. He brought two new visitors with him, Ramnath Mishra, a seeker, and Shantikumar Vaidya.

HATHA YOGA AND SIDDHA YOGA

Mishra: *What is the importance of the* khechari *mudra in yogic practice?*

Baba: There are two types of *khechari mudra*: the outer *khechari* and the inner *khechari.* Hatha yogis sometimes cut the fraenum under the tongue in order to practise *khechari mudra.* This is the outer *khechari* brought about by external means. In contrast, *khechari mudra* occurs spontaneously with the grace of the Guru. During *sadhana,* the tongue sometimes rolls back and presses against the upper palate or even extends up and back into the nasal pharynx. This is the spontaneous, inner *khechari.* It is the true *khechari mudra,* the one considered to be significant in yoga.

Mishra: *What is the place of* ashtanga *yoga (Patanjali's eight-limbed yoga) in Siddha Yoga?*

Baba: Siddha Yoga comes very easily to one who has already practised *ashtanga* yoga. Generally, he will not experience any difficulties in *sadhana;* but even if he does, they will be comparatively minor because, through the practice of *asana, pranayama* and so forth, his *nadis* are already purified. One who has not purified the *nadis* encounters a lot of difficulties in *sadhana* such as diarrhoea, cough and body aches. Purification of the *nadis* occurs automatically in Siddha Yoga. As the *nadis* are purified, even the clothes and sweat of the seeker no longer have a bad odour. One starts regulating one's food intake naturally, eating just the right amount of food required by the body, never too much or too little.

Mishra: *What is the correct time for meditation?*

Baba: Since hatha yoga is a yoga of self-effort and discipline, many rules and regulations must be observed whereas in Siddha Yoga, it is not necessary to establish a set time for meditation. In this yoga, meditation happens naturally whenever you want it, regardless of time or place.

Since this yoga is not antagonistic to the life of a householder, one need not give up his home and family. This yoga removes obstacles; it does not create them. This yoga does not obstruct anyone's daily life. On the contrary, it is helpful. In this yoga, the seeker mentally renounces everything with ease.

Mishra: *Does the sleep state continue during wakefulness?*

Baba: Yes, it is called *jagriti turiya*. With passage of time, this state becomes more and more steady. Eventually one remains in it all the time. Then even if he is abused, he will not get disturbed. Moreover, his state also affects everyone in his company. Even the trees, plants and flowers are affected.

I fully believe in Patanjali's yoga; nevertheless, Siddha Yoga is superior and easier to practise. In this yoga, a seeker does *sadhana* spontaneously and cannot give it up. Whenever anyone asks me for initiation, I tell him, "Come and stay here; you will receive it automatically." Many people receive initiation as soon as they arrive here. Initiation given intentionally by touch is inferior to that received automatically by staying in the ashram. I do not have to initiate anyone. The Divine Shakti Herself does it. This initiation is beyond all differences of caste, sect and religion. The seekers here include Jews, Christians, Hindus, Parsis, Jains and others.

Mishra: *Do you give discourses?*

Baba: I speak according to the needs of the seeker and the subject under consideration.

Mishra: *Is it essential to have kumbhaka in yoga sadhana.?*

Baba: It need not be practised with effort in Siddha Yoga; it takes place automatically.

Mishra: *Do prana and apana keep functioning during kumbhaka in Siddha Yoga?*

Baba: *Kumbhaka* is of two types: One is external and requires effort; the other is internal and takes place automatically. The inner *prana* is subtler than the outer *prana*. When you have *kumbhaka* of this subtle *prana,* the movement of *prana* and *apana* continues inside the *sushumna*. This *kumbhaka* is permanent and gives the seeker satisfaction and happiness. When the internal *kumbhaka* occurs, just a small part of the *prana* goes out.

This subject cannot be understood intellectually either through discussion or by reading books. It is understood only by direct experience.

Thursday, June 30, 1966

Today a bus driver came to the ashram with some relatives and friends.

THE PATH OF DEVOTION

Bus Driver: *For the past year or two, I have completely lost interest in everything worldly. I don't feel like*

*working or doing anything else. I can't hold down a
job and feel like leaving my present job as a bus driver.
My relatives noticed my condition and arranged a marriage for me two months ago, but I still have absolutely
no interest in anything. I only feel like secluding myself and practising* bhakti *(devotion). I have been
doing* japa *of Bhagavati Ma for a long time.*

Baba: *Bhakti* is of two kinds. One kind is that which
is suggested to you by your own mind and the other is
that which is prescribed by the Guru or the scriptures.
If you follow the path shown by a Guru who is
thoroughly versed in the scriptures and who is also adept
in the life of the world, then you will find the true way
of *bhakti*.

Marriage is determined by one's destiny and a
householder's life does not come in the way of *bhakti*.
Sri Siddharudha Swami, who initiated me into
Vedanta, was visited by many people like you who
complained that their family life was creating difficulties
in their *sadhana*. Swamiji used to show them the
hundreds of stoves for cooking food in the ashram, telling them that he, a *sannyasi*, had an even larger family
than they.

Remain intoxicated with devotion to God, but at
the same time, love your wife and make her your
partner in devotion. Merely chanting the name of
Rama or Krishna with closed eyes is not real devotion.

Bhagavati Ma, whose name you have been using
for *japa*, has full knowledge of your life in the world
and will not let it affect your devotion. After doing
your driving duty, do *bhakti* as well as attend properly
to your household. Bhagavati lives with Shiva. Has
any harm come to their life together? Remain devoted
to Bhagavati with great love and, along with that, also
do your other work.

Sunday, August 21, 1966

A student from the family of Sri Chandrashekhar Bharati, Shankaracharya of Sringeri Math, who gave up that position as soon as he attained realization, came to Baba today. Barrister Nain and other devotees were also there.

TRUE SAMADHI

Student: *I have heard and also read that if one remains in* samadhi *for 21 days, the body drops and one attains liberation. Is this true?*
Baba: A person's body may drop after a 21-day *samadhi*, but the future of his soul depends on his *karma* and his destiny. If he has any remaining *karma* in store, he will have to take another birth. There are many cases, however, of yogis who remained in *samadhi* for more than 21 days without dropping their bodies. Two examples are Ramana Maharshi and Bhagawan Nityananda.

This kind of *samadhi* is not necessary to attain Brahman. One whose destined *karmas* are attenuated goes into *samadhi* spontaneously as the example of Jadabharat illustrates. But how many such persons can there be? You should talk about ordinary seekers.

Samadhi can be understood only by direct experience. It is *samadhi* when '*dhi*' (*buddhi*, or intellect) attains '*sama*' (equanimity). In *samadhi*, a *jnani* experiences this entire world as full of God. He considers this very world to be the attributeless Brahman and acts accordingly in his daily life. He proclaims that what is considered non-existent exists. While living his daily life, he is fully aware that he is superimposing this world on Brahman. Whatever he does, whatever he sees, is all Brahman and nothing else.

There are no objects in his mind so what should he
meditate upon? There are no thoughts in his mind
so what mental waves should he eliminate? He sees
the entire world as that Brahman who is one without
a second. He is always in the same state wherever he
may be, whether at home or in a forest. He is liberated
even while living in the world. This is the highest
kind of *samadhi*. In hatha yoga, however, one has to
continually practise *kumbhaka* and enter into *samadhi*
through effort, and even then, its duration is limited.

THE MIND

Student: *What is the mind?*
Baba: The mind is a vibration of the Self; the Self is
its support. As we go on doing *sadhana* and our intellect becomes extremely subtle, then we can know the
mind. Just as I know myself, it is also possible to know
the mind. The mind itself is comprehensible and it
also comprehends other objects just as the sun illumines
itself as well as illuminating the world.

So long as we do not understand the mind, we think
that it is merely mind; but once we understand its true
nature, we realize that, in reality, it is Chiti (Consciousness). It is Chiti who vibrates in the form of the
mind. The *nirvikalpa* (thought-free) becomes *savikalpa*
(with thoughts). The *savikalpa* state is to make worldly
activities possible.

By what means do you know that you went into
samadhi and experienced bliss? It is only by the vibration of the mind that these experiences are known.
You are not the mind; the mind is yours. Just as such
objects as your house, clothes and ornaments belong to
you, similarly, the mind also belongs to you and helps
you in your daily life. Even saints and great beings

who have attained *jivanmukti* require the help of their
minds to teach their disciples and write profound books
on *jnana*.

GOD ALONE IS EVERYWHERE

Nain: *Which is the correct understanding: "I exist," or
"I do not exist"?*
Baba: A seeker is confused about such matters only
during the period of *sadhana*. After realization, he
knows, "I alone exist and none else."

This world is a manifestation of God. Just as the
body with its various constituents such as blood, bones,
flesh and hair is formed from one semen, similarly, this
world with its diverse objects has emerged from the one
Consciousness. Though there are diverse names and
forms, only one God pervades all. Everything is composed of Chiti; hence, there is unity in diversity. The
world has emerged from Truth and will merge back
into Truth. That (the world) which did not exist
in the beginning and which will not exist at the end,
cannot be said to exist in between either. This is the
truth. If anyone views it otherwise, his vision is faulty.

There are two types of understanding: one is gross,
superficial, or outer; and the other is subtle, or inner.
Subtle understanding is to know the true nature of
things. Superficial, or gross, understanding perceives
the same object in many different ways. Generally,
everyone perceives an object after superimposing himself (his own preconceptions, prejudices, etc.) onto that
object. For example, a man was once relaxing under
a tree. A student of the *Bhagavad Gita* happened to
pass by and said to himself, "This man appears to be a
sthitaprajna (one with steadfast knowledge of the
Truth)." After some time, a *vaidya* (Ayurvedic doctor)
passed by and he thought, "This man seems to be suf-

fering from some disease. That's why he is lying
unconscious under this tree." A little while later, a
thief passed by and he surmised, "This man must have
committed a theft last night. That's why he is sleeping." Still later, an exorcist passed by and he presumed
that the man was afflicted by a ghost. When the man
got up, someone asked him, "Why were you lying under
that tree?" He answered, "I just wanted to rest for a
while."

This story is similar to that of the five blind men
who came across an elephant. Each of the five men
gave a different description of the elephant depending
on which part of it he had felt. Truth is not like this.
After realizing the Truth, one sees nothing but the
kingdom of God everywhere. During the period of
sadhana, one is trapped in such dualities as heaven and
hell, *prakriti* and *purusha,* etc., but a *jnani* sees everything as one.

Nain: *The scriptures say that there is neither bondage
nor liberation for the Self.*

Baba: That is very true. Bondage and liberation are
relative terms adopted only for the purpose of discussion and argument.

Nain: *Why are there discussions and arguments?*

Baba: You will understand this when you get into the
state free from debate.

Nain: *Why do we experience pleasure and pain?*

Baba: Pleasure and pain are apparent in a particular
state. Pleasurable and painful events occur even in the
lives of great beings, but since they are beyond that
state, they are not affected by them. Pleasure and pain
seem very important to a seeker, but are insignificant
to a *jnani.*

Student: *Can a man become a doctor or an engineer in
his next life if he cherishes such a desire at the time of*

death?

Baba: That is what the scriptures say.   This world has been described as an embodiment of desire and one takes birth only because of desire.   If you ask a child what he would like to be when he grows up, he would say a doctor, a barrister and so forth.   What he says is based on his awareness about his previous life.   As he grows up, an urge arises within that he should become such and such.

Thursday, September 22, 1966

Baba has been in Bombay for the past four days.   At about four in the afternoon, Rasik Kadakia, Rajendra Mahant and other seekers came for his *darshan* and *satsang.*

Rasik: *After realizing the Self, can one give an experience of the Self to others?*

Baba: Yes, he can give the experience to one who is worthy and deserving of it.   He who has seen the Self can show It to others, but he who wants to see must have the right vision.   One man sees It and he shows It to a second man, who, in turn, shows It to a third man; this verily is the Guru-disciple lineage.

Rajendra: *Swami Vivekananda did not write anything about his experiences.*

Baba: Other disciples of Ramakrishna Paramahansa have written about their experiences.

Rajendra: *But does this indicate that Swamiji did not have any experiences?*

Baba: No, it doesn't.   It is a saint's personal choice whether or not to relate his experiences to others.

Rajendra: *Even Sri Shankaracharya did not give an account of his spiritual experiences.*

Baba: Have you read the acharya's own books? Read
Saundarya Lahari. What is contained there could not
have been written without personal experience.

Saints like Tukaram, Jnaneshwar and Kabir all
wrote about *swargaloka* (heaven), *sahasrara, nada,
bindu* and *kala*. Did they write without having experienced these things? A detailed description of the
awakening of Kundalini is given in the sixth chapter
of *Jnaneshwari*. Could all that be false? Read Vivekananda's introduction to *Raja Yoga* in which he has
written about Kundalini.

One day a *sannyasi* who was here said, "I do
not believe in the Kundalini." I replied, "Who cares
what you believe? It is immaterial whether or not you
believe in Kundalini. Just because you don't believe
in Her doesn't mean that Kundalini does not exist."
Rasik: *A friend of mine says that only a celibate can
become a Siddha. What would you say about that?*
Baba: Saints can be either *sannyasis* or householders.
Householder saints can achieve everything according to
the *varnashram,* the four stages of life. Maharshi Vyas,
Kabir and Tukaram were all householders. Ramana
Maharshi renounced his home and Bhagawan Nityananda was an *avadhut*. He had neither a home nor a
family, nor did he need them. For householder saints,
worldly dealings are a part of their normal daily activities. They do not do these activities for gratification
of the senses or for material enjoyment and pleasure.

इन्द्रियाणि इन्द्रियार्थेषु वर्तन्त इति धारयन्

"They act with the awareness that only the sense organs
are being engaged in the sense objects to perform their
work." Again, this is not your friend's subject and he
has no competence to make a judgment in this matter.
This is the subject of the scriptures and *acharyas*.

Rasik: *Can astrological predictions come true?*
Baba: If the inspiration of a pure mind combines with
the science of astrology, they come true.
Rasik: *Can a true Guru destroy the* karmas *of his
disciple?*
Baba: It is rare good fortune to get such a Guru. If
you have incurred heavy debts and a millionaire like
Birla becomes your friend, he can pay off all your debts.
Similarly, if you seek refuge in a Guru, the burden of
your *karmas* is relieved. He elevates you to such a
state that outwardly you may be undergoing any amount
of trouble or hardship, but inwardly you remain blissful and undisturbed.

WHAT IS TO BE RENOUNCED

Rajendra: *Is it essential to give up the material world
to achieve God?*
Baba: If you want God-realization and liberation, give
up the one thing that really needs to be given up: the
idea of "I" and "mine," the idea that you possess that
which really does not belong to you. A saint sings as
follows:

नहिं मिले धन त्यागे, नहिं मिले रामजी जान तजे।
नारायण तो मिले उसी को, जो देह अभिमान तजे॥ टेक॥
सुत-दारा या कुटुम्ब त्यागे, या अपना घर बार तजे।
नहिं मिले प्रभु कदापि, जगत का सब व्यवहार तजे।
कंद मूल फळ खाय रहे, और अन्न का भी आहार तजे।
वस्त्र को त्याग नग्न हो रहे, और घर की नार तजे।
तो भी हरि नहिं मिले यह त्यागे, चाहे अपने प्राण तजे।
नारायण तो मिले उसी को, जो देह अभिमान तजे॥

Ram is not attained by renouncing wealth or life;
Only he attains Narayana who renounces the pride
   of his body.
God can never be attained by renouncing all

worldly affairs,

By renouncing wife, children, family or household
matters,

By eating only roots, tubers and fruit, and renouncing other foods,

By renouncing clothes and going about naked, by
giving up women.

Even by renouncing one's own life force, Hari is
not attained.

Ram is not attained by renouncing wealth or life.

Only he attains Narayana who renounces the pride
of his body.

To renounce that which really does not belong to you,
but for which you have acquired the idea of my-ness
is like giving someone else's cow in charity and then
looking upward expecting an airplane to take you to
heaven.

This world created by God is not meant to be
renounced. If it were, why would God have created
it at all? What is the purpose of giving it up? It is
like leaving one house just to take up residence in
another or like taking off one set of clothes just to put
on another. How can that be called renunciation?
It is like going to the barber shop for a haircut and
afterwards declaring, "I have sacrificed my hair." After
a few days, your hair will grow back again. Similarly,
that which you give up now will eventually return and
present itself to you again. You need a house to stay
in, you need clothes to protect the body and you need
food to sustain the body.

What did you bring with you when you were born?
Nothing! You came into this world naked, with empty
hands, without even teeth; yet now you lay claim to so
many objects, saying, "This is mine and that is mine." In

fact, nothing belongs to you. In the end, you will leave the world exactly as you entered it. Therefore, give up the idea of my-ness, not the world. A woman saint named Jaydevi says :

मैं-मेरा संसार है, अन्य नहीं संसार ।
मैं-मेरा जाता रहे, बेड़ा है भव पार ॥
बेड़ा है भव पार, जहाँ न दुःख जरा है ।
सुखसागर भरपूर, एक सा नित्यभरा है ॥
जयदेवी तज मोह, देह भी नहीं तेरा ।
क्यूं करती अभिमान, 'गृह मेरा, धन मेरा' ॥

"The world consists of the idea of "I" and "mine"; apart from this idea, no world exists. Give up the idea of I-ness and my-ness and you will have achieved liberation. After crossing this ocean of transmigratory existence, you will reach a place where there is no pain, sorrow or misery. It is an ocean of bliss, ever full of happiness and contentment. O Jaydevi, give up attachment to the things of this world. Even this body does not belong to you. Why then do you say with pride, 'This wealth is mine and this house is mine'?"

Sunday, October 16, 1966

Many devotees attended *satsang* today including Barrister Ramanlal Vyas.

THE IMPORTANCE OF PRANA

Ramanlal: *Recently, after reading* Hathayoga Pradeepika, *a question arose in my mind as to why so much importance is given to* prana *and* pranayama *in hatha yoga.*

Baba: *Prana* is the most important thing in this world.

The *Kathopanishad* says, "यदिदं किंच जगत्सर्वं प्राण एजति निःसृतम् ।" "All that lives in this world has arisen from the vibration of *prana*." Because *prana* is the first cause of creation, the *Upanishads* accord importance to the worship of it.

Life is sustained by the presence of *prana* in the body. When *prana* leaves, the body dies. Many different *pranas* function in the body. The five principal *pranas* are *prana, apana, samana, vyana* and *udana;* the five subsidiary *pranas* are *naga, koorma, kookar, devadatta* and *dhananjaya. Prana* moves through the 72,000 *nadis,* purifying the body. The mind becomes quiet through control of *prana.*

HATHA YOGA MATURED INTO RAJA YOGA

Ramanlal: *Since hatha yoga is concerned with the body and the Self is separate from the body, then how can one attain knowledge of the Self through hatha yoga?*
Baba: You are right. Hatha yoga has no connection with the Self. The Self is non-dual, unattached and completely independent. The purpose of hatha yoga is to purify the body and the mind. The Self is always pure; It never becomes impure or tainted so there can be no question of purifying It.

As the name signifies, hatha yoga is practised through discipline. It requires effort; it has certain prescribed rules, methods and times for practice. Its main aim is to keep the body fit so that one may enjoy bodily pleasures and comfort. Hatha yoga makes the body healthy and strong. As a result, one appears younger and lives longer. It is said, ' शरीरमाद्यं खलु धर्म साधनम्'। "You need a healthy body to do *sadhana.*"
Ramanlal: *Is hatha yoga the same as raja yoga?*
Baba: No, they are different.
Ramanlal: *Then why does* Hathayoga Pradeepika *refer*

to hatha yoga as raja yoga?
Baba: It makes no such statement. Read it again carefully. It says that hatha yoga takes you toward raja yoga.
This means that after hatha yoga has been practised
systematically, it eventually matures into raja yoga. It
says, ' बिभ्राजते प्रोन्नतराजयोगमारोढुमिच्छोरधि रोहिणीव "Hatha
yoga is the stairway for those who wish to ascend to
the great height of raja yoga." Just as after high school,
there is college; similarly, mastery of hatha yoga leads
to raja yoga.
Ramanlal: *Can a householder practise yoga?*
Baba: Yes, you are already practising it every day, but
you have not given it any conscious thought. You sit
in a particular traditional way; that is *asana*. You eat
at a certain time, sleep at a certain time and go to the
office at a certain time—that is *yama* and *niyama*. *You*
concentrate on your work; that is meditation.

Wednesday, October 19, 1966

Dr. Vipinbhai Modi and his family, who come every
Sunday for Baba's *darshan*, were at the ashram today as
well. The doctor's wife, Hansaben, has great interest in
spirituality and sometimes asks Baba questions.

THE GOAL OF ALL RELIGIONS IS THE SAME

Hansaben: *People initiated into one religion or sect
wear white clothes while those initiated into another
wear yellow or saffron clothes. What is the reason for
these differences? What is the significance of the colour
of clothes?*
Baba: During his *sadhana,* a saint sees only a particular
colour in meditation and then wears clothes of that

colour.   Later, his disciples follow his example and start
wearing the same colour.

There may be sects, many religions, but they all
have the same final goal, which is to know the Truth,
to know the Self.   After this goal is achieved, all religions and sects are seen as one, undivided by superficial
differences.   . .

God is changeless, formless and unattached.   He
has no name.   One has to adopt some path in order to
realize Him.   It may be Hinduism, Islam, Jainism or
Christianity.   The paths may be different, but their
goal is the same.   Once the goal is reached, the path
has no further use.   We serve food on a leaf plate, but
after the food has been eaten, the leaf plate is of no
more use and we throw it away.   Another example: You
came here by means of a car, but in order to enter the
ashram, you had to leave the car outside.

Initially, when a seeker begins to meditate, he
adopts some name or form of God for *japa* and meditation.   It is by means of God with attributes that a
seeker eventually attains the goal of realizing God
without name or form.

Tuesday, November 8, 1966

This morning at 9 o'clock, Professor Umedbhai Maniar
came to the ashram with Mr. Umashankar Joshi, his
daughter, Swati, and another friend.   Umashankar is a
well known scholar and poet.   Currently, he is head of
the Linguistic. Studies Department at Gujarat University
and, on December 1st, he will become Vice-chancellor
of the University.

All the visitors went out to the garden where Baba was
sitting and Professor Maniar introduced everyone to him.

Baba talked to them lovingly and started showing them the garden.

Baba: The leaves, fruit and other parts of these trees have so many uses. They often have medicinal value. The juice of guava is an antidote for liquor intoxication. A particular kind of abdominal pain can be cured by applying the leaves of swallow wort on the stomach.

Umashankar: *Yes, Baba, my father used to put them on his stomach.*

Baba: And if you walk around the swallow wort, you obtain wealth, but this is known only to the Marwaris (merchant community), not to others. (laughter)

Umashankar: *Yes, because they not only worship Narayan, they also worship Lakshmi Narayan (Goddess of Wealth).*

Baba and the visitors discussed various topics in this way as they walked to the *satsang* hall.

KASHMIR SHAIVISM

Umashankar: *I read the book* Pratyabijnahridayam *on Kashmir Shaivism, but I could not understand it.*

Baba: Such mystical books can be understood only by the grace of the Guru or God. It is stated in the very beginning of the book that :

शक्तिपातोन्मिषितपारमेश्वरसमावेशाभिलाषिणः कतिचित्
भक्तिभाजः तेषाम् ईश्वरप्रत्यभिज्ञोपदेशतत्त्वं मनाक् उन्मील्यते ।

"Only a few seekers who are full of devotion and who have a desire to achieve oneness with the Supreme Self can, after *shaktipat* initiation, begin to grasp the teachings give herein."

Umashankar: *Yes, the essence of the entire Shaivite doctrine has been given in just twenty sutras.*

Baba: You have studied the book quite thoroughly; you

even remember the number of *sutras* it contains. These
few *sutras* express the entire essence of the philosophy
that everything in the world is Consciousness. This
Consciousness, or Chiti, is absolutely independent and
creates this manifold world. She possesses the power
to create many from one and one from many. This
same Chiti dwells in man in the form of Kundalini.

Umashankar: *Yes, She dwells in human beings in a
contracted form.*

Baba: She is also all-pervading.

Umashankar: *Everything is covered with impurities.
Even the individual soul is said to be covered with
impurities.*

Baba: Yes, as long as the divine Shakti is not awakened,
man remains a *jiva* (individual soul) ; after Her awakening, he becomes Shiva.

'अयं शक्तिदरिद्रः संसारी उच्यते, स्वशक्तिविकासे तु शिव एव ।

"Man without Shakti is a victim of transmigratory
existence. When his own Shakti unfolds, verily he
becomes Shiva."

Umashankar: *This scripture can be understood only
with the help of the Guru.*

Baba: One needs a teacher to learn even the normal
things of daily life so why wouldn't one need a teacher
for this? Various arts and sciences such as driving,
cooking, carpentry, etc., are all learnt either by observing someone else or through instruction. In the same
way, spiritual knowledge has to be learnt from a
Guru. The Guru is said to be the grace-bestowing
power of God. 'गुरुर्वा पारमेश्वरी अनुग्राहिका शक्तिः '

Umashankar: *The Guru is also the same Chitshakti.*

Baba: Yes, the Guru is that power which bestows the
grace of God on the disciple. God bestows His grace
through the Guru. One of the *Shivasutras* says, गुरुरुपायः।

"The Guru is the means."

Umashankar: Gururupaya; *that is, you must go to the Guru to receive this Shakti.*

Baba: Yes, as soon as the disciple receives this Shakti, his *sushumna* begins to open and his own Shakti is activated. Then the seeker experiences great inner bliss. Another sutra says, 'मध्यविकासात् चिदानन्दलाभः' "By the opening of the middle one (*sushumna*), one obtains the bliss of the Self." In this connection, I will give you an illustration from Jnaneshwar Maharaj. In his book *Amritanubhava,* he writes about one of the *Shivasutras,* ' ज्ञानं बन्धः' *jnanam bandaha.* This is quite surprising because he had no direct knowledge of the *Shivasutras;* what he has written about them came from inner omniscience arising from *shaktipat.*

Umashankar: *Is the tradition of* shaktipat *still alive, or has it come to an end?*.

Baba: It has not ended, nor will it ever come to an end. Jnaneshwar Maharaj has very clearly indicated his own lineage: Adinath, Matsyendranath, Goraknath, Gahininath, Nivrittinath and then Jnaneshwar himself.

One must understand this science thoroughly. What can a *sadhu* achieve just by piercing his ears, applying sacred ash, wearing a loincloth and repeating *shiva gorakh? Shiva gorakh* is not a mantra. The Guru's name is not the Guru mantra. The mantra given by the Guru is the Guru mantra. You must discover which mantra the Guru repeated to achieve perfection. Many people are displeased with me because I do not chant my Guru's name, but *om namo bhagavate nityanandaya* is not a mantra, just as the names of Tulsidas, Mira and Kabir are not mantras; they are only names.

Umashankar: *Is it necessary to follow a technique in this branch of knowledge?*

Baba: You must know certain essential things such as

who the Guru is, what Kundalini is, what *shaktipat* is,
the meaning of Chitshakti and so forth.

Umashankar: *Is it good to awaken the Kundalini
through hatha yoga?*

Baba: Kundalini should never be disturbed or
provoked. She must never be subjected to any force;
otherwise, negative results will ensue. The simplest
method of awakening Kundalini is by receiving the
Guru's grace through *shaktipat*. There will be no
obstacles on this path.

Another satsang took place in the evening.

Umashankar: *If all the work is performed by Chitshakti,
then Shiva has no significance.*

Baba: Yes, that is so. It is said in *Saundarya Lahari*:

शिवः शक्तया युक्तो यदि भवति शक्तिः प्रभवितुम् ।
न चेदेवं देवो न खलु कुशलः स्पन्दितुमपि ॥

"Shiva is able to create the universe only when united
with Shakti. Without Shakti, He cannot even vibrate."
Shiva without Shakti is like a corpse.

According to Shaivite doctrine, Parashiva, Shiva and
Shakti are the three main principles. Parashiva is attributeless, motionless and of the nature of supreme bliss.
He is supreme existence and supreme knowledge. The
first wave arising in Him as *idam* (this) is Shiva; the
vibration of that wave is Shakti. She is also known as
Parashakti or Paravak. She has three aspects: will, knowledge and action. The ecstatic dance of Shiva and Shakti
brings this world into existence. The myriad forms
seen in the world are Shakti's own forms.

Once when Dr. Brahm Prakash, director of the
Atomic Energy Plant in Trombay, was here, he explained that, according to the principles of physics, all matter
is energy. I replied, "Then there is no difference at
all between your doctrine and ours. What you call

energy, we call Brahma or Chitshakti."
Umashankar: *The philosopher and the scientist have come very close to each other.*
Baba: Yes, you're right.

Wednesday, November 9, 1966

At 7:30 this morning, everyone again gathered in the hall. Yesterday evening, Shrimati Rajeshwariben, the wife of Dr. Brahm Prakash, brought a copy of *Gita Panchashati*, a collection of poems by Rabindranath Tagore, to *satsang*. At Baba's request, she recited two of the poems.

INSPIRED POETS AND ORDINARY POETS

Umashankar: *Akha, a great Gujarati poet-saint and* jnani, *used to say that a* jnani *should not be called a poet because a* jnani *has gone far beyond a mere poet.*
Baba: There are two types of poets: inspired poets (वरकवि) and ordinary poets (नरकवि). Those who write from divine inspiration or those who have received the grace of the Guru are inspired poets. Tukaram, Jnaneshwar and Sundardas were inspired poets. Those who write with effort by applying the intellect are ordinary poets. Only the poems of inspired poets appeal to me. I read only those.
Umashankar: *He who has received the grace of God is an inspired poet. A Gujarati proverb says, "The poet reaches a place that the sun cannot reach and the realized one reaches a place that the poet cannot reach."*

SHABDA BRAHMAN (THE SOUND-FORM OF THE ABSOLUTE)

Umashankar: *It has been said that the sound 'aum' can be heard even in the water flowing from the tap. The*

world has emerged from pashyanti *(vibration of sound)*.
Baba: In the Sanskrit alphabet, the vowel 'a' is inherent
in every letter from 'ka' to 'ksha.' This is the same 'a'
that is in the sacred syllable *aum*. Sound at the *para*
stage (the subtlest level of sound) is devoid of attributes or manifestation; at the *pashyanti* stage, it starts
vibrating; at the *madhyama* stage, it assumes a subtle
form; and at the *vaikhari* stage, it finds complete
expression.

Aum, or *ham,* occurs in every word or sound. It can
be heard in the gurgling of a stream, in the roaring of
the sea and in the gentle dance of raindrops. You utter
ham even when you lift a bucket or some weight. The
entire world has emerged from *aum*. Our *prana* inces-
santly repeats the sound of *so'ham*.

हकारेण बहिर्यांति सकारेण विशेत्पुनः ।
हंसहंसेति मंत्रोऽयं जीवो जपति सर्वदा ॥

The incoming breath makes the sound *'ham'* and the
outgoing breath makes the sound *'sa.'* We are constantly doing japa of this mantra, *hamsa, hamsa.*

Umashankar: *This is known as* shabda brahman, *the
sound-form of the Absolute. Even the Bible says that
the world came into being out of "the Word" and there
is also a theory regarding the process of dissolution.*
Baba: The world will dissolve in the same way in which
it was born. Its sequence of evolution was from ether,
to air, to fire, to water, and finally, to earth. At the time
of dissolution, it will merge back in the reverse order.

SHAKTIPAT INITIATION

Umashankar: *Is any special technique involved in*
shaktipat *initiation?*
Baba: Initiation takes place spontaneously; nothing
special has to be done. Even without the Guru's con-

:scious knowledge, his Shakti may enter an earnest seeker.
Sometimes I get signals like those of a radar in my
heart. Then I start looking around and, if I find some-
·one swaying, I know that he has received *shaktipat;* that
is, he has been initiated. If germs like those of tuber-
·culosis can infect people so easily, why shouldn't the
particles of this all-pervading Shakti also be contagious?
In the presence of one whose Shakti is fully awake, one
·quickly experiences Shakti's effects.
Umashankar: *Is the process the same for everyone?*
Baba: Yes, the same.   All the saints have the same
·degree from the same university.   Truth is only one.

Saturday, November 26, 1966

An American woman, Manjushri (formerly Irene Wol-
fington), has been staying in the ashram for two or three
·days. She has been in India for the past three years,
visiting many ashrams and meeting numerous saints and
:sages; but she has not found what she is seeking. She is
now living the life of a sannyasini in the Bajarang Cave
·on Mt. Abu. This morning she asked Baba some questions.

KNOWLEDGE OF THE GURU IS ESSENTIAL

Manjushri: *If we initially received Shakti from one
Guru and for some reason its unfoldment is obstructed,
and then another Guru reawakens the Shakti, will any
harmful results ensue?*
Baba: All Gurus are one; throughout the entire world,
the Guru principle is only one.   The Shakti dwelling
in each and every individual is also one and the same,
:and all Gurus awaken the same Shakti.   Different
Gurus do not awaken different Shaktis.   Before asking
this question, however, you must first know who the

Guru is. Do not limit the Guru to the frame of the gross body.

Manjushri: *If one has received guidance from more than one Guru, then it is very difficult to serve or worship all of them at the same time.*

Baba: Why do you give importance to the outer form of the Guru?

Manjushri: *Since it is God Himself who guides us in the form of the Guru, then why does God turn against us? It is God's duty to put us on the right path.*

Baba: God never turns against us. We feel so because of our own mental defects, not because of any fault on the part of God or the Guru. If we err in our own actions, we feel that the Guru turned against us. If you do not have thorough knowledge of the Guru, you will have many occasions to feel victimised.

Manjushri: *If the Guru's physical form is not important, then that means a Guru is not necessary. Isn't it possible to progress without a Guru?*

Baba: Love God, contemplate Him, sing His glories. Eventually, you yourself will become a Guru. Remain where you are and keep doing whatever you are doing now. This is the best course for you.

Manjushri: *I believe in devotion to the Guru and in surrendering completely to him.*

Baba: Very good, but along with devotion you must also have knowledge about the Guru; otherwise, you may lose your faith. It is very good to have faith in only one Guru. There is a story in the *Mahabharata* about Eklavya who imbibed all of his Guru's knowledge and expertise in archery solely through devotion to him.

Manjushri: *Yes, but I am not at all satisfied with that example. How can a Guru harm his disciple? Dronacharya asked for Eklavya's thumb and thus deprived him of his art. Was that proper behaviour for a Guru?*

Baba: The saints and sages in those days were the protectors of the world. Dronacharya was Guru to the king. He was as adept in worldly matters as he was in archery and spirituality. He acted after considering what Eklavya deserved. Eklavya was a boy from the Bhil tribe. He had faith and devotion, but he lacked discrimination. Instead of using his skill in archery at a proper time and place, he used it on a dog. If higher knowledge and expertise fall into the hands of unworthy individuals, it is likely to be misused to the detriment of society. For example, atomic energy can be used for the world's benefit and also for its destruction. For this reason, the Guru imparts his knowledge only to a worthy disciple.

SADGURUNATH MAHARAJ KI JAI

GLOSSARY

abhanga : a devotional song composed in the Marathi language.

abhaya mudra : a symbolic gesture formed by raising one hand with the palm outward, meaning "Do not fear."

acharya : one who teaches the scriptures.

agama : divinely revealed scripture which has been handed down from teacher to pupil through the ages.

ajna chakra : the spiritual centre located between the eyebrows. The awakened Kundalini passes through this *chakra* only by the command (*ajna*) of the Guru, and for this reason, it is often called the *guru chakra*. When *shaktipat* is given, the Guru often touches the seeker at this spot.

apana : one of the five major pranas; the incoming breath.

arati : the waving of lights, incense, camphor, and other things before a saint or idol as an act of worship.

Arjuna : a famous warrior and one of the heroes of the *Mahabharata* epic. It was to Arjuna that Krishna imparted the knowledge of the *Bhagavad Gita.*

asana : various bodily postures, practised to strengthen the body, purify the nerves, and develop one-pointedness of mind—the yoga scriptures describe eighty-four major *asanas*; a seat or mat on which one sits for meditation.

ashram : an institution or community where spiritual discipline is practised; the abode of a saint or holy man.

astra : weapon, missile.

atma : the Self.

avadhut : a saint who has transcended body-consciousness and whose behaviour is not bound by ordinary social conventions.

ayurveda : (lit. knowledge of life) : ancient Indian science of medicine that teaches that good health depends on maintaining the even balance of the three bodily humours : wind, bile and phlegm.

Baba : a term of affection for a saint or holy man, meaning "father."

Bhagavad Gita : a portion of the *Mahabharata* and one of the great works of spiritual literature, in which Lord Krishna explains the path of liberation to Arjuna on the battlefield of the war described in the epic poem.

bhajan : devotional verse or hymn.

bhakta : a devotee, a lover of God; a follower of bhakti yoga.

bhakti : the path of devotion leading to union with God; the state of intense devotional love for God or Guru.

349

bindu : (lit. a dot, a point) : the compact mass of Shakti gathered
into an undifferentiated point, ready to manifest as the
universe; a form made of light (Blue Pearl); the material
cause and substance of creation.
Brahma : the creator of the universe.
brahmin : the first caste of Hindu society, the members of which
are by tradition priests, scholars, and teachers.
Brahman : Vedantic term for the Absolute Reality.
brahmachari : a student engaged in scriptural study and the
practice of celibacy.

Chaitanya : Consciousness.
chakra (lit. wheel) : in human body, there are seven major
energy centres, or nerve plexes, called *chakras* that are
located in the subtle body.
Chit Shakti (Chiti) : the power of Self-revelation by which the
Supreme shines by Itself; Universal Consciousness.

darshan : seeing God, an image of God, or a holy being.
dharma : righteousness; religion; the path to Truth.
dhyana : meditation.

Eknath Maharaj (1528-1609) : householder poet-saint of Maharashtra, renowned for his scriptural commentaries and
spiritual poetry.

gopis : the milkmaids of Vraja, childhood companions and devotees
of Krishna; revered as the embodiments of the ideal states
of ecstatic devotion to God.
gunas : the three basic qualities of nature, which determine the
inherent characteristics of all created things. They are
sattva : purity, light, harmony; *rajas* : activity, passion; and
tamas : dullness, inertia, ignorance.
Guru : a spiritual master who has attained oneness with God and
who initiates his disciples and devotees into the spiritual
path and guides them to liberation.

hatha yoga : a yogic discipline by which the *samadhi* state is
attained through union of *prana* and *apana* (outgoing and
incoming breath). Various bodily and mental exercises are
practised in order to purify the *nadis* and bring about the
even flow of *prana*. When the flow of *prana* is even, the
mind becomes still. One then experiences equality-con-
sciousness and enters into the state of *samadhi*.

japa : repetition of mantra.
jiva : individual soul.

jivanmukti : the state of liberation while still in the physical body.

jnana yoga : the path of knowledge; the yoga of attaining supreme wisdom through intellectual inquiry.

jnani : an enlightened being; a follower of the path of knowledge.

Jnaneshwar Maharaj (1275-1296) : foremost among the saints of Maharashtra and a child yogi of extraordinary powers. He was born into a family of saints, and his elder brother Nivrittinath was his Guru. His verse commentary on the *Bhagavad Gita, Jnaneshwari*, written in the Marathi language, is acknowledged as one of the most important spiritual works. He took live *samadhi* at the age of 21 in Alandi, where his *samadhi* shrine continues to attract thousands of seekers.

Kabir (1440-1518) : a great poet-saint who lived his life as a weaver in Benares. His followers were both Hindu and Muslim, and his influence was a strong force in overcoming religious factionalism.

karma : physical, mental, or verbal actions; accumulation of past actions.

karma yoga : the yoga of performing selfless actions as service to God.

Kashmir Shaivism : non-dual philosophy that recognises the entire universe as a manifestation of Chiti, or divine conscious energy. Kashmir Shaivism explains how the formless, unmanifest Supreme Principle manifests as the universe. The authoritative scripture of Kashmir Shaivism is the *Shiva Sutras*.

kripa : grace.

Krishna (lit. the dark one, the one who irresistibly attracts): an incarnation of God whose life story is described in the *Shrimad Bhagavatam* and the *Mahabharata* and whose spiritual teachings are contained in the *Bhagavad Gita*.

kriya : a gross (physical) or subtle (mental, emotional) purificatory movement initiated by the awakened Kundalini. *Kriyas* purify the body and nervous system so as to allow a seeker to endure the energy of higher states of consciousness.

kumbhaka : voluntary or involuntary retention of breath.

kumkum : a red powder, made from turmeric, used for putting the auspicious mark between the eyebrows in remembrance of the Guru and for ritual worship.

Kundalini (lit. coiled one) : the primordial Shakti, or cosmic energy, that lies coiled in the *muladhara chakra* of every individual. When awakened, Kundalini begins to move upward within the *sushumna*, the subtle central channel, piercing the *chakras* and initiating various yogic processes that bring about total purification and rejuvenation of the entire

being. When Kundalini enters the *sahasrara*, the spiritual
centre in the crown of the head, the individual self merges
in the universal Self and attains the state of Self-realization.

lakh : 100,000.
Lama : Tibetan Buddhist monk.

Mahabharata : an epic poem composed by the sage Vyasa that
    recounts the struggle between the Kaurava and the Pandava
    brothers over a disputed kingdom. As the vast narrative
    unfolds, a storehouse of secular and religious lore is
    revealed. The *Bhagavad Gita* occurs in the latter portion
    of the *Mahabharata*.
mahasamadhi (lit. the great *samadhi*) : a yogi's conscious exit
    from the body at death.
mala : a string of beads used for repetition of mantra.
mantra : cosmic word, or divine sound; name of God.
math : ashram.
maya : the force that shows the unreal as real and presents that
    which is temporary and short-lived as permanent and ever-
    lasting.
muladhara chakra : spiritual centre at the base of the spine where
    the Kundalini lies dormant.
mullah : a Muslim priest.
muni : Jain holy man.

nada : metaphysically, the first movement of Shiva-Shakti toward
    manifestation. In yoga, the unstruck sound experienced in
    meditation.
nadi : subtle channel within the body through which *prana* flows.
Narada : a divine *rishi*, or seer, who was a great devotee and
    servant of Vishnu. Author of the *Narada Bhakti Sutras*, the
    authoritative text on bhakti yoga.
Narayana : a name for Vishnu.
nirvikalpa samadhi : superconscious thought-free state.

om : the primal sound; sound or vibration from which the entire
    universe emanates. It is the essence of all mantras.
om namah shivaya : a mantra meaning "salutations to Shiva";
    Shiva denotes the inner Self. It is known as the grea*t*
    redeeming mantra because it has the power to grant worldly
    fulfillment as well as spiritual realization.

prakriti : primordial nature; the natural force that manifests the
    universe; also, the world of matter. In Kashmir Shaivism,
    prakriti is identified with Shakti.
prana : vital force; specifically, the vital air in the breathing pro-
    cess; the outgoing breath.

pranam : obeisance.

pranayama : the regulation and restraint of breath.

Pratyabhijnahridayam (lit. the heart of the doctrine of recognition) : a concise treatise of twenty *sutras* by Kshemaraja that summarises the Pratyabhijna philosophy of Kashmir Shaivism. In essence it states that we have forgotten our true nature by identifying with the body. Realization is a process of recognising our true Self.

Puranas (lit. ancient legends) : sacred books containing stories, legends, and hymns about the creation of the universe, the incarnations of God, and the instructions of various deities, as well as the spiritual legacies of ancient sages and kings. There are eighteen *Puranas*.

purusha : the individual soul; the form of the Supreme Principle that resides within a human being. In Kashmir Shaivism, the *purusha* is identified with Shiva.

Radha : the childhood companion and consort of Krishna who is celebrated in Indian tradition as the embodiment of devotion to God.

raja yoga or *ashtanga* yoga (lit. eight limbs of yoga) : the eight-fold yoga expounded by Patanjali in the *Yoga Sutras*, the authoritative text on raja yoga. The eight steps are :

1. *yama* (self-restraint) : non-injury, truthfulness, non-stealing, celibacy and non-acquisitiveness.
2. *niyama* (daily observances) : purity, contentment, austerrity, study, and surrender to God.
3. *asana* : steady and comfortable posture.
4. *pranayama* : the regulation and restraint of breath.
5. *pratyahara* : withdrawal of the senses from their objects.
6. *dharana* : concentration, fixing the mind on an object of contemplation.
7. *dhyana* : meditation, the continuous flow of thoughts toward the chosen object.
8. *samadhi* : superconscious state in which the mind merges with the object of meditation; meditative union with the Absolute.

rajas : activity or passion (one of the three gunas).

Rama : an incarnation of God whose life story is told in the Ramayana epic; a name of the all-pervasive Supreme Reality.

Ramayana (lit. history of Rama) : the oldest of the Sanskrit epic poems written by the sage Valmiki. Celebrates the life of Rama. The story tells of the abduction of Sita, Rama's wife, by the ten-headed demon king Ravana, and how Rama, with the help of Hanuman and the monkey kingdom, fought and conquered Ravana. Also rendered into poetic Hindi 400 years ago by Tulsidas.

Sadguru : a true Guru.

sadhana : the practice of spiritual discipline.

sadhu : holy man or spiritual seeker.

sahasrara : thousand-petalled spiritual centre at the crown of the head where one experiences the highest states of consciousness.

samadhi : a state of meditative union with the Absolute.

samadhi shrine : site where a saint has taken *mahasamadhi*; the tomb of a saint, which is alive with the spiritual power of the saint who is buried there.

sannyasa : the fourth stage of traditional Indian life; the time of complete renunciation in which one is freed from all worldly obligations and responsibilities in order to devote one's life to the pursuit of Self-realization.

sannyasi : a monk or ascetic; one who has taken the formal vow of renunciation.

satchidananda : the nature of the Supreme Reality. *Sat* is being, that which exists in all times, in all places, and in all things; *chit* is consciousness, that which illumines all places, times and things; *ananda* is absolute bliss.

satsang : a meeting of devotees for the purpose of listening to scriptural readings, chanting, or sitting in the presence of a holy being; the company of saints and devotees.

sattva : purity, light, harmony (one of the three *gunas*).

Shakti (also known as Chiti, Chit Shakti, Kundalini) : the divine cosmic power that projects, maintains and dissolves the universe.

shaktipat : the transmission of spiritual power (Shakti) from the Guru to the disciple; spiritual awakening by grace.

Shankaracharya (788-820) : one of the greatest of India's philosophers and sages, who expounded the philosophy of absolute non-dualism (Advaita Vedanta). In addition to his writing and teaching, he established *maths* (ashrams) in the four corners of India.

Shiva : a name for the all-pervasive Supreme Reality; one of the Hindu trinity representing God as destroyer; the personal God of the Shaivites. In His personal form, He is portrayed as a yogi wearing a tiger skin and holding a trident, with snakes coiled around His neck and arms.

Shiva Sutras : a Sanskrit text that Shiva revealed to the sage Vasuguptacharya. It consists of seventy-seven *sutras*, which were found inscribed on a rock in Kashmir. It is the major scriptural authority of the philosophical school of Kashmir Shaivism.

Shrimad Bhagavatam : the most popular devotional scripture in India, containing many legends, stories, and the life and teachings of Krishna; composed by Vyasa.

Siddha : a perfect being; one who has attained the highest

state and become one with the Absolute.

Siddha Yoga : the yoga that takes place spontaneously within a seeker whose Kundalini has been awakened by a Siddha Guru and that leads to the state of spiritual perfection.

siddhis : supernatural powers attained through the practice of yoga.

so'ham (lit. I am That) : the natural vibration of the Self, which occurs spontaneously with each incoming and outgoing breath. By becoming aware of it, a yogi experiences the identity between his individual self and the Supreme Self.

Sundardas (1596-1689) : a renowned Hindu poet-saint born in Rajasthan.

Surdas (1479-1584) : blind poet-saint. Devoted to the child Krishna, he spent his life in the district on the banks of the Yamuna River where Krishna lived and sported with the *gopis*.

sushumna : the central and most important of all *nadis* located in the centre of the spinal column extending from the base of the spine to the top of the head. The six *chakras* are situated in the *sushumna* and it is through the *sushumna* channel that the Kundalini rises.

sutra : an aphorism, or pithy saying.

seva : service to the Guru.

swami : title given to a sannyasi; one who has taken the vow of renunciation.

tamas : inertia or dullness (one of the three *gunas*).

tantra : an esoteric spiritual discipline in which Shakti, the creative power of the Absolute, is worshipped as the Divine Mother through the practice of rituals, mantras, and *yantras* (visual symbols). The goal of *tantra* is to attain Self-realization through Kundalini awakening and through uniting the two principles—Shiva and Shakti.

tapasya (lit. to heat up) : austere or ascetic practices, which purify the mind and give control over the senses.

Tukaram Maharaj (1608-1650) : great poet-saint of Maharashtra; author of thousands of *abhangas* (devotional songs).

tulsi : a plant sacred to Vishnu; a type of basil, leaves of which are used for worship.

Tulsidas (1532-1623) : North Indian poet-saint and author of *Ramayana*, the life story of Lord Rama written in Hindi, which is still one of the most popular scriptures in India.

turiya (lit. fourth) : the transcendental state, the fourth state of consciousness beyond waking, dream, and deep sleep in which the true nature of reality is directly perceived; the state of witness-consciousness.

Upanishads : the teachings of the ancient sages that form the knowledge or end portion of the Vedas. The central teaching of the *Upanishads* is that the Self of a human being is the same as Brahman, the Absolute. The goal of life, according to the *Upanishads*, is realization of Brahman.

vaidya : Ayurvedic doctor.

Vedanta : a philosophical school founded by Badarayana that contains the philosophical teachings of the *Upanishads* and investigates the nature and relationship of the Absolute, the world, and the Self.

Vedas : very ancient and authoritative revealed scriptures of India.

Vishnu : a name for the all-pervasive Supreme Reality; one of the Hindu trinity, representing God as the sustainer; the personal God of the Vaishnavas. In His personal form, He is portrayed as four-armed and holding a conch, a discus, a lotus, and a mace.

Vitthal : (lit. the place of the brick) : Krishna went to the house of Pundalik, who asked Him to wait while he tended to his ageing parents and threw a brick for Him to stand on. The form of Krishna standing on a brick is known as Vitthal. His image is enshrined in Pandharpur, a famous place of pilgrimage in Maharashtra, and has been worshipped by the poet saints of Maharashtra and Karnataka.

yamas and *niyamas* : (see raja yoga).

yajna : ritualistic sacrifice; any work done in the spirit of surrender to God.

yoga (lit. union) : the state of oneness with the Self, God; the practices leading to that state.

yuga : an age of the world.

yogi : one who practises yoga, one who has attained the goal of yogic practices.